D1153073

98

GILL'S STUDIES IN IRISH LITERATURE
Terence Brown, General Editor

BRIAN MOORE
A Critical Study

GILL'S STUDIES IN IRISH LITERATURE

BRIAN MOORE

A Critical Study

JO O'DONOGHUE

GILL AND MACMILLAN

Published in Ireland by
Gill and Macmillan Ltd
Goldenbridge
Dublin 8
with associated companies in
Auckland, Delhi, Gaborone, Hamburg, Harare,
Hong Kong, Johannesburg, Kuala Lumpur, Lagos, London,
Manzini, Melbourne, Mexico City, Nairobi,
New York, Singapore, Tokyo
© Jo O'Donoghue 1990
Print origination by Irish Typesetters
Printed by Billing & Sons Ltd, Worcester
All rights reserved. No part of this publication may be copied,
reproduced or transmitted in any form or by any means,
without permission of the publishers.

British Library Cataloguing in Publication Data
Donoghue, Jo
Brian Moore: a critical study. — (Gill's studies in Irish literature).
1. Fiction in English. Canadian writers. Moore, Brian, 1921–
I. Title
813.54
ISBN 0-7171-1713-8

LEABHARLANNA ATHA CLIATH
BALLYROAN LIBRARY
ACC. NO.   0717 117138
COPY NO.   TF 1004
INV NO/91   301A
PRICE IR£   30.00
CLASS   823.914MOO

For
Richard

Contents

Acknowledgments

Introduction

Acknowledgments

I should like to offer thanks to Professor Terence Brown of Trinity College, Dublin, for his encouragement and guidance in the preparation of this critical study, to my husband, Richard Parfrey, for technical and moral support and to Sean McMahon, who read the manuscript and offered many helpful suggestions.

Introduction

I think it was Greene who said that the governing passion lends a unity to any shelf of books.[1] Brian Moore

A man's whole art may be rendered down, by analysis, to variations upon a single theme.[2] Elizabeth Bowen

BRIAN MOORE was born in Belfast, Northern Ireland, on 25 August 1921, the fourth child in a family of nine. His father, James Brian Moore FRCS, was a surgeon at the Mater Hospital in Belfast. His mother, Eileen McFadden, came from Donegal. His father had married when he was fifty and died when Moore was eighteen.

Moore was educated at St Malachy's Diocesan College in Belfast, whose ethos he describes as very harsh, clerical and old-fashioned. He was, he says, frequently caned for academic failure as well as for misdeeds. This kind of Catholic education of the 1930s in retrospect appears nightmarish to Moore and was the theme of his second novel, *The Feast of Lupercal* (1957). His evocation of Ardath College, a thinly disguised St Malachy's, is informed by great bitterness. Because his father had put himself through medical school on scholarships in the 1890s and still remembered his French irregular verbs at the end of his life, he was a daunting role-model and academic success was greatly prized in the Moore household. There was also the perception—not surprising at the end of the great depression decade of the 1930s—that academic achievement was the only safe route to a respectable career and prosperous standard of living. Moore remembers both his parents as being very anxious for him to succeed at school. In the end his weakness at mathematics prevented him from matriculating and he left school to join the Air Raid Precautions Service (ARP) at the beginning of the Second World War. It was a disappointment to his parents and to himself that he did not follow other members of his family to The Queen's University of Belfast and to this day the author frequently adverts ruefully to this period of his life, describing himself as a 'dropout' and an academic 'failure'.

While a teenager in the 1930s, Moore became mildly involved in the left-wing politics that were popular at the time, sold *Socialist Appeal* on street corners and joined the Belfast Theatre Guild. This aspect of his adolescence and the period he spent with the ARP during the war feature largely in his fifth novel, *The Emperor of Ice Cream* (1965), which is among the most directly biographical of his works.

In 1943, Brian Moore left Belfast and became a civilian employee of the British Ministry of War Transport. He was stationed in Algiers, Naples and Marseilles. He returned briefly to Belfast at the end of the war, but then got a job with UNRRA (The United Nations commission for the resettlement of refugees). His work took him to Warsaw and then he travelled as a free-lance reporter in Scandinavia and France. This period of his life has furnished him with little material for fiction, although he has traced part of the inspiration for his recent novel of Eastern Europe, *The Colour of Blood*, to a meeting with Cardinal Wyszynski of Poland in the late 1940s.

Brian Moore returned briefly to London in 1948 but then left Europe immediately for Canada. He has therefore lived away from Ireland for over forty years. In the eleven years he lived in Canada, he bought time to write serious fiction by working in succession as a proof-reader, a reporter and a pseudonymous thriller-writer. In order to write his first serious novel, *Judith Hearne*, he lived for several months in a log cabin in the Lawrentian Mountains. When *Judith Hearne* was published in 1955, it was a critical success, earning praise as a first novel and comparison with Françoise Sagan's *Bonjour Tristesse*. *The Feast of Lupercal* followed in 1957.

Although Brian Moore is a Canadian citizen and has sometimes been identified as a Canadian novelist, he has lived in the United States since 1959. In that year, he held a

Guggenheim fellowship and moved from Canada to New York. He went to California to write a film for Alfred Hitchcock, later became an adjunct professor at UCLA and eventually settled in Los Angeles. He now lives with his wife in Malibu, from where he makes frequent trips to Europe. Though he has been so long an exile, his themes and characters have almost always had an Irish connection. He seems to have remained identifiably Irish and he is regarded by many critics as Ireland's finest living novelist. He has been the recipient of many literary awards, including the Fiction award of the Governor-General of Canada, 1961 and 1975, the W. H. Smith award, 1973, the James Tait Black Memorial award, 1975, the Royal Society of Literature and Heinemann awards, 1986, and the *Sunday Express* Book of the Year award, 1987.

Brian Moore has published sixteen novels and one work of reportage, *The Revolution Script*, in a little over thirty years, from *Judith Hearne* in 1955 to his most recent work, *Lies of Silence* (April 1990). During that period he has attracted a considerable amount of critical attention, not all of it favourable, particularly in Canada and the United States, his adoptive countries, and more recently in Ireland. His work has been interpreted in many ways: he was claimed as an adoptive Canadian who dramatised the trauma of exile; he has been acclaimed as a novelist especially sensitive and attentive to the female psyche. Criticism of his work, whether in short articles or extended studies, tends to concentrate on the themes and the moral preoccupations of his novels rather than attempting any artistic evaluation of his techniques.

Thus, among the most significant interpreters of his work as a whole, Hallvard Dahlie focuses on 'his preoccupation with the loser, with the marginal character, with the individual at crisis';[3] John Wilson Foster in one of the earliest serious studies of Moore[4] and again in his book on Ulster fiction,[5] expands the idea of the individual in crisis to propose an anthropological model of 'the individuals' rejection by the community' because they fail to weather 'rites of passage' into maturity. The validity of this approach is testified to by Moore's own remark that he deliberately puts his characters into crisis in order that they should be tested in some fundamental life-searching way in a very limited period of time. Other studies have put forward other theories; for instance, in her 1974 monograph on Moore,[6] Jeanne Flood proposes a Freudian interpretation of Moore's main themes, with particular reference to *I am Mary Dunne*.

The lack of concentration on aesthetic approaches to Moore's work is probably due to several factors: firstly, because he has been and is still regarded by many as a novelist who is only barely 'serious' and scarcely literary at all (he has been too 'popular' to be 'serious' and simultaneously, to his own chagrin, too 'serious' to be a bestseller); secondly, because his is the kind of art that conceals its art. His literary persona is self-deprecatory. Thus, one of his warmest and most consistent English admirers, Christopher Ricks, entitles a very early article on his work 'The Simple Excellence of Brian Moore'[7] and praises him for writing 'transparently'. This view of Moore is recurrent, particularly perhaps among his promoters, who seem to feel the need to explain or even to apologise for what they perceive as Moore's quality of accessibility. In keeping with this tradition, Michael Paul Gallagher, in a valuable recent article, writes of Moore in almost the same terms as did Ricks twenty years earlier, approvingly but guardedly. He considers Moore:

> a marvellously transparent and non-intellectual dramat-
> iser of some key philosophical issues of our time: issues
> of epistemology (what can I believe in any more?); issues
> of psychology (who am I any more?); issues of ethics
> (what am I doing here?).[8]

The first half of this sentence is in curious contrast with the second. The implication seems to be that Moore is a serious, philosophical writer unknown to himself, or maybe despite himself, that he takes on board such heavyweight considerations by accident, or that he is a serious novelist masquerading as a popular or middle-brow one.

However, Gallagher's abiding interest in Moore's work and the importance he attaches to what he has identified as Moore's central theme have created one of the most useful critical approaches to his work. Moore's most consistent concern in his thirty years of writing novels has been belief or faith in its widest sense and that this is the theme that gives his work both coherence and significance. He has, himself, repeatedly testified to his conviction of the importance of having something to believe in. First, there is belief for its own sake:

> I've always been interested in the fact that people must believe in something—nuclear disarmament, love as a regenerating force, politics, anything.[9]

> When I discuss belief I discuss it as a question of what stops us from the *accidie* of despair, of saying we're only here to reproduce our species.[10]

Then later in Moore's work, religious faith is seen as a form of belief:

> I found, when I started to write, I became very interested in the question of faith.[11]

> . . . the virtue of having a belief in something. I began to see and to feel, as I do now, that the great lack of modern life is the lack of a belief in something greater than ourselves.[12]

Belief can mean anything an individual holds dear, an ideal, an inspiration, a goal, but it can also mean religious belief. Moore has not always perceived institutional religion (Catholicism) as a valid focus of belief, but his hostility to religion and to Catholicism in particular has gradually disappeared and he now sees spiritual faith, not just as another kind of belief but as the highest kind there is.

Moore's first two novels, *Judith Hearne* and *The Feast of Lupercal*, which are set in Belfast of the 1950s, convey a bitter and passionate rejection of the repressive Catholicism of that era and that city. This implies an assertion by Moore of the essential right of the individual to pursue a private belief and the necessity of his doing so. The protagonists of both these novels are denied this right by the Catholic Church which has formed them and which continues to dominate them, and by the society in which they live. Moore's preoccupations and style mark him in some ways as a 'Catholic' novelist, because he can be compared with other writers who were or are obsessed, in their different ways, by the effect of Catholic faith on the individual. The creation and development of such restricted and repressed characters as Judith Hearne and Diarmuid Devine are certain to have consequences for the author's style. The prevalent mode in these early novels is one of realism and the 'voice' of the protagonists is captured by a widespread use of free indirect speech which distances the authorial perspective, ironically, from that of the protagonists, while maintaining a degree of sympathy for their plight.

Of the large number of books written by Moore in the 1960s and 1970s, the best and most interesting are *An Answer from Limbo*, *I am Mary Dunne* and *The Doctor's Wife*. The protagonists of these novels are free in the sense that they have rejected the values of their families and of the Catholic religion, and have chosen exile in order to pursue their own personal beliefs. These beliefs are secular, but absorbing, even consuming, and are conveyed very much, in metaphorical terms, as quasi-religious. However, Moore, having placed his protagonists in a position of freedom, begins to ponder in these novels the morality of such secular beliefs and the consequences for the protagonists themselves of devotedly pursuing these beliefs. His disillusionment with the selfishness of much of what passes for belief begins in this period of his work and leads to the renewed respect for a higher religious faith. It is also to this secular period that

Moore's most famous novels with female protagonists belong. He broadens the scope of the term 'belief' to include sexual love, which for these women is all consuming, but which is shown to have its own pitfalls and terrors. The techniques used by Moore in these three novels are among his most interesting: he experiments particularly with perspectival modes, *I am Mary Dunne,* for instance, being written completely in first-person interior monologue. Moore dramatises guilt and anguish by a variety of methods, including a cinematic technique of shifting multiple perspectives in *The Doctor's Wife.* By the time that novel was published, it had become clear that Moore had achieved complete mastery of his art and that he could successfully create a fictional world using any number of different types of protagonists, settings, forms and techniques.

Three of Moore's more recent novels, all published in the 1980s — *The Temptation of Eileen Hughes, Cold Heaven* and *Black Robe* — mark another new departure. It is evident in these works that the author's disillusionment with secular and selfish materialism is complete. Moore returns to the possibility of religion as belief by means of the intermediate stage of mystical obsession in *The Temptation of Eileen Hughes.* With a new respect for the unselfishness of religion, unimaginable in the attitude of the author of *Judith Hearne* and *The Feast of Lupercal,* he explores the possibility of spiritual belief in contemporary society and in the missionary world of seventeenth-century Canada. Though the authorial viewpoint is still predominantly sceptical, there is a considerable degree of openness to the faith of others. The technique of these novels involves variations on realism, but with an underpinning of symbolic or metaphysical commentary which Moore uses to convey the idea of the supernatural in the secular world.

Thus Moore's attitude to belief, to religious faith and to moral questions will be seen to have developed through three stages: complete rejection of Catholicism in the early novels; an investigation of the values of personal secular beliefs in the middle period (the novels of exile of the 1960s and 1970s), with which beliefs the author gradually becomes disillusioned; finally, a return to an open interest in Catholicism. Though Moore continues to assert that, on a personal basis, he cannot share religious faith, he now sees such religious belief not only as one form of personal belief among many, but as something higher. For those who can experience it in its true, unworldly form (and, according to the evidence of Moore's novels, this is a rare phenomenon), spirituality is the highest, most rewarding, most selfless and most moral form of belief known to man. Now Moore's attitude to the faith of others is wistful rather than hostile. The change in Moore's attitude to belief and religion has been radical, but has happened gradually, over the thirty-year period in which he has been writing novels that deal with the themes of belief and faith.

The Colour of Blood (1987) may be seen as a development of the faith theme and also as evidence of a movement into a new genre, the contemporary political thriller. As a thriller, this novel is concerned less with the psychology of the protagonist and the meaning of his faith than with the public and political aspects of the Church as an institution, since Cardinal Bem is the head of that institution in his country. Until the publication of *Lies of Silence* in 1990, this novel was the most meaningful comment made by Moore on the religious and political situation in Northern Ireland since the early Belfast novels. *The Colour of Blood* is the first novel where the existence of religious faith is totally accepted in a protagonist; it is a *donnée* in the case of Cardinal Bem. Though not by any means Brian Moore's most impressive novel, *The Colour of Blood* is of interest both as a development of the theme of faith in his work and as a preparation for the direct engagement with the current situation in Northern Ireland in *Lies of Silence*.

Moore has declared that a novelist's function does not include commenting on actualities or getting involved in political issues. His own excursion into reportage, with *The Revolution Script*, was heretofore the exception to this.

Furthermore, he has put on record his own unwillingness and inability to write a novel about contemporary Belfast, the city of his birth, which he left for good in the 1940s. But in 1990, he contravened these self-imposed strictures by producing a novel, *Lies of Silence*, that deals directly with the political reality in Northern Ireland. The novel's framework is a week in the life of a Catholic hotel manager in Belfast. Michael Dillon is forced to come to terms with terrorist violence, Orange bigotry, the security forces and various shades of nationalist and republican opinion – all of these things impinging on his personal life which is itself in crisis. With this novel Moore returns to the elemental theme of his early novels – what will the individual do when faced with a crisis? – and deals in quite a different way from ever before with the topics of institutional religion and personal belief. Though this novel, in the thriller genre like *The Colour of Blood*, is, as one might expect, taut, skilfully constructed and compulsively readable, there is nothing of *simplisme* about it. Indeed, Michael Dillon is a character who has to evaluate his own deepest beliefs, not once, but several times during the time-span of the novel. Through Dillon, a character as apolitical as only a middle-class Catholic from Northern Ireland can be, Moore expresses political viewpoints surprisingly trenchant. *Lies of Silence* is a moral study, not didactic, but encompassing much more human and political complexity than does the normal thriller's moral universe.

As a novelist, Brian Moore always creates a plausible world by the techniques he employs. He is a master of plot, extremely skilled in his exploitation of different points of view, and, above all, *interesting*. Though he never produces novels of great length, his works are consistently thought-provoking, ambitious, experimental, at least in his pairing of technique and subject matter. He is never a miniaturist; his works are too serious for that. His latest novel, *Lies of Silence*, shows his artistic courage in approaching subject matter that, until recently, he himself would not have considered possible.

SECTION I

The Early Belfast Novels

1
Beleaguered Catholicism

IT may be argued that none of Moore's protagonists is free, though the search for freedom and self-expression is one of his major themes, and that fatalism or determinism is one of the most consistent attributes of his writing. Although this argument contains a great deal of truth, it is nevertheless possible to illustrate that only in Moore's first two novels, the novels of Belfast life in the 1950s, is his picture of life so bleakly pessimistic as to appear totally deterministic. Both *Judith Hearne* and *The Feast of Lupercal* are anti-religious and anti-Catholic because religion, far from liberating or empowering Judith Hearne or Diarmuid Devine, is the power that enslaves them. It is not merely a spiritual slavery, though that too exists, but because the society they live in (the Catholic portion of Belfast society) has adopted completely the tenets of Catholicism, particularly the repression of sexuality, and has hardened and codified these tenets into social interdiction. It is a slavery of the whole personality and even of the unconscious psyche.

Although all of Catholic Ireland was rigidly and puritanically religious in the 1950s, and this is testified to by the writers of the period, Moore's novels bear witness to the fact that a unique set of circumstances obtained in Northern Ireland. The title of John Cronin's 1969 article 'Ulster's Alarming Novels' indicates the writer's perception of the embitterment that was pervasive in Ulster fiction of the previous decades. In Cronin's opinion, writers such as Moore, by dwelling morbidly on bigotry and frustration, failed to transcend the sectarian divide:

> Ulster's malaise is nowhere more clearly exposed than in its novels where the region's odious sectarian split is

depressingly and constantly depicted and images of solitude, despair and frustration abound. Northern Ireland's dreary doctrinal duality has invaded even its literature, the one place where we might have looked for a vision capable of transcending an intolerable situation. You will look in vain in the novels of Ulster for the healing wisdom which a truly great novelist can bring . . .

Ulster, with its segregated schools, its residential ghettos and its neanderthal politics produces novelists who reflect its sectarian schizophrenia. Catholic novelists emerge as either elegiac or embittered, the work of the former being characterised by a plangently mournful quality as with Michael McLaverty, that of the latter by a mordant savagery as with Brian Moore . . .

A region's literature ought to transcend its habits; the failure of Ulster writing in this respect is an index of the place's cultural primitivism.[1]

This severe criticism of Moore may be justified as regards his early novels, but is certainly not so for his work after *An Answer from Limbo*. Moore's embittered attitude towards Belfast society found expression, it is certainly true to say, in novels of extreme hostility, but it could equally be argued that if all writers sought to 'transcend' [the region's] habits, to paraphrase Cronin's words, there would then be grounds for accusing them of escapism. The question of whether it is proper for a writer to transcend his society or to reflect his society will always be a subject of debate. In *Judith Hearne* and *The Feast of Lupercal* Moore certainly chose to reflect his society, both as a means of exorcising his personal bitterness towards Northern Ireland and towards Catholicism in particular, and as a means of making a political statement. His religious and political vision may, in this instance, appear completely negative, but if these early novels are examined in association with his later work, then it can be seen that he does assert a positive value as well. *Judith Hearne* and *The*

Feast of Lupercal assert a positive value negatively, as it were. What is present in these early novels is religion; what is lacking are freedom and genuine belief. All of Moore's novels, in one way or another, explore the search for belief. The negative beginning is Moore's way of casting off religious attitudes that he, at the time of writing the novels, saw as being completely negative and life denying.

In both these early novels, but especially in *The Feast of Lupercal*, can be seen the defensiveness of a beleaguered minority which is conscious simultaneously of the reality of its political impotence and of the myth of its religious superiority. Reality and myth become fused, and the result is exemplified by the weird mixture of inferiority and religious superiority which characterises Diarmuid Devine's meetings with Protestants and his love for a Protestant girl. Looked at like this, the situation can be stated simply, if perhaps unsubtly (from a reading of Moore's novels only, not of any wider area): Catholics fear Protestants who are more powerful politically and economically; Catholics, like all those who are in some way powerless, take their revenge: they despise Protestants for not being blessed with the one true faith, suspect all Protestants of being depraved and immoral and seek to preserve their own racial and religious purity by keeping their club as exclusive as possible. Thence the obstacles, amounting almost to an interdiction, put in the way of Catholics who contemplate marrying Protestants, as Diarmuid Devine feebly does in *The Feast of Lupercal*.

A second element of repression which shapes the lives of Moore's Belfast protagonists is the influence of the majority religion to which they do not belong, but which controls the public aspects of their lives. Moore's bitterness in the novels is therefore not directed solely at Catholicism, though it is primarily so, but indirectly at the majority religion. His detailed focus is on Catholicism, but inasmuch as his novels are political, his criticism also encompasses indirectly the religion that controls the institutions of the state: 'I felt, and I feel that both Protestantism and Catholicism in Northern

Ireland are the most desperate tragedies that can happen to people . . . I feel there should be a pox on both their houses.'² In a way, the Belfast Catholics who are Moore's protagonists could be said to have the worst of both worlds: the paranoia of the minority within their own community; the dour Sabbatarianism of the majority imposed from outside. *Judith Hearne*, in particular, is coloured by this dismal atmosphere, because Judith is forced by the misery of her circumstances to spend so much time out of doors. Of his own experience of living in Belfast, Moore has said: 'I found it a very repressive place to live' and 'We all lived in a Catholic ghetto at that time.'³ An examination of *Judith Hearne* and *The Feast of Lupercal* will show protagonists trapped beyond all hope of escape by the cultural, economic and religious conditions of their time; in other words, trapped in a Catholic ghetto of the mind.

Judith Hearne and Diarmuid Devine are certainly weak characters who would be failures in any society, but in the novels, Moore goes to great lengths to show them as products of their particular society. Since childhood they have been shaped in compliancy, moulded by expectations, shown no way of change, even discouraged from contemplating change. Change is dangerous; the option of change denotes freedom. It is the object of society in these novels to prevent both freedom and change. The fact that all societies are to some extent interested in preserving the status quo and resistant to change highlights rather than excuses the extraordinary conservatism of the society in question here. John Wilson Foster makes just this point in his study of Ulster fiction:

> Devine's faintheartedness and Judith Hearne's timidity and plainness suggest that they would be losers wherever they lived. But if there is a terrible inevitability about their fates, the specific counts on which the community indicts them are wholly unreasonable and

are themselves indictments of an unchanging static society.[4]

In fact, to extend Foster's legal metaphor, the community is guilty on two counts, one obvious, one more deep-seated. It creates Judith Hearne and Diarmuid Devine and then punishes them for being what they are.

To look closely at these two early novels is to realise the extent of Moore's hostility to traditional Catholicism and to the kind of society that it formed. The bitterness and despair of these novels also come into sharp relief when they are compared with his later novels and when Judith Hearne and Diarmuid Devine are contrasted with other Moore protagonists. In his later works, Moore is interested in showing the limiting factors which prevent people from following beliefs which are important to them, but a simple comparison will reveal how free all these other protagonists are, even in their apparent lack of freedom, when compared to the Belfast protagonists. This may appear paradoxical, since in the first two novels, Moore is dealing with pressures of society and religion, which, in theory can be cast off, rather than with more subtle factors of psychology or personality. In theory, Judith Hearne or Diarmuid Devine could leave Belfast and free themselves at once from the tyranny of Catholicism and from their minority status. In practice, society's greatest deprivation has been to deprive them even of the volition to do this. These characters can be said to be non-starters, whereas to look at two novels where other forms of determinism are in operation, *Fergus* and *I am Mary Dunne*, is to notice, instead, protagonists whose freedom is obstructed in some way, but who are certainly not deprived of all freedom. In *Fergus*, one sees the inescapable psychic influence of the family at work: this is a theme Moore takes seriously, yet he treats it, in this novel, largely in a comic manner. In *I am Mary Dunne*, the ineluctable fact of her gender oppresses Mary, because she perceives herself as a victim of her body and of the men she has married. Yet what emerges from these novels is that no one factor will impede the convinced individual in the pursuit of his beliefs, if not in their fulfilment. The whole of society combines to produce just this impediment to belief in *The Feast of Lupercal* and to prevent Judith Hearne from having or even envisaging an alternative belief in *Judith Hearne*. Catholicism is shown, therefore, in a completely negative light, shown as caring only for the observance of religion rather than for fundamental belief and as simultaneously preventing development in any other direction.

Perhaps paradoxically for a novelist so inclined to perceive his protagonists as unfree, Moore's novels do not contain the element of religious determinism that connotes the absence of free will. Time and time again, in his later novels, his protagonists refuse to believe or cease to believe or have serious doubts about their faith. This is true of characters in religious life like the Abbot in *Catholics* and Father Laforgue in *Black Robe* just as much as of representatives of secular post-Christian America like Marie Davenport in *Cold Heaven*. Judith Hearne ceases to believe, but if she merely expressed her unbelief quietly to herself in her dingy bedroom, there is no sense conveyed in the novel that divine retribution would fall on her. Her unbelief has consequences for herself and for others that are connected with society rather than with spirituality. Her loss of faith is a manifestation of the despair that arises out of loneliness, penury and the resultant alcoholism. When her hope crumbles, she has no defences which would keep her respectable and tolerable in society. Faced with the full horror of her situation and unable to delude herself any longer, she screams, shouts abuse and becomes hysterical in her behaviour. She undergoes what might be termed a breakdown, which is not surprising; since reality is so horrible as to defy contemplation, she turns her back on it altogether. Thus, she breaks one of the deepest taboos of her society: that one must stay quiet, respectable and in control and above all respectful to the clergy. The scene she makes in the church and the fact that she has become a burden is of much more concern to the people involved than the fact that she has lost her faith.

Much of the interest in Moore's novels over the past thirty years has focused on his attitude to Catholicism in its public manifestations and to the question of individual belief. He is frequently considered a 'Catholic' novelist, but he is surely an enigma or even unique in being a 'Catholic' novelist who has lost his faith and who therefore is much more interested, on the whole, in people who lose or have lost theirs. He is himself aware of the strangeness of this situation: 'this seems rather odd, because I keep writing about Catholicism all the time'.[5] By this remark, he appears to recognise that even when he is not writing officially or overtly about Catholicism, he is still writing about it—in other words, if not about the presence of Catholic belief, then about its absence. Though Mauriac is a novelist with whom Moore has been compared and with whom he has compared himself, Moore is the living denial of Mauriac's conviction about himself and other Catholics that 'He had not been free to choose or reject Catholicism for he was born a Catholic.'[6]

Moore chooses, instead, to adopt the point of view of another 'Catholic' novelist, Graham Greene, with whom he has been compared, a point of view in its way just as fatalistic as Mauriac's, but more Calvinistic, carrying echoes of predestination. 'Graham Greene says that faith is a gift and I believe that he is absolutely right. And I felt it was a gift that I wasn't given.'[7] This remark, which Moore made recently and which contains a certain element of wistfulness, certainly does not reflect the full complexity of his relationship with Catholicism. Perhaps lack of faith was an element, but there is certainly also evident in his earlier comments and in these early novels, an emotional rejection ('Like most children who turn from religion, my motives were emotional and confused.')[8] which changed into bitterness. This is the reason for the overwhelming sense of bitterness, meanness and despair in *Judith Hearne* and *The Feast of Lupercal*. The awfulness of

Catholicism emerges so strongly from these novels that it is difficult to imagine the writer ever becoming reconciled with any aspect of the religion. And yet, this did happen: Moore reaches a *rapprochement* with the idea and values of Catholic belief, if not with the belief itself. But he approaches it as a free agent, just as he has his protagonist, Marie Davenport, do, in one of his most recent novels of faith, *Cold Heaven*.

As a Catholic writer, Moore's position is unusual or even unique in that his later *rapprochement* with Catholicism seems largely a result of his disillusion with secularism. It is interesting in this respect, to compare Moore with Evelyn Waugh, a 'Catholic' novelist who exhibits in his novels a combination of the zeal of the converted and a hankering after ancient nobility, and finds both the zeal and the nobility exemplified in the rarified English Catholic aristocracy. Waugh wrote that he saw *Brideshead Revisited* as 'an attempt to trace the divine purpose in a pagan world' where people escape from God, or appear to do so, in order to follow secular desires, but God brings them back with 'a twitch upon a thread'.[9] Moore does not have this perception of God's omnipotence or of the ultimate and tragic absence of free will on which Waugh's vision of human life is predicated (for Charles Ryder and Julia Flyte in *Brideshead Revisited*). Indeed, Moore has explicitly rejected comparison with Waugh and with some justification: not only does he not attach any credence to the 'twitch upon the thread' idea, but he is libertarian in his attitudes in a manner conspicuously not shared by Waugh or, indeed, with other Catholic writers of Waugh's generation. Of Waugh, Moore has said: 'I consider him a total shit politically and a total sycophant in many ways, an aper and a toady to the British class system.'[10] While Moore read Auden (who served in a republican ambulance brigade) and Clifford Odets and Louis MacNeice in the 1930s, Waugh was announcing his support for Franco's rebellion in Spain. While it would be simplistic and untrue to say that all Catholic writers are as reactionary as Waugh or his contemporary Roy Campbell (who fought on the Francoist side) or as the crypto-Fascist French writer, Claudel, another convert to Catholicism, the Spanish Civil War did tend to align traditional Catholics on the traditional Catholic side, the Francoist. This is Moore's recollection of the late 1930s:

> Well, the left-wing thing was in the air at that time. I remember getting *The Faber Book of Modern Verse* and trying to find out more about people like Auden and Isherwood. At the end of the Thirties political discontent was popular the way rock music is popular today and I latched on to this at once . . . So that led me, while I was still at school, to the Belfast Theatre Guild—people like Bernard Barnett and Harold Goldblatt who were Jews. It was great for me. It was very liberating.[11]

Though Moore is inclined, with hindsight, to treat this boyish enthusiasm lightly, his conception of political activity as 'liberating' is very significant. It is a freely chosen belief, an alternative to Catholicism, both as a faith and as an alternative political structure, a different way of ordering the world. In another interview Moore identifies, more seriously, a 'political' purpose in his early writing:

> I do believe that for a novelist to have something to react against, to have something to fight against, to be dissatisfied, to be an outsider, to be a person who has some almost moralistic mission to correct what he considers to be an injustice or a wrong way of living, is probably his strength, will start him writing and may even keep him writing.[12]

Moore has written little that has an overtly political subject, with the exception of the little-read *The Revolution Script* (1971), which he himself does not regard highly, and he has returned to such matters only in his most recent novels, the contemporary political/religious parable, *The Colour of Blood* and also *Lies of Silence*. But given the political climate of his youth and the stance he took in the 1930s and 1940s, it should not be ignored that in *Judith Hearne* and *The Feast of Lupercal*,

Moore treats Catholicism as a political system, that is political in the widest sense, relating to the role of the individual in the community. He made a revealing remark to this effect in an interview given shortly after the escalation of the present Northern troubles:

> I don't think the real issue is religious. The analogy in the States is the poor whites and the blacks: most Ulster Protestants are the poor whites and the Catholics are the blacks.[13]

To call Moore a 'political' religious novelist is not to label him narrowly, but to define his tendency as libertarian. He does not share with other 'Catholic' writers such as Waugh, Mauriac, Greene or Claudel, a preoccupation with the great Catholic legacy of guilt and sin; nor, as has been demonstrated, does he bring to his writing a perception of the inescapable grasp of Catholicism and of the reach of God's power. In his early novels, spirituality is not his interest: Catholic society is. It is therefore as a libertarian that it is interesting to consider Moore's attitude to religion. As a libertarian he rejects religious totalitarianism along with the bigotry that is symptomatic of all totalitarian systems but which is particularly enhanced by the political climate of Belfast. In later works he also rejects the totalitarianism of the secular cult of self-gratification with which the modern world has replaced Christianity. The increased tolerance of Catholicism as well as his disillusion with the secular world have induced Moore again to become interested in and sympathetic towards Catholicism. However, it is fundamental to his ideas and to his writings that he lacks and has always lacked two primary characteristics of the typical 'Catholic' writer— firstly, a very sceptical attitude towards free will, and secondly, a sense of the inevitability of sin which derives from the Manichaean doctrine of duality and which is so striking, for instance, in Graham Greene's novels. It is these two characteristics that set truly Catholic novelists apart

and give them a definite—albeit morbid and pessimistic—
fascination even for unbelievers. But, lacking these attitudes,
Moore has his own interest and his own originality in writing
about Catholicism. Those who consider Moore an apostate to
unbelief in his most recent novels, tend, therefore, not to
have taken into account how closely his abhorrence of
Catholicism depended on the particular circumstances of
mid-century Catholic Belfast. If those circumstances no
longer obtained, his bitterness towards Catholicism would
not be so great. Secondly, his rejection of Catholicism was
emotional and perhaps therefore reversible, as opposed to
intellectual and irreversible. One could not imagine such a
backsliding on the part of, for example, a rigorous Utilitarian
intellectual such as James Mill whose attitude to Christianity,
strongly inculcated in his son, is described by that son, John
Stuart Mill, in his *Autobiography*:

> Think (he used to say) of a being who would make a
> Hell—who would create the human race with the infal-
> lible knowledge, and therefore with the intention, that
> the great majority of them were to be consigned to
> horrible and everlasting torment . . . My father was as
> well aware as anyone that Christians do not, in general,
> undergo the demoralising consequences which seem
> inherent in such a creed, in the manner or to the extent to
> which might have been expected from it. The same
> slovenliness of thought, and subjection of the reason to
> fears, wishes and affections, which enable them to accept
> a theory involving a contradiction in terms, prevents
> them from perceiving the logical consequences of the
> theory.[14]

The flexibility of thought which can accommodate contradic-
tions and paradoxes can be found not only in those who
adhere to Christian belief but in those who reject it on
emotional grounds but find themselves attracted to it again at
a later stage. It is precisely such an accommodation of

paradox that is at the heart of Moore's *Cold Heaven*; it is probably the only spirit in which an unbeliever can write of belief. (It is also the spirit of poetry or creativity, memorably characterised by Keats as 'negative capability', rather than of the political economy which was the interest of James Mill.)

Judith Hearne and *The Feast of Lupercal* can be read as political novels because they are concerned with the way people live in a society that is hidebound by repression. Neither Judith Hearne nor Diarmuid Devine is a rebel, but both are in different ways outcasts, because, through no fault of their own, they fall foul of society's strictures: Judith, because she is the victim of despair, Devine, because he falls in love with a girl of the enemy camp, a Capulet to his Montague. It is much more plausible, psychologically, that they should be totally defeated by society than that they should rebel or escape. Moore is an emotional humanist rather than a rigorous intellectual. He rejects the tyranny of Church-dominated society, exploring in his early novels the stultifying effects of such a society on the individual. In doing this, he appears to be rejecting Catholicism, but it must be remembered that it is a particular type of Catholicism that he is rejecting. It was many years before Moore became so disillusioned with the new tyranny of secular materialism that he began to look elsewhere for moral values and self-transcendence. He found these, to some extent, in Catholicism of a more liberal kind. For Moore in his most recent novels, Catholicism and belief have become more compatible, although not always in an orthodox or predictable way.

A pillar of Moore's artistic structure in all his novels is the question of personal belief.[15] From the point of view of the first two novels, belief is impossible. Catholicism is possible, certainly, but for Moore, the essence of belief is not that one is born into it and somehow fated to have it, but that it is freely chosen; in *Judith Hearne* and *The Feast of Lupercal*, Catholicism is not freely chosen. If the Catholic faith is a 'gift' and not a 'choice', as Moore, according to the remark quoted earlier, seems still to think, a paradox arises here: can one freely choose a 'gift'? Or does the freedom arise in the ability to accept or reject that 'gift'? In any case, the Catholicism of the first novels is not free and is not based on any deep personal faith on the part of the protagonists. It is, instead, inculcated from an early age and imposed by society. For Judith Hearne and Diarmuid Devine, real belief is impossible. Judith is too caught up in poverty and too desperate for illusion even to envisage a belief. A belief involves some knowledge of oneself; Judith has none. Devine is prevented from prosecuting his belief, his love for Una Clarke (which in any case, is partly founded on delusion and a romanticisation of himself) by the taboos of his society and of his job. Despite the differences between the two characters—Devine, because of his sex and his economic sufficiency, is less pathetic and powerless than Judith—the difference is primarily one of degree, not of essence. Moore certainly conceived of the two novels as depicting the same type of character, imprisoned in the same society. For him, the first led to the second:

> I felt that in *Judith Hearne* I had written about somebody losing faith and it then occurred to me to ask what was the education, the religious education and the background, which maybe destroyed that woman's life—she was a 'Sacred Heart' girl. And so I became interested in a schoolmaster character and in how much that kind of education makes cowards of us all—because we have to live in the community, we can't just walk away from it.[16]

This remark exactly sums up Moore's preoccupations in these early novels: the political sense of the powerlessness of the individual in Catholic society: the individual who is powerless not only in the actual, but fated to be powerless, indeed reared and educated to be powerless. This 'cowardice' prevents his protagonists from pursuing an alternative belief by keeping them shackled to the observance of a form of Catholicism which has no real spiritual meaning, but exists only as a political tyranny.

2

Religion without Belief—
Judith Hearne

MOORE has spoken and written of *Judith Hearne* as a novel of faith and also as a novel of failure. It represents the religious 'climate' of Belfast in the 1950s, as perceived by the wounded sensibilities of the involuntary exile. For Moore, the writer who has escaped, it is an evocation of what he has escaped and also of the factors which made it imperative for him to escape. It is greatly coloured by personal bitterness.

> I discovered in writing it what I really felt about my past. I left Ireland with the intention of not going back, but my reasons became clear only when I wrote that first novel. It was then that my bitterness against the bigotry in Northern Ireland, my feelings about the narrowness of life there, and, in a sense, my loneliness when living as an exile in Canada, all focused to produce a novel about what I felt the climate of Ulster to be.[1]

The bitterness in the evocation of the climate of Ulster is conveyed by many different elements: Judith's own lack of a steadfast personal faith and the manner in which faith for her is tied up with gentility and tradition; the anti-clericalism of Moore's depiction of the Catholic clergy as represented by Father Quigley; the attitudes of Judith's community to her and especially the hypocrisy of the righteous Catholics in Mrs Rice's boarding-house; the sordid detail of Judith's life and the techniques used by the author to convey her 'voice'.

Judith's attitude towards religion is itself revealed as being based on observance rather than belief. Religion is not something that inspires her or influences the way she behaves, but something that for her, for most of the novel, is an accepted and unquestioned part of conventional life. Thus does Moore highlight the difference between real personal belief and mere organised religion. In the chapter where Moore shows Judith and Madden going to Mass together, he analyses the religious attitudes of both. This is Judith's:

> She was not, she sometimes chided herself, a particularly religious person. She had never been able to take much interest in the Children of Mary, the Foreign Missions, the decoration of altars or any of the other good causes in which married and single ladies devote themselves to God and his Blessed Mother. No, she had followed her Aunt's lead in that. Church affairs, her aunt once said, tend to put one in contact with all sorts of people whom one would prefer not to know socially. Prayer and a rigorous attention to one's religious duties will contribute far more towards one's personal salvation than the bickering that goes on about Church bazaars. Miss Hearne had her lifelong devotion to the Sacred Heart. He was her guide and comforter. And her terrible judge. She had a special saint, to whom she addressed her novenas: Anne, mother of Mary traditional recourse of spinsters desperate for marriage]. She used to have a special confessor, old Father Farrelly, Rest in Peace. She had never missed Sunday Mass in her life, except for real illness. She had made the Nine Fridays every year for as long as she could remember. She went to evening devotions regularly and never a day since her First Communion had she missed saying her prayers.
>
> Religion was there: it was not something you thought about, and if, occasionally, you had a small doubt about something in the way Church affairs were carried on, or something that seemed wrong or silly, well, that was the Devil at work and God's ways were not our ways.[2]

The attitude revealed in this passage is a most joyless mixture of snobbery, devotionalism and observance without any solid basis or any real sense of transcendence or spirituality. In this passage is evident the meanness of Belfast lay Catholicism: to alter Moore's analogy quoted earlier, poor whites looking down on poorer whites. The social outlet which is an important function of religion in a community — and in the aftermath of the changes of Vatican II, the lay community is seen as having a vital importance in Catholic parish life, going far beyond altar flowers or church bazaars — is denied Judith by her Aunt d'Arcy's interdiction: for Judith, who has no real friends, it might have been worth risking the 'bickering that goes on about church bazaars' in order to meet like-minded devout ladies. The phrase is, however, a criticism of Catholicism in two ways, a double-edged sword. It criticises not only snobbery but the prevailing lack of charity and unity which gives the likes of Aunt d'Arcy an excuse to distance herself. This snobbery is, in a way, an inverse reflection, a consequence of Protestant bigotry: Aunt d'Arcy's friends, the Breens and the O'Neills would be representatives of the numerically small Catholic professional elite to which Moore's own family also belonged and whose values are reflected by the authoritarian father-figure, the censorious and successful doctor or solicitor in so many of his novels. Aunt d'Arcy would therefore be anxious to avoid contamination by the Catholic *hoi polloi*, and this is the attitude she has passed on to Judith. This exclusiveness is a negation of everything that is valued by Christianity, and, furthermore, these snobbish values have done nothing but disservice to Judith in her normal social intercourse. It is an example of the true basis of religion being stood on its head in order to accommodate and even to foster illusory feelings of superiority.

The second element of Judith's religion, devotionalism, is a quality that has traditionally been much promoted by the Catholic authorities. (This is no longer the case.) It was part of an outlook that saw religion as being primarily an external matter of people being on their knees in the church, preferably all at the same appointed time. Encouraging large attendance not just at Sunday Mass, but at Mass at other times (Judith mentions the devotion of attending Mass on nine consecutive first Fridays in honour of the Sacred Heart) and at devotions, was part of the hierarchy's tactics to emphasise communal prayer at the expense of personal communion. The communal element consisted either in repeating prayers by rote or assisting, uncomprehendingly, at a Mass in Latin. For the Catholic clergy, it had the advantage of keeping the congregation docile by denying them any individual voice. Devotionalism also took the form of establishing a particular personal attachment to a saint or saints (here Saint Anne) or even the deity. Judith's oleograph of the Sacred Heart is a talisman that goes everywhere with her. She invests him with human qualities which reveal more of her own needs than any sense of a deity. For her, he is an incompatible combination of best friend, counsellor/therapist and 'terrible judge'. As the novel progresses and Judith indulges repeatedly and desperately in the deadly sin of gluttony (drunkenness), it appears increasingly obvious that the Sacred Heart cannot sustain this triumvirate of roles. When this image of the Sacred Heart which she has created and sustained fails, she has no basis for believing in him any longer. She has no sense of God. She makes demands—that she should be furnished with a sign—that cannot possibly be met.

On the second occasion Judith is shown at Mass, after James Madden has rejected her with brutal frankness, religion is shown to be of no comfort to her. Now it is just observance without even the pretence of devotion: 'The Our Fathers and Hail Marys stumbled through her mind, repeating themselves until they were meaningless, as hurried and without devotion as the mumbled responses of the altarboys.' (139) Indeed, there is no true piety anywhere in the novel. The official representatives of the Church, the altarboys and the priest, simply go through the motions:

> The priest rushed ahead to the Offertory. (60) After mumbled prayers for the dead . . . (65) As Father Quigley droned . . . (65) Then he began in rapid Latin . . . (66)

No doubt there are many fervent, spiritual and charitable Catholics, and no doubt there were many such in the Belfast of the 1950s, but they certainly do not play a role in this novel. Moore might well be accused of bias in his one-sided portrayal of Catholicism. For the author, the same artistic problem could be said to exist here as in his novels with religious themes, *Cold Heaven* and *Black Robe*: how can an unbeliever represent the reality of religious belief? It is certainly much easier to seize on the negative aspects, many of which undoubtedly presented themselves especially at that time, than to do what Moore has done more recently — that is to say, to validate religious and transcendental experience without sharing it. It is very easy to denigrate religion by seizing on the external aspects of devotion and observance that exist without an accompanying fervent belief and especially easy in an Irish context, to criticise the over-powerful clergy. But if faith is by its nature personal and by its essence not susceptible of communication or explanation, the unbeliever, in a sense, should tread warily when trying to convey it. Moore comes to terms with this problem in his most recent novels and writes successfully about characters with a genuine gift of faith, even if he cannot attempt to analyse that faith. But such is his bitterness in his two early novels that the bitterness applies to all aspects of religion, the personal and the institutional.

In *Judith Hearne* the depiction of Father Quigley, which is so harsh as to be savage, shows that anti-clericalism is the strongest element of the criticism of Catholicism in the novel. As illustrated earlier, Father Quigley's prayers in English and in Latin, are cursory and mumbled, but his homily is most enthusiastic. This can be seen even from Moore's choice of the contrasting adverb 'slowly' to describe the priest's mounting of the pulpit, his orchestration of his appearance and the deliberate drama of his production with which even the weather conspires: 'this sombre preliminary lighting.' (61–62) The Mass is a routine, but the sermon is a dramatic event. Moore conveys this event in a passage of literary bravura: the dramatic lighting, the priest's Jesuitical 'hollow-cheeked' asceticism; the effectiveness of the accusing 'long spatulate' finger; the intemperance of the harangue with which he lashes his congregation; the incongruous combination of threats of hell-fire and a housewifely concern for the cleanliness of his church. Above all, what emerges is the priest's complete assumption of power over his congregation. Irony too is evident when he climaxes his denunciation with '"They don't have time for God"', (64) in view of the verbs and adverbs used by Moore both before and after the sermon to show Father Quigley's own haste in the conduct of the Mass. The whole scene is so violently anti-clerical that it seems that Father Quigley is, if not a caricature, a combination of all the worst defects observed or imaginable in a Catholic priest. If it were not so serious, this portion of his sermon would appear almost laughable, but it is bitter comedy:

> They've got time for sin, time for naked dancing girls in the cinema, time to get drunk . . . time to spend hours making up their football pools, time to spend in beauty parlours, time to go to foreign dances instead of *ceilidhes*, time to dance the tango and the foxtrot and the jitterbugging, time to read trashy books and indecent magazines, time to do any blessed thing you could care to mention. Except one.
> They-don't-have-time-for-God. (64)

Foreign means bad; Gaelic means Catholic. Twenty years earlier clerics all over Ireland were fulminating against barn and cross-road dances as hotbeds of vice; in the 1950s Irish dances are the lesser of two evils. The falling off in the general moral tone of Father Quigley's parishioners which is to be inferred from their betrayal of their Gaelic/Catholic heritage and their indulgence in 'foreign' pastimes and

'foreign vices' must be resisted. Observance and the appearance of devotion must be reinforced or imposed. Again, it is a
curious clerical irony that Father Quigley should make assumptions about the fidelity to Catholic doctrine of his
congregation, assumptions based on the outward evidence of
their leisure activities, while being anxious, later on in the
novel, to ignore Judith's genuine confession of loss of faith.
On an individual basis, he is quite unequipped to deal with
such a confession. He has been trained to be interested only
in the political control that comes from the browbeating of the
masses, not in the trauma of a pathetic spinster. During her
confession to him, Judith realises this:

> But she stopped speaking. She had seen his face. A
> weary face, his cheek resting in the palm of his hand, his
> eyes shut. He's not listening, her mind cried. Not
> listening! (172)

Judith is so obviously punctilious and scrupulous that he has
no fears for her. His main requirements are the observance,
the punctuality and the unquestioning obedience of all the
members of his Catholic congregation.

Moore's criticism of Father Quigley, which continues and
intensifies in the penultimate section of the novel—that of
Judith's breakdown—should not really be seen as criticism of
an individual, because a priest, after all, must also be
considered a person with human feelings. As criticism of an
individual, it is as intemperate as the priest's own sermon
and might be considered an artistic flaw. But it is really a
criticism of the whole repressive Catholic system whose
failings one man is made to embody. This aspect emerges
strongly from the contrast between the intolerant and unsympathetic Father Quigley who witnesses Judith's hysteria and
the chastened priest who visits her in Earnscliffe Home near
the end of the novel. In the earlier instance, his reaction to
her despair is gruff: '"Now, you listen to me . . . go home
and sober up and examine your conscience while you're at

it."' (206) and he is quite unable to view the human misery he sees in front of him from a point of view other than the confessor's. Confession and guilt are what he offers her when she needs sympathy: '"You should be grateful that God hasn't punished you worse, mortal sin on your soul and you not in a fit condition to receive absolution."' (207) He is much more humane towards Judith on his final appearance in the novel, but even here, the form his humanity takes is an indictment of the bankruptcy of the religion he promotes. After helpless attempts to offer spiritual comfort, he falls back on the same confession which was all he could offer her at the time of her breakdown: '"Well, if I were you, I'd make an effort to go as soon as you feel up to it. I'd be very glad to hear your confession now, if you like."' (215) He sees no way of treating her illness except as guilt. For the reader, if not for the broken, alcoholic Judith, the irony is bitter: some weeks earlier, the same priest had refused her guidance, comfort or even a proper hearing in confession. It is symptomatic of the blinkered nature of his views and his training. Earlier, there was no sin, merely scruples; now he has the security of the sin of blasphemy to guide him in his treatment of this woman. She has committed the sin of blasphemy in the church and he will be happy to revert to his traditional role, the role in which he was trained: he will be the confessor, the judge who takes the place of God; she will be the sinner looking for absolution. The institution of confession has traditionally been the strongest means used by the Catholic clergy of maintaining control over the individual, rather than the masses. In this ritual, the priest is always in the position of power, the sinner is always the supplicant. This is the role in which Father Quigley has been trained.

For the unscrupulous, on the other hand, confession is merely an exercise in hypocrisy. Judith's is not the only version of Catholicism that Moore gives in the novel. James Madden, sadistic sensualist and bully, goes to Mass and places himself in 'an attitude of prayer'. He is a cynical

Catholic of the type that flourishes in an atmosphere that lays the main emphasis on outward observance and devotion. James Madden thinks:

> This was religion. Religion was begging God's pardon on a morning like this one when the drink had made your mouth dry and the thing that happened last night with the serving girl was painful to think about. It was making your Easter duty once a year, going to Mass on Sunday morning. Religion was insurance. It meant you got security afterwards. It meant you could always turn over a new leaf . . . Mr Madden rarely thought of Purgatory, of penance. Confession and resultant absolution were the pillars of his faith. He found it comforting to start out as often as possible with a clean slate, a new and promising future. (58)

Madden is a rationaliser *par excellence*. He has been reared to fear the judgment of God, so despite the lack of any real belief, he continues to abide by the confession/absolution model. For him, confession consists of the cathartic element only. The high ideals of penance and absolution are degraded by his phrase 'as often as possible with a clean slate'. There is authorial irony in this passage, in the movement from free indirect speech to convey Madden's thought to the distancing effect of 'Mr Madden rarely thought . . .' This depiction of Madden's 'philosophy' reinforces the picture of official Catholic belief and observance created by the characterisation of the religion of Judith and the ministering of Father Quigley.

To compound his condemnation of Catholicism in the novel, Moore shows both the Catholic clergy and the Catholic laity as being sectarian. Again, Father Quigley represents the clergy. A small but telling detail is the thought that Moore puts into Father Quigley's head as he prepares to turn Judith from the presbytery: because the taxi-driver calls him: 'Sir' and not 'Father', he thinks 'The taxi-man was a Protestant. Nice thing for him to see.' (206) and a little later 'it was very awkward in front of the Protestant taxi-driver'. (207) The obsession of the Catholic Church with appearances and with regimentation and its siege mentality are nowhere better represented than by these slight remarks.

With this example from the clergy, it is no wonder that the laity have such defensive attitudes. Sectarianism is evident at the breakfast table in Mrs Rice's house, when Lenehan, in the arid currency of bigotry, accuses Madden of being an 'Orangeman' rather than an 'Irishman'. (40) Moore chooses Lenehan and Miss Friel at the breakfast-table on this and subsequent occasions to represent two strands of Catholic opinion, both equally narrow-minded. His is the Catholic = Gaelic version of nationalism while she represents pious rather than political bigotry; above all, she is concerned with upholding temperance and what she sees as exclusively Catholic values. Neither character is developed to any great depth, but Moore has considerable skill in creating life-like and convincing minor figures. Belfast Catholicism at its most virulent comes out in the round-robin sequence in chapter 6, which Moore uses to represent the views of the other occupants of the house on Judith, and where Miss Friel and Lenehan give vent to their pious or nationalistic bigotry: (Lenehan): 'I tell you the most of the Catholics in this town are bloody little West Britons', (81) (equating of Catholic with nationalist/Irishman), and (Miss Friel): 'When I think that most of the publicans here are Catholics, it makes me see red.' (81) (the myth of the religious and moral superiority of Catholics). In the terrible breakfast-table scene (127) after Judith's lapse into drunkenness, when she has to undergo her earthly 'penance' or 'passion' in one of the many possible interpretations of the title, charity and compassion are very far from her companions' minds: '"A nice thing for a Catholic house"', says Miss Friel, showing the same horror of any sign of weakness in the Catholic chain-mail of religious superiority. Mr Lenehan can only leer in hypocritical 'sympathy', rejoicing, no doubt, to see this 'castle' Catholic brought so low. This is indeed what John Wilson Foster calls a 'compassionless Church and a compassionless society'.[3]

Both the Church and the community are too busy being defensive and keeping moral subversion at bay to have time for compassion. The lack of human sympathy that characterises the society is signalled very early in the novel by the description of the dining-room and its occupants as they appear on the morning of Judith's first breakfast in Mrs Rice's house. On pages 22 to 23, Moore's highly metaphorical style is not used to suggest any beauty or relief in the dreary life of Judith Hearne. In Mrs Rice's dining-room, the sideboard 'blossoms', but with ugly empty articles rather than flowers; the table is an island; the chairs ride 'like ships at anchor'; tea is dispensed at a 'little fortress'. The list of similes is long, but adds up to a gloomy picture of a dining-room that deprives people, not just of any interesting or nutritious food, but also of human conviviality. If the chairs are like ships, the passengers can do little more than hail each other or fire broadsides, and this is exactly what they do. Similarly, when Moore uses similes to describe human beings, the consequences are far from flattering. Mrs Rice's hair is 'like a forkful of wet hay', in keeping, one supposes, with her rural Donegal origins; Miss Friel's hair is like a fox-terrier's and so is her nature; Mr Lenehan is given a 'sickled' smile and an 'imprisoned' tie, to indicate a personality that is repressed, but malicious when roused.

One of the most memorable aspects of the novel is Moore's representation of the *texture* of a life that is subject to such forces and conducted in such a society, and also of the point of view of the protagonist who is the victim of the forces of repression, primarily religious, but also societal. 'Dismissive bitterness . . . is Brian Moore's consistent attitude to Belfast', says John Cronin. '*Judith Hearne* [is] a bleak and powerful depiction of a lonely middle-class Catholic . . . Everywhere in this powerful book there is loneliness and despair.'[4] The technique Moore uses to convey this tone or attitude is one of realism: the 'voice' of the main protagonist (and, to a lesser extent, that of James Madden) is set up, sometimes in harmony with, sometimes in counterpoint to this social realism. This realism is so harsh, so unrelieved, so much directed at revealing the helplessness and hopelessness of Judith's plight, that there are times when it would seem to merit the epithet 'naturalistic'. Moore, however, lacks the pcooimiom about human nature (ac oppored to human society and religion) that is so evident in truly 'naturalistic' novelists, and does not share their scientific basis for a belief in biological determinism. He has little sense of evil, except as it is embodied in institutions, and he is much more inclined to see his early protagonists as victims who, in other circumstances, would not be victims. What Moore's *Judith Hearne* shares with French naturalism and also with the 'naturalism' of English authors like Gissing and Orwell can be defined by borrowing a phrase of Terry Eagleton's, used in the context of the English novel: 'a drably detailed, grimly unselective reproduction of "life as it is" — of the seedy realms of routine social existence'.[5] *Judith Hearne* and *The Feast of Lupercal* also share a certain deterministic perception or assumption: 'It is part of the philosophical assumptions of naturalism, that men are passively bound to their situations by only partially controllable forces.'[6]

The phrase 'grimly unselective' may be taken as a key element of description of Moore's portrayal of Judith's life in *Judith Hearne*. To attempt to define the type of realism used by Moore in *Judith Hearne* and also in *The Feast of Lupercal* it is necessary to compare it with other kinds of realistic writing. For instance, many critics have drawn a comparison between Moore's first two novels and the realism of Joyce's *Dubliners*. But the phrase 'grimly unselective' cannot be applied to the short stories of Joyce. 'Grimly selective' might be a more apt phrase, because the stories in *Dubliners* are characterised by a thoughtfulness and a distancing of the author from the subject that raise them to the level of masterpieces. This level is never reached by Moore in *Judith Hearne* or *The Feast of Lupercal* despite the undoubted merits of these novels, because the author is too closely involved with the society he is describing and because his bitterness emerges too strongly. In Moore's own estimation, his exile increased the extent of his bitterness rather than providing a sense of detachment.

Moore himself acknowledges both his debt to Joyce as a model and Joyce's unique genius: 'Yet for the rest of us, failed heirs, false heirs, Joyce remains our mentor: he who helped us fly past those nets of home, fatherland and church, who taught us the rebel cry of *non serviam*.'[7] This remark identifies Joyce as being a liberating influence on a generation of Irish people, and particularly on the many Irish writers who chose to write about Ireland from the point of view of the exile. Moore also specifically notes the technical influence of Joyce on his first two novels. He describes Judith Hearne as:

> a character as foreign to me as Bloom must have been to Joyce, but a character which, in some way, was then my lonely self. The novel, when I look back on it now, is directly influenced by Joyce in many other ways. Interior monologue is central to the exposition: there is even an awkward chapter, a round-robin of interior monologues (or commentaries by minor characters on the main character).[8] [This characterisation of interior monologue as the primary mode of *Judith Hearne* is not completely exact; the technique has elsewhere been otherwise described by Moore.]

Critics have joined in seeing similarities between Joyce's techniques and Moore's. In two extended critical articles published in the same year, Derek Mahon and Kerry McSweeney comment on the influence of Joyce on Moore. Mahon sees Joyce's obsession with paralysis and death as being comparable with Moore's concern with 'the immutability of his Belfast society, and with the effect of this stagnancy on its inhabitants'.[9] Kerry McSweeney sees both

Judith Hearne and *The Feast of Lupercal* as having been influenced by *Dubliners* in that the protagonists of both novels are 'outcast from life's feast', like Mr Duffy in 'A Painful Case'.[10] However, a close study of the techniques of these novels will show that, though Moore's preoccupations—his hostility to traditional Catholicism and his vision of Ireland as restrictive and oppressive—may have been shared with Joyce, his kind of realism has little in common with the realism of *Dubliners* from the point of view of style. Perhaps Moore himself, writing in another context, pinpointed the essential difference when he said that he admires Joyce for his 'celebration of the commonplace'.[11] There is little celebration, in any sense of that word, in either *Judith Hearne* or *The Feast of Lupercal*.

A passage taken from Joyce's 'A Painful Case' will highlight the differences that exist between that story and *Judith Hearne*, between Mr Duffy and Judith, between Moore's kind of realism and Joyce's, and, very significantly, between the respective authorial attitudes to the protagonists in the novel and story. There is a similarity between Mr Duffy's fate and Judith's; it is true that both end up being 'outcast from life's feast', but for different reasons. Judith is a helpless victim; Mr Duffy's lifestyle is doggedly deliberate. This is Mr Duffy's room:

> The lofty walls of his uncarpeted room were free from pictures. He had himself bought every article of furniture in the room: a black iron bedstead, an iron washstand, four cane chairs, a clothes rack, a coal scuttle, a fender and irons, and a square table on which lay a double desk.[12]

Unlike Mr Duffy, Judith Hearne is, to borrow Michael Paul Gallagher's phrase, an 'imaginist'.[13] The contrast is constantly drawn between the squalor of her surroundings and her expectations, her delusions, her disappointments and her disillusion. The description of Mr Duffy's room, above, is characterised by deliberate choice — that the walls were 'free' from pictures, that Mr Duffy himself had chosen all the furniture to be adequate but not excessive. In the paragraph, each noun is qualified by a single adjective, denoting material, colour or usage, except for 'fender', which does not require an adjective, and 'chairs', where number as well as material is shown. By contrast, the following paragraph of description of Judith's room seems almost excessively detailed. It is also very significant that the room is described, as Judith sees it when she wakes up for the first time in her new lodgings, so it is filtered through her consciousness:

> A chair, broadbeamed, straightbacked, sat in the alcove by the bay window, an old pensioner staring out at the street. Near the bed, a dressing-table, made familiar by her bottle of cologne, her combs and brushes and her little round box of rouge. Across the worn carpet was a wardrobe of brown varnished wood with a long panel mirror set in its door. She looked in the mirror and saw the end of her bed, the small commotion of her feet ruffling the smooth tucked blankets. The wardrobe was ornamented with whorls and loops and on either side of the door mirror was a circle of light-coloured wood. The circles seemed to her like eyes, mournful wooden eyes on either side of the reflecting mirror nose. She looked away from those eyes to the white marble mantelpiece, cracked down one support, with its brass fender of Arabic design. Her Aunt D'Arcy said good day in silver and sepia-toned arrogance from the exact centre of this arrangement, while beside the gas fire a sagging green-covered armchair waited its human burden. The carpet below the mantelpiece was worn to brown fibre threads. She hurried on, passing over the small wash-basin, the bed-table with its green lamp, to reach the reassurance of her two big trunks, blacktopped, brassbound, ready to travel. (19)

This passage is notable, especially in contrast with Joyce's work, for its lack of economy. Instead of the 'scrupulous meanness' of *Dubliners* (Joyce's own phrase),[14] one sees an enthusiastic evocation of sordidness in Moore's work. Most nouns are defined by two or more adjectives or longer adjectival phrases. The carpet is described twice, the wardrobe is the subject of a detailed and extended description. The language is frequently metaphorical; the chair 'sat' like an old pensioner; the armchair 'waited' its human burden. Here the personification adds to the gloom: the chair is alone and rejected; the armchair is alone and abused. The most extended metaphorical passage concerns the configuration of the wardrobe: 'the circles seemed to her like eyes, mournful wooden eyes', a phrase which prepares the way for the human photograph eyes of Aunt d'Arcy looking down at her from the mantelpiece. The difference arises mainly from the fact that Mr Duffy in 'A Painful Case' is in control of his environment; Judith is not. He has created his room; she has to suffer hers. The second difference is that Judith is an imaginist and self-delusionist; Mr Duffy is the epitome of realism. He cannot even imagine a romantic attachment, which is why he takes fright at Mrs Sinico's advances; Judith convinces herself of romantic possibilities on no evidence or on the slightest of evidence.

The paragraph is part of Judith's process of familiarisation. Hence the imagery, as she is fond of giving human characteristics to inanimate objects to alleviate her loneliness. This is what M. J. Toolan calls 'a recurrent device: the investing of a material object with the power to reflect and articulate at least part of the psychic condition of the central character'.[15] The imagery, however, actually contributes to the reader's sense of Judith's loneliness (the pensioner image) and the repression of her life (the sense of being watched by the 'eyes' of the wardrobe as well as by the eyes of her dead aunt). It is important to her that she should already have made some small impression on her environment: her feet ruffle the blankets; her trunks and box of rouge are signs of her presence. The realism of *Judith Hearne* consists therefore in the technique of accumulating detail rather than selecting detail. David Daiches, in his study of *Dubliners*, characterises Joyce's realism, on the contrary, as 'patterned realism':

> Joyce's realism in *Dubliners* is not therefore the casual observation of the stray photographer, nor is it the piling-up of unrelated details . . . [it is] the work of an artist whose gift of observation, tremendous as it is, is never allowed to thwart his literary craftsmanship—his ability to construct, arrange, organise.[16]

Furthermore, Judith's environment as well as her hopes and memories are almost always conveyed not in detached third-person narrative, but filtered instead through her consciousness.

McSweeney and Mahon, in the comments quoted above, are of course right to compare the outcome of 'A Painful Case' with that of *Judith Hearne*. In a memorable phrase from the end of Joyce's story, Mr Duffy 'gnawed the rectitude of his life: he felt that he had been outcast from life's feast' (114) and, again, 'No one wanted him: he was outcast from life's feast.' But, even if he regrets it now, he has chosen that fate in the interest of preserving the inviolable order of his life: 'Mr Duffy abhorred anything which betokened physical or mental disorder.' (106) He has made a moral choice: 'Why had he sentenced her to death? He felt his moral nature falling to pieces.' (114) The remarkable impact of this story derives in great measure from its dispassion and lack of melodrama. *Judith Hearne*, on the contrary, is passionate, in every sense of the word used in the title, and it is also melodramatic in a way that true realism of the naturalistic mode would never be. The similarity in the fates of the characters is the only valid point of comparison between Moore's novel and Joyce's story. That is not to say that Moore's novel should be more like Joyce's work: the differences between them are a result of Moore's perception of Judith's helplessness and of the inevitability of her fate. Because of this perception he uses a different technique to convey her point of view.

The 'unselective' realism of *Judith Hearne* also marks Moore's writing off from what is commonly perceived as the style of 'Catholic' writers, with its emphasis on individual guilt. It is partly Moore's perception of the helplessness of Judith that leads him to choose a style which concentrates so much on her surroundings. That aspect of his style for which the phrase 'grimly unselective' has been adopted, emerges very strongly when the novel is contrasted, for example, with Mauriac's *Thérèse Desqueyroux*. This novel, like *Judith Hearne*, has a female protagonist, but unlike Judith, Thérèse is a young woman of passion and guilt, a sinner in true Catholic style. Mauriac concentrates on individual guilt, although the intelligent Thérèse is also the victim of repressive forces, this time of the *mores* of the materialistic bourgeois pine-tree proprietors of Les Landes, the society into which she was born and where she was married. In the novel, Thérèse is given a passionate association with the intuitive and sensuous things of the earth which defies conventional bonds and which sets her apart from the practical mentality of her family and her husband. This sensuousness is, of course, linked with evil and guilt. The recurring images of the earth, of soil, of darkness and of light are carefully chosen. This is a short evocation of some of the feelings of Thérèse after she has been acquitted of attempting to poison her boorish husband, although everyone, including the husband, knows she is guilty:

> *L'odeur de fournil et de brouillard n'etait plus seulement pour elle l'odeur du soir dans une petite ville . . . elle fermait les yeux au souffle de la terre endormie, herbeuse et mouillée.*[17]
> [The scent of the bake-house and the fog were no longer for her just the scent of the evening in a small town . . .

> she closed her eyes to feel the breath of the sleeping
> earth, grassy and moist]

Thérèse's sensuous identification is with that part of the
natural world which remains untainted by the business of
making money from pine-trees. This identification liberates
her. Her passion is evident in her sensuous association with
the physical world. Judith Hearne's 'passion' is a lonely
passion: for her, there is nothing to identify with, in friends,
church or society. There is no sense of nature, or of any
elemental force in *Judith Hearne*, or, indeed, in most of
Moore's novels until the most recent ones. A cold, alien,
urban environment, devoid of beauty and affection is the fate
of his early protagonists. For Judith Hearne, there is no
passion like that of Thérèse to urge her to revolt; Judith's
'lonely' passion instead brings her to breakdown. Where
Thérèse acts, Judith merely reacts or is acted upon.

Judith Hearne comes closer to sharing the unselective realism of Orwell's *A Clergyman's Daughter*, although that novel
is immensely inferior from the point of view of plot, characterisation and verisimilitude. Though Orwell's setting is
the English lower-upper-middle class and thus the members
of that society are much more conscious of being 'shabby-
genteel', his novel shares with *Judith Hearne* the sense of
people being imprisoned by financial and social circumstances which are almost unbearable, but which it is completely beyond their power to change, partly because they
have been shaped and deprived of volition by the very
environment which now traps them. Like Moore in *Judith
Hearne*, Orwell dwells repeatedly and lingeringly on comfort-
less interiors, whether squalid or genteel, as in the following
description of the rectory dining-room which is occupied by
Dorothy Hare and her father, the clergyman:

> It was a smallish, dark room, badly in need of repaper-
> ing, and like every other room in the rectory, it had the
> air of having been furnished from the sweepings of an

antique shop. The furniture was 'good' but battered beyond repair, and the chairs were so worm-eaten that you could only sit on them in safety if you knew their individual foibles.[18]

For outspoken and consistent bitterness, however it is really only to Irish authors that one can look for attitudes similar to those displayed in *Judith Hearne* and *The Feast of Lupercal*, because the particular sense of repression found in Irish writers arises in a society subject to the domination of the Church (a different perception of repression would result from a system of temporal or political tyranny). In John McGahern's *The Dark*, the author conveys a much stronger sense of sin and guilt than Moore, in such a manner, perhaps, as to remind one of Mauriac. But the oppression of the individual is again the aspect that emerges most strongly. Family life is brutal; poverty brings not hunger but blindness to opportunity and the violent frustration of a father who once, too, was head of the class. The novel contains sickening scenes of brutality of various kinds and gains its impact and intensity from being narrated exclusively by the adolescent protagonist. If the protagonist manages to escape his environment at the end, which Judith will never do, this makes McGahern's novel more optimistic. The bitterness of *Judith Hearne* is more diffused, more focused on the whole of society rather than on the claustrophobia of family life and Moore's novel does not convey the same recurrent immediacy of pain as does McGahern's.

If Moore does not write quite like Joyce, or Orwell, or Mauriac, or yet again, McGahern, how then does he create the effects which make *Judith Hearne* such a powerful and depressing novel? He uses the first few chapters, on the occasion of Judith's moving lodgings once again, to show the circumstances in which she lives. There is a lingering concentration on squalor: the stains in the carpet and the worn patch show that the house has seen great numbers of people passing through and that, like Judith herself, it has seen better days. Time moves slowly in the opening chapters: we see Judith's Friday, Madden's Saturday, Sunday for both of them before the novel moves on more swiftly. There is an intense concentration on the small details of life like Judith's *toilette*, her clothes, her hair-brushing and also on her sensations, especially cold and hunger. Alternating with the realistic details are Judith's moods and actions of self-delusive optimism. She sees herself as a gypsy, as a *femme fatale* in a black and red dress, as a 'lady' with good jewellery and good grammar, though her watch has long since ceased to work, and though James Madden can hardly appreciate her good education, so lacking is he himself in culture.

For Judith, the typical Friday is a dull day of idleness and hunger. Her perception of Belfast is coloured by her boredom and her desire to spend as little as possible on food and this is the perception that is passed on to the reader, because her point of view is the central one. The city also provides the frame for the rejection of Judith, a rejection that is becoming increasingly common in her life, but that the reader suffers for the first time with her: the library attendant is not friendly; little Tommy Mullen rejects her kiss as all men have done and his mother dispenses with her piano lessons. Because the scene is presented through the filter of Judith's hurt and indignation, the reader initially accepts her version of events: that the children she has tried to teach have been undisciplined and unmusical, though later events will show that Judith's misfortunes in this respect are not the result of some kind of conspiracy against her, but the consequence of her own shortcomings.

Moore uses James Madden to provide a kind of sub-plot commentary on Judith's situation as well as for his role in the plot. A good deal of time is spent on him at the beginning of the novel. He is a character like Judith in some ways, despite the gulf between them from the point of view of sensibility and of morality. The description of his Saturday reinforces one's image of her Friday. He has money, so his idleness takes a different form: where she goes to the library, he drinks. She is rejected by the librarian; he is exploited, then abandoned by Major Mahaffy-Hyde. There is a wider perception of the grey damp misery of Belfast through the eyes of James Madden, because he can afford to see more of it and because of his nostalgia for New York. Over the lives of both Judith and James Madden, though not always in their own perception of their lives, there is a pervasive sense of depression and cynicism. The author's attitude towards the life led by Judith, Madden and most of the other characters is clear. Is it worth living like this? Judith and Madden have idleness forced upon them; Bernie Rice is idle by choice. Characters are bitter, negative or vengeful, like Lenehan or Miss Friel. Over the whole of Judith's world hangs a miasma of frustration, of people not being free to do what they want, or of people being forced to do what they do not want to do. In the only other world she knows, the O'Neills' comfortable middle-class home, there is genuine family affection, but she is excluded from this more positive atmosphere by the lack of any real affection between her and the O'Neills. The chasm of loneliness between Judith and her so-called friends is emphasised by the children's mockery of the expressions she uses, like 'It's only me!' (72) and 'Two is my absolute limit.' (77) In the world she belongs to, family relationships are like that between Mrs Rice and Bernie, where she panders to him and he exploits her, or like the negative, hostile, destroyed relationship between James Madden and his daughter.

Plot, realistic detail, other characters' attitudes, all tell much about the author's attitude to his protagonist, but the technique Moore uses to convey the character of Judith in this novel is also of considerable importance. The style of *Judith Hearne* and Moore's other early novels differs from that of classical realism because of the technique used by Moore to dramatise the voice of the protagonist, or protagonists (here James Madden as well as Judith Hearne), so that the reader identifies very closely with the character's aspirations. At the same time, through direct descriptive writing, or through using the point of view of other characters, Moore sets up, in counterpoint, an ironic commentary on the illusions or delusions of, for instance, Judith Hearne. He switches very subtly, in mid-chapter, in mid-paragraph, sometimes even in mid-sentence, from description to the third-person consciousness of the protagonist, then to the third-person consciousness of an outsider, then sometimes even to a first-person style. Capturing the voice of the character was a very important commitment for Moore in his early work:

> My original notion of fiction — an idea that I don't think of so much now — was that it was all voice, that unless you caught the voice you never had the character. Judith Hearne . . . is not written in the first person, although people think it is; that was the inspiration I had in that first novel. That while it seems a third-person narrative it is always coloured by the words *she* would use, the type of thoughts she might have and so you are not conscious of any third person or first person: you only hear *her* voice. And if her voice is strong enough then the lesser characters will seem right too and the whole piece will have the ring of a first-person narrative.[19]

When Moore thus captures the voice of Judith Hearne, he is using free indirect speech (*erlebte Rede*), developed especially by nineteenth-century writers like Flaubert (but already used extensively by Jane Austen, particularly in *Persuasion*) who wished to cultivate a style that was personal yet impersonal.

The aim was to speak through the protagonist without the limitation of using a first-person narrative, and without the direct intrusion of the author. Stephen Ullmann, in his *Style in the French Novel*, quotes Flaubert's remark: '*L'auteur, dans son oeuvre, doit être comme Dieu dans l'univers, présent partout et visible nulle part*' and remarks 'free indirect speech is the exact equivalent, on the linguistic plane, of this withdrawal of the author from his work'.[20]   Thus, in *Judith Hearne*, Moore dramatises the response of Judith and of others. The verbs and pronouns are those of indirect speech, but the whole is not subordinate to the author—or does not appear to be subordinate—in the way that recounting of the experience would be. In his book on the functions of free indirect speech, Roy Pascal notes this effect:

> While simple indirect speech tends to obliterate the characteristic personal idiom of the reported speaker, free indirect speech preserves some of its elements—the sentence form . . . intonation, and the personal vocabulary—just as it preserves the subjective perspective of the character.[21]

The impression thereby conveyed is one of immediacy.

This free indirect style provides an expression of the inner life of the character, but not an uncritical one; it suggests that there is another way of evaluating what the character says, from the outside. Roy Pascal considers free indirect speech to be 'the dual voice of character and narrator together which may be heard as a tone of irony or sympathy, of negation or approval, underlying the statement of the character'.[22] Thus, while it would appear from Moore's remark above, that he is expressing loyalty to his protagonist by using this style, in fact this is not always the case; there is frequently a tension set up between his character and the world she lives in and the people she associates with. Moore uses this style much more in his early novels than he has subsequently done; it is a way of sympathetically showing a character while at the same time exposing her faults, her misconceptions and her delusions. In the case of Judith Hearne, her faults, her misconceptions and her delusions are the result of the blighted life that has been created for her by circumstances largely outside her control—in short, a determined life. By the same technique, Flaubert creates in Emma Bovary a character whose faults are manifest, but with whom the reader none the less sympathises. George Eliot uses a similar method to express the noble but fallible character of Dorothea Brooke in

Middlemarch, as Derek Oldfield points out in his work on the language of the novel.[23] The fact that the style can be used to depict heroines as different as Emma Bovary and Dorothea Brooke and with such a varying degree of authorial sympathy or approbation shows the flexibility of this medium and its usefulness in conveying an equivocal authorial viewpoint. Ullmann believes that 'anguish finds its natural expression in this medium'.[24] Anguish is certainly one of the predominant emotions of *Judith Hearne*.

Free indirect speech is not the only means of conveying anguish: for instance, Moore uses a more direct first-person narration to convey anguish in *I am Mary Dunne* and a more impersonal third-person technique in *The Doctor's Wife*, but Mary Dunne and Sheila Redden are altogether different heroines. They are articulate, emotionally independent, the product of quite a different culture from that which formed Judith Hearne and Diarmuid Devine. They are both chronologically and geographically at a great distance. It seems that nowhere does Moore convey a pathetic helplessness better than through the free indirect speech of *Judith Hearne* and, to a lesser degree, of *The Feast of Lupercal*. He achieves this effect by alternately taking the reader inside the head of Judith and out again, to show that the world does not see Judith as Judith sees herself. An equivocal sympathy is both the reason, in the author's attitude, and the result, in the reader's perception of the use of this style.

Chapter 5 of *Judith Hearne* provides a good illustration of the way Moore uses free indirect speech along with more objective narrative and dialogue to show Judith's reactions to the O'Neills, their reaction to her and the self-delusion which allows her to come to their house, Sunday after Sunday on the pretext of being a friend of the family. They, in courtesy and kindness and in full consciousness of their good fortune and superiority, allow her to continue in her self-delusion, but they have reduced the inconvenience of her visit to a minimum for themselves: the father flees to his study; the children escape to work or friends; Mrs O'Neill endures longest, but she too, finally, takes refuge in sleep. After presenting the picture of the comfortable drawing-room and recounting the arguments advanced by the young O'Neills in order to enable them to avoid Judith's company, Moore shows Judith coming up the stairs. Already, the reader is aware of how much the family represents what Judith lacks in her own cold impoverished life and how much pride she is prepared to sacrifice in order to sit, eat and drink with the O'Neills on Sunday afternoon. In the short passage that follows, there are many elements at work and a very varied stylistic approach:

> She climbed the stairs slowly, giving Kevin time to escape to the chilly solitude of the attic and his chemistry set. Just like his father, she thought, seeing his small legs scuttle around the curve of the bannisters, two flights above her. Always running off to work or something or other. Dear Owen, the child takes after him.
>
> The drawing-room door was ajar. I wonder how many of them are in? Una and Shaun, and perhaps little Kathleen. And Moira herself, half asleep already. She knocked lightly on the drawing-room door.
>
> 'It's only me!' she called. (72)

The passage begins with an apparently straightforward description, 'She climbed the stairs', but with the adverb 'slowly' comes, in reality, an authorial intrusion. The second half of the first sentence contains a multitude of implications. Kevin escapes a fate worse than cold and solitude, the boring company of Judith Hearne, but she connives at his escape. She will not, of course, admit it, even to herself, but she is aware that her Sunday arrival is the signal for the family to escape. That is why she ascends the stairs 'slowly'. The continuation of these painful Sunday visits depends on her turning a blind eye to such escapes and avoiding embarrassment at all costs; Moira O'Neill, for her part, plays her role in the conspiracy by trying to ensure that there is no obvious outbreak of insubordination or mockery among her children, though this becomes harder to ensure as the children get older.

In the second sentence of the passage, there is a change to free indirect speech: 'Just like his father, she thought'. Here the verbs and pronouns are those of indirect speech, but the thought is as much the thought of Judith as if it were expressed in the first person. The thought is a self-delusive one: she pretends to believe that Kevin's flight to the attic is not a result of her visit, but of his natural conscientiousness. It is not that she is deliberately pretending, but that the quality of her thought is subconsciously self-delusive. For such a character as Judith, condemned to poverty and unpopularity and with few redeeming features, such self-delusion is absolutely essential if she is to survive at all. The clichés of her vocabulary infiltrate her thought here: one of her more embarrassing characteristics for the reader is her constant habit of calling the members of the O'Neill family 'dear', when they to her or she to them are anything but 'dear' and when the children register their lack of affection for her in one of the few ways allowed them in civilised family life—by refusing to consider her as anything other than 'Miss Hearne'. In that short set of sentences conveying Judith's thought, there is also an implied hostility to or downgrading of Moira O'Neill: the child takes after his father, who is clever and studious. The implication is that the mother is neither of those things.

In the second paragraph of the quoted passage, it can be seen how smoothly and imperceptibly Moore changes from the third-person free indirect speech to the first person, then into straightforward narrative, though here again the adverb 'lightly', used to describe the manner of her knocking, suggests her hesitation and diffidence on entering the room. Finally, her 'It's only me', as well as echoing the earlier mockery of the children, moves the emphasis from the ponderings of Judith coming up the stairs and hesitating at the door to the fact that this is a social visit that she is paying.

The effect of this passage (and there are many such in the

novel) is to underline the isolation of Judith. The author withdraws and allows Judith to condemn herself to the reader out of her own thoughts and out of her own mouth, with her repetition of the set-phrase greeting so reviled by the young O'Neills. Moore has shown us her life, what she is and what has made her what she is, and this is what he continues to do throughout the novel. The person she is, as the action of the novel unfolds, the person who is desperate enough to invent a friendship where none exists and to invent a love-affair where none was intended, is shown not just through her speech, nor even primarily through her speech, but through the inward 'voice' that Moore was so anxious to capture, the voice that expresses her fears, her justifications and especially her delusions and unfounded hopes. In an early article on Moore, Philip French wrote of the style of this and other early Moore novsls:

> All except one of Moore's books is written in the third person but always giving the impression of a first-person narrator, as if one were standing behind a character and yet at the same time seeing events through his eyes. The effect is that the style of the book is strongly coloured, but not dominated, by the sensibility of the central character . . . Using this form Moore can if he wants switch unobtrusively or abruptly into showing us another point of view.[25]

What French says is true, but does not take into account the different effects achieved by this method. Moore uses a narrative technique in *Judith Hearne* which creates a 'determined' protagonist, a protagonist who is unfree and helpless. Therefore, even while he is showing the reader her outlook on religion and the world *through* her sensibilities, Moore frequently shows Judith's limitation as an agent of perception, of thought, or even of feeling by using free indirect speech. The Judith Hearne whose life £nd characteristics were determined by factors and people outside her own control is, on the whole, no more capable of thinking clearly than she is of doing anything drastic to remedy her intolerable situation.

Viewed in this light, the disaster that befalls Judith at the end of the novel is some sort of victory, though perhaps a Pyrrhic one, a victory for her thought processes and freedom of mind at the expense of her physical and mental balance. At last, she tells Moira what she really thinks of her; she employs a similar method of straight-talking with God and with the priest. At the end of the novel she is, for the first time, at one in her own perception of herself with the way others see her: she is friendless, alcoholic and her fate is too terrible to imagine. Even given that she is drunk for most of her last day at large in the world, there is a big difference between the Judith of chapter 5 and the Judith who goes so unprecedentedly to visit Moira O'Neill on a weekday forenoon (chapter 17). Her adventures during that day's odyssey, in the O'Neills' house, in the presbytery and in the church are described through the eyes of others: Moira O'Neill, the taximan, Father Quigley. Here and subsequently, Moore gives the floor, so to speak, to more characters than he has done in the novel up to now. Judith speaks, or shouts or rants, but there is a complete change from the mixture of self-pity and self-delusion that was her currency while she connived at her own humiliation because she still thought that she had something to lose. The 'voice' of Judith becomes more raucous, more disturbing and much less ladylike at the end of the novel, but it is a much more honest and braver voice.

It is significant also to note that Moore uses the same technique of a mixture of first-person 'interior monologue' (Moore's own phrase)[26] and free indirect speech to show the thought processes of the secondary protagonist, James Madden, whose story is parallel to, though different from, Judith's. There is a similar discrepancy between the manner in which James Madden views himself and the way the world sees him. He too is a victim, though not the victim of so many determining forces as Judith; he too oscillates between self-pity and optimistic self-delusion. The voice of Madden is a blustering boastful one: 'Hell, I got dough. I can get on a boat and go anywhere.' (45) But he cannot, because he has nowhere to go and no one to go with. His problems may not be the same as Judith's, but they are real, none the less. He fools himself into thinking that he has power, but he is powerless. He continually fools himself, never more so than when he manhandles Mary in lust and calls it chastisement.

Moore's technique in creating both these characters in *Judith Hearne* arises out of his perception of them as helpless victims. They are bored, lonely and afraid; Judith Hearne's refuge is in self-delusion from the beginning of the novel, and later in drink; James Madden's, in a combination of drink and self-delusion all through the course of the novel. They are not evil; Judith, in fact, is conspicuously moral. In the novel, Judith's loss of faith is only a symptom of the despair that strikes her when she realises that she has nothing to hope for in life. Moore's theme in this first novel is repression. His depiction of Belfast Catholicism is motivated by his sense of its effect on his own life and by his abhorrence of it as a quasi-political tyranny. From the evidence of the novel, it is certainly not a religion conducive to the retention of belief, or conducive to the development of Christianity in its members. Both the Catholic Church and Catholic society are bigoted and inhumane. The novel can be seen, quite simply, as completely hostile to Catholicism; that religion, according to Moore, has no virtue as a system of ordering belief or mediating belief to the ordinary person. It is, instead, a negative force inasmuch as it has reference to belief; it prevents its adherents from believing in anything else, while denying them, simultaneously, the joy and the fulfilment that should come with belief.

3

The Making
of an Ulster Catholic—
The Feast of Lupercal

AS IS the case with Judith Hearne, powerlessness is the main characteristic of the protagonist of *The Feast of Lupercal*, Diarmuid Devine. His experience of an educational system dominated by the clergy has moulded Diarmuid Devine both as a pupil and as a master. Moore is nowhere more anti-clerical than in *The Feast of Lupercal*. Not only are the clerics who feature in the novel bigoted and intolerant, but they are also devious, self-seeking and power-hungry. None of them has the saving grace of self-forgetful zeal, a quality that is so noticeable, despite all his faults, in a later Moore protagonist, Father Laforgue in *Black Robe*. The Catholic laymen who are in the power of the clergy are only less despicable because they are the victims of the system, not its masters. Tim Heron and the other teachers and Devine himself are the products of clerical hegemony.

If the novel appears to exaggerate the ugly side of Catholic education, it is because Moore retains a great deal of bitterness towards the system of religious education to which he himself was subjected. He was educated at St Malachy's, Belfast's Diocesan College, and vividly remembers the brutality and repression of his school life:

> We were educated at St Malachy's in a very harsh, old-fashioned clerical atmosphere. We were caned for everything. We weren't caned just for misdeeds, we were caned when we got our exercises wrong, or when we couldn't conjugate verbs properly. That sort of education

by rote made me hostile to the people who were doing it.[1]

Moore's perception of his own education remains that of the sensitive, suffering adolescent. Because he left Belfast and Northern Ireland as a young man and never returned, he was never to see any justification for it or any extenuation of it as an adult. The consequences of such an unenlightened, clergy-dominated system of education are shown in graphic, even grotesque detail in *The Feast of Lupercal*: the violence in the classrooms which makes the pupils hate the masters and fight back by any devious means in their power; the inevitability of the masters becoming bullies since only violence guarantees respect; the filth and squalor. But, and this is for Diarmuid Devine a far more serious matter, the influence of such an educational system extends far outside the school and long after schooldays are over. It imposes and perpetuates a sort of religious apartheid, which makes Diarmuid Devine look on the Protestant Una Clarke as a representative of some rare, foreign and dangerous species and puts the onus on him to prove the innocence of his dealings with such a depraved creature. It deprives him of freedom; it deprives him of choice; it deprives him of the right to believe in all but the narrow Catholic sense, if we are to apply Moore's own criterion and describe sexual love as a form of belief. The formation Devine has undergone makes him paranoid, furtive, guilty without cause, not because of any instability or neurosis in himself, but because the school, the attitudes of the boys, of the masters and of the religious authorities that run the school all add up to a sort of religious and social McCarthyism. Depriving him of freedom, this also deprives him of all human dignity.

Father McSwiney, the Dean, is the most powerful representative of the Catholic establishment in the novel, though he is punished for his ambition and insubordination at the end. When Devine comes face to face with him, he is not only intimidated by the considerable force of the man's personality, but cowed by years of conditioning. The Dean is an authoritarian father-figure to him, just as the whole community of priests, teachers and boys is like an extended family, where every member will be looked after as long as he does not transgress. Devine thinks: 'Father McSwiney seemed an impossible opponent, remembered from childhood, twice as large as life. There was no hope of changing that authoritarian mind.'[2] Devine resents being treated like this, not for the last time in the novel, but it is, on the whole, an impotent resentment: 'Dammit, he was a grown man now, why should a priest still make him feel like a wee boy?' (45) He gives in on this occasion as he has always done.

Devine is granted temporary courage because for the first time in his life, he makes an attempt to believe in something outside himself and the system—he falls in love with Una Clarke. In chapter 3, he becomes braver than he has ever been before, albeit in minor ways, and the elation caused by his new-found confidence lasts through the early stages of his courtship of Una: 'It's astonishing the confidence she gave me; I was a different man.' (55) But it also takes courage to prosecute a belief, especially if that belief breaks the most dearly-held taboos of one's particular society. Devine becomes nervous as soon as he is threatened, when Tim Heron finds out that he is seeing Una. He realises: 'The men who ran Ardath did not believe in words of honour, they did not consider human intention a match for the devil's lures' (81) and that they would regard his relationship with Una as 'materialistic values, self-love, neglecting your duty as a Catholic'. (82)

Devine has never really behaved as an adult and his weakness and cowardice ruin his chances of success not just *vis-à-vis* the school establishment, but also with Una. He is eventually punished for a sin that is no sin, because when it comes to the point of going to bed with Una, he is 'sick as a boy who had not prepared: the role had been reversed, he was victim, he would be punished for his failure'. (148) When Tim Heron canes Devine in the school grounds and Devine is

again described as 'victim', the reader remembers the earlier
'failure' of Devine. In the mind of the reader, therefore,
Heron is punishing him for his real failure of courage as well
as for the partly imaginary and wholly exaggerated transgres-
sion with Una. His final interview with the principal of the
college, the doddery old man who really wields the big stick,
is the ultimate degradation for Devine. Power knows when to
humiliate by violence, when to impose itself by subtler
means. Despite Devine's 'moment of defiance' (228) where he
asserts publicly '"I'm a grown man. I will not be treated like a
schoolboy"' (228) and '"I have been treated like a schoolboy.
A schoolboy!"' (231), he allows himself to be treated precisely
so. It suits the authorities to be lenient, to close ranks around
him and to ignore the rumours, because his disgrace would
disgrace them all. He will not be allowed the dignity of
resigning and, even worse, he will be forced to feel relief and
gratitude towards the powers that have shown mercy to him:
'It was a relief, in a way.' (235)

The Feast of Lupercal, though a deeply pessimistic novel,
where the protagonist's weakness arouses feelings of contempt and irritation in the reader, does show a development
in Moore's ideas on freedom. It does not have quite so
deterministic an outlook as *The Lonely Passion of Judith Hearne*.
On the surface, Diarmuid Devine has enormous advantages
over Judith Hearne: he is well educated and economically
secure. Though he is frequently shown in situations of acute
embarrassment or else trying to bolster his ego by self-
delusion or disguise, he is not a powerless individual. He
exercises power in the classroom, though it is the power of
the bully, aided by the big stick, and he exerts a certain mild
and halting influence in his drama group. When Moore wrote
the novel, this is how he felt about Diarmuid Devine: 'I feel
equal sympathy with this hero, but the odds are not stacked
against him so much [as against Judith Hearne]. He has more
free choices and therefore it is harder to be compassionate
with him.'[3] He may be more free, and the fact that he makes

an attempt to exercise that freedom in pursuit of Una Clarke immediately puts him in a different category from Judith Hearne, but how free, in fact, is a man with the tradition of years and the whole power of the Catholic community, lay and clerical, against him? Furthermore, Devine's economic 'independence' can only make him dependent on his employers. The novel is a black and gloomy picture of an individual's powerlessness.

Moore has repeatedly asserted that he has not exaggerated the violence of the education he received and it is the memory of the effect of it on his adolescence that colours this novel. He describes it, literally, as a nightmare:

> I used to have a recurring dream. That I was late for school again, running up the long avenue towards a schoolmaster waiting at the top for me with his cane. And I would cry out, you can't cane me, I'm married now, I have a child, I'm wearing a Brooks Brothers suit . . . I wrote about it in *The Feast of Lupercal* and I've never had the dream since. Like Hemingway said, my analyst is my Remington number five.[4]

A nightmare quality pervades *The Feast of Lupercal*, because the novel draws on Moore's memories of a system founded on violence, actual or implied, and the protagonist, who has striven all his life to avoid giving offence, finds himself eventually a victim of this violence. The educational environment of the pupils, though it has the advantage of being of relatively short duration, is certainly nasty and brutish. In the physical sense too, there is a concentration on lavatories, with their attendant filth and graffiti: some of the most important scenes in the novel take place in the lavatories, because they are ideal places in which to eavesdrop, whether unintentionally, as Devine does in the opening scene, or deliberately, when Father McSwiney spies on the three pupils. Eavesdropping and overhearing are the pivotal functions of the plot. The 'sweating green walls, snuffling radiators, window sills which blew cold draughts into the back of the neck' (160) make Ardath sound like a penal institution or Jane Eyre's Lowood, but as Devine observes, perfectly respectable Catholic professionals, farmers and shopkeepers actually pay for their sons to be brutalised and kept cold, dirty and ignorant. The beatings have definite undertones of sadism especially on the occasion when Father McSwiney canes the three gossipers: 'Father Mac was panting now, like a man threshing corn.' (97) and 'Afterwards, he shut the door and dropped the cane on his desk. He looked a lot calmer now, a little tired. He accepted a cigarette from Father Creely's case.' (97) Then he has a whiskey.

In the contest between the individual and the power of the Catholic hierarchy and educational establishment, the individual, Diarmuid Devine, stands very little chance. In this he is like Judith Hearne. His 'voice', too, is like that of Judith Hearne, presented in free indirect speech. Like Judith Hearne's, it is the voice of the 'determined' character who has been made weak and unfree by the combination of personality, habit, education and by the highly repressive social and educational system presided over by the Catholic clergy and which it would take a much stronger man than Devine to resist. Again, like Judith, Devine has a different idea of himself from the perception others have of him and this is brought out by Moore when he shows Devine observed by dispassionate outsiders, like the rather Dickensian dancing-master, Martin McDade, and the draper Mr Parton. It is conveyed most strikingly in the opening pages of the novel, when Devine hears himself being called an 'old woman'. (11) He is shocked when his young colleague continues: '"How can you expect the likes of Dev to understand what a fellow feels about a girl?"' What is 'the likes of Dev'? Is it what Dev is, how he appears, or how he appears to himself? Certainly the comprehensive descriptive paragraph which follows is more likely to establish the reader's impression of him in accordance with the manner in which young Connolly perceives him, rather than as Devine's own shocked response would insist:

> He was a tall man, yet did not seem so: not youthful, yet
> somehow young; a man whose appearance suggested
> some painful uncertainty. He wore the jacket and waist-
> coat of a business suit, but his trousers were sag-kneed
> flannels. His black brogues clashed with loud Argyle
> socks. The military bravura of his large moustache was
> denied by weak eyes, circled with ill-fitting spectacles.
> Similarly, his hair, worn long and untidy behind the
> ears, thinning to a sandy shoal on his freckled brow,
> offset the Victorian respectability of waistcoat, gold
> watch-chain and signet ring. (12).

Devine is caught in the old world, but belongs to the new:
the 'Victorian' waistcoat, his father's chain and signet ring,
which we later see to be his talisman, and the Victorian
moustache, all mark him as being attached to the past. Even
his age appears indeterminate; he is in a limbo between old
and young. Moore is at great pains in the somewhat laboured
prose of this passage to show Devine as a person shaped by
his past, his parents, his weak personality, his career (which
is responsible for the 'respectable' but worn and shabby
clothes he wears), but the appearance of Devine also manifests a conflicting desire for some kind of independence. The
length of his hair and the loudness of his socks make a
sartorial statement. It is the Devine of the long hair and the
gay socks, and who fancies himself still young, who is
appalled to hear himself called an 'old woman'.

The reader's full image of Devine is formed partly by such
descriptive passages, but more often by Devine's view of
himself presented in free indirect speech. His confidence is
shaky and though he is annoyed at the inference in Connolly's remark 'that he was some ninny, incapable of getting
a girl' (14), his annoyance and hurt stem partly from his
suspicion that Connolly may be speaking the truth. But to
himself, he only half admits the truth, shying away from it in
an effort to comfort himself. In the following passage he

allows consideration of the boys in front of him to deflect his attention from himself. It is a typical example of Devine's reliance on half-truths, self-justification and rationalisation:

> As for girls, well, he had never been a ladies' man. He was not ugly, no, nor too shy, no, but he never had much luck with girls. It was the education in Ireland, dammit, he had said it many a time. He had been a boarder at this very same school, shut off from girls until he was almost a grown man . . . No wonder these boys weren't fit to go out with girls when they left school. (15)

In this passage, he reduces success 'with girls' either to luck, which he did not have, rather in the way a person would complain of never having won the prize bonds; he also casts a subtle aspersion on those men, who unlike himself are 'ladies' men', as if this designation entailed being a heartless Lothario. It is significant how quickly he dismisses the charge of being 'ugly' or 'shy'. The speed with which he dismisses these elements suggests confidence, but this confidence is feigned, not real, and the intensive 'too', coming before 'shy' undermines the force of his rebuttal. He is right to blame the education he has received, but it is not by any means the only reason for his failure: other men have emerged from Ardath and undertaken matrimony. Otherwise Catholic education would have quite an unacceptable effect on the Catholic population. The boys who face him may not be 'fit to go out with girls', but most of them will do so.

Similarly, the early description of him by the author can be contrasted with Devine's own image of himself in the bathroom. Moore uses the same device of the protagonist looking at herself in the mirror in *Judith Hearne* in order to show the disparity between illusion and objective reality. In the mirror, Judith Hearne sees herself as a chocolate-box princess or as a sultry gypsy-girl. Diarmuid Devine does not go to such extremes; he merely presents to himself a kinder, more optimistic vision of his appearance. The language of his self-appraisal in this passage, far from being honest, plays down the negative aspects and highlights those features which he (mistakenly, he realises later) considers attractive:

> His hair was getting just a wee bit thin on top. He remembered when it used to stick up like a whin bush. But it was no use . . . Oh, well, he was not such a bad-looking cuss; he had seen worse in his day. He bowed to himself and gave his moustache a military twirl. After all, he was off to a party that very night. There would be lots of girls there, you would imagine. (20)

The emphasis is on the reductive 'just a wee bit' and, rather than consider his approaching baldness for any length of time, Devine drifts into nostalgia for the hair he once had. In this passage of first-person consciousness presented in the guise of third-person narrative, Moore captures very well the natural human tendency to slide away from unpleasant thoughts and the drifting nature of any kind of human thought as one looks into a bathroom mirror. But Devine is shown to be unrealistic, in the light of the earlier objective description of his appearance and in the light of his past experience at parties. Why should he think that he will be any more successful with girls now than he has ever been? He euphemises his bald patch and in Prufrockian style, uses his moustache to boost his morale. Devine in this role presages the hero of Moore's next novel, Ginger Coffey, who depends a great deal on his military moustache and his virile charm.

The other major technique used by Moore to show Devine as a 'determined' character is the voice of the public man, not the voice that speaks aloud, but the voice that represses what the protagonist really feels in the interest of peace or of a demeaning form of self-preservation. Except when he is in the classroom, Devine's voice is timid and conciliatory. In the classroom, buttressed by the cane, Devine knows himself; he knows the effect he has and his pupils know him too. Elsewhere, this is his voice: 'Still, there was no use offending him. Let it pass.' (23) Devine is not a saint: the quoted remark

shows, not that he is infinitely tolerant, but that he sup-
presses hostility because he feels it not to be 'useful'. In Irish
idiom, the phrase 'there is no use' suggests not the idea of
usefulness in its normal sense, but instead conveys the sense
of an activity being counter-productive, or even unwise.
Therefore, though Devine is frequently capable of being
vehement in his private reactions—he uses phrases like
'dammit' and 'what the blazes'—the conciliatory inner voice
of caution always interjects in time to prevent any public
expression of annoyance. For instance, at the party, he thinks
about Tony Molony: 'a conceited little Dublin cockerel
. . . the soul of vulgarity, so he was' (26) but he resolves to
appear friendly: 'a fellow had to live with him. No sense
cutting a man dead, was there, just because you didn't like
his manner?' (26) Devine is constantly repressing his true
feelings: 'Look who's talking, Mr Devine thought. But he did
not say it.' (27) At the same time, Devine displays a great
sensitivity to what others think of him, despite the bravado of
his private thoughts and a corresponding readiness to interpret remarks, which might be innocent, as being unflattering
to himself. His conciliatory nature makes him kind even to
people like Geoghegan, the despised gym master ('Mr
Devine, who did not like to hurt any man's feelings, never
had the heart to put Geoghegan in his place') (86) and
attractive to Una, who needs emotional nurturing after her
failed and illicit love-affair, but it also makes him unable to
assert himself, even to protect his own integrity. A weak
character to start with, years of pleasing people and the fear
instilled in him by the Church and his society have made
Devine like this.

The great difference between Devine and Una can be
attributed to this conciliatory voice of his; even if the forces of
the Catholic establishment and unfortunate circumstances
had not combined to separate them, their relationship is
doomed because of what he is. Not only is there a religious
difference, which may make him feel morally superior but
does nothing to enhance his social confidence ('in Mr

Devine's world, Protestants were the hostile establishment, leaders with Scots and English surnames'), (37) but Una is also frank and outspoken.

Even Una Clarke's appearance is rebellious, young and boyish. From the beginning, she is perfectly frank about her own frankness. She admires people like Joan of Arc, '"people who defy people and do what they think is right"'. (62) The reader has very little access to Una Clarke's mind, but it is not necessary, as she is so frank and open in expressing her ideas. Her remarks convey a basic misunderstanding of the kind of man Devine is: '"I've often noticed how humble you are with people"' (137) and '"I haven't gone out with many boys . . . And none of them were ever as thoughtful as you."' (139) She mistakes his weakness for humility and his constant appeasement for kindness. Not until the end of the novel, when she has suffered because of his weakness and her feelings have clarified into half-contemptuous pity, do we have direct access to Una's point of view: 'he was so hopeless . . . Poor Dev, she wondered now what she'd ever seen in him.' (238–9)

The relationship with Una Clarke transforms Devine, but only on the surface. The expensive new clothes and the clean-shaven upper lip are not enough; he is still the same fearful and timid Devine. Self-justification is still the predominant note in his voice, when, near the end of the novel, he betrays Una. His desire to defend her is outweighed by a lifetime of deference and self-protection. Here Moore uses free indirect speech to great effect, to show the inner conflict experienced by Devine and how he decides that deception, in this case, is the better part of valour:

> But I am a liar, Mr Devine remembered guiltily. No, not a liar, I'm just trying to calm him down. No sense upsetting him, is there? A little white lie never hurt anyone. (157)

and

But what could I do? I didn't know what story to tell him. I had to say something. (158)

A lie is not really a lie when it is used for the purpose of 'calming someone down'. All his life, Devine has been able to avoid 'upsetting' people by hiding his real feelings and by placating them. To avoid 'upsetting' Tim Heron now, it is worth betraying Una. Devine reduces this betrayal of her in his own mind to that most minor and necessary of social sins, a 'little white lie'. In the second comment above, the plea is of helplessness. To tell the truth is unthinkable. Devine makes his inability to invent a story (presumably a virtue of one who is not a 'ladies' man') into an excuse for a downright untruth. Given that he incontestably has 'to say something' it is only in his own cowardly consciousness that he has to tell a lie. He ignores the third possibility, that of telling the truth.

A novel like *The Feast of Lupercal*, where the reality of the protagonist is so far from his conception of himself, is bound to be full of irony. Devine sees his relationship with Una through a rosy glow of pure love and chivalry. He sees himself as the soul of integrity, which he undoubtedly is, in the sexual sense, and is infuriated to hear of Una's involvement with a married man—infuriated that is, with the married man who, he thinks, has seduced her. But he is about to treat her just as shabbily. Just as the married man yielded to the pressure of maintaining respectable matrimony, so Dev will offer Una as a sacrifice to his terror of scandal and the power of the Catholic establishment in his life. Later he atones for his betrayal but it is too late.

Una's comments on her married lover, from whom she presumes Dev to be very different, in fact provide an ironic description of him for the reader who knows more than she does. Take such remarks as these:

That's what's worried me all along. I'm the one who's taken all the risks in this thing. (75)

He's just like a lot of Irishmen I know. He pretends to be a wild Celt but he's frightened to do anything his neighbours wouldn't approve of. (75)

That's one of the things I like about you, Dev. You're honest. You'd stand by your principles. (76)

The reader knows that the first two remarks describe Devine and Una's relationship with him exactly, but in the third, when she thinks she is describing Devine, she is actually pinpointing the quality which he most lacks, moral courage. Una speaks in unconscious irony; as far as she is concerned, the trustworthy, sincere Devine is the opposite of her married philanderer, but the way she presents him to herself is not the way he really is. Devine has only a partial knowledge of himself: his past experience and his present behaviour should tell him that he is not one to take risks, but his self-knowledge comes only at moments and certainly not at heady moments like this. From the first description of Devine and from the first moments of the novel, when he deludes himself by asserting to himself that he is not what Connolly thinks he is, the reader is witnessing a determined character.

Therefore, though the point of view of the novel is predominantly Devine's, this does not mean that Moore is altogether sympathetic to his protagonist. He needs to show a character who is unfree and who has developed by now certain entrenched characteristics—moral faintheartedness and constant appeasement of everyone; he needs to show the influences that have gone into making that character and that continue to exert a huge pressure on it. In the sense of understanding, the author is sympathetic, but in the sense of condoning, he is not. Thus, side by side with the realistic evocation of Catholic Belfast and Ardath College is presented the voice of the protagonist: rationalising, justifying, excusing himself, betraying, often embarrassed, always weak. Most of all, it is the voice of a protagonist who does not know himself as he is.

The Feast of Lupercal marks a widening of Moore's theme,

from the claustrophobia of Judith's life to a concern with the Catholic influence on education and the broader society. Whereas Judith and those with whom she lives are the losers in 1950s Belfast, this second novel is peopled by solid middle-class citizens, secure in their positions. But all of the Catholics, and not just the timorous Devine, allow themselves to be intimidated or bullied by the powerful men in soutanes; whether in the school, the drama-group or the parish. Devine is completely denied the right to follow his own personal belief in loving Una Clarke, but he makes it easy for those who dominate him. At all times, he himself is conscious that the relationship is unsuitable or indecorous. He is aware that he will be judged harshly for it, and is ready to judge Una as immoral or promiscuous in accordance with the prejudices of his own religion about the members of the majority faith. Like Judith Hearne, he is not capable of serious rebellion. He is even less defiant than Judith; whereas she gets drunk and forgets herself, he has too much to lose and is glad to submit cravenly. His dignity and integrity he regards as expendable, but this is not surprising as those qualities are not given a high priority in the system in which he was educated and in which he has worked all his life. In fact, there is a systematic recurrent effort designed and maintained by the clerical masters of Ardath to prevent any individual, master or boy, from valuing his own independence and maturity. Devine and the other masters, in their turn, enforce this system just as much as the priests when they have power in the classroom.

If anything, *The Feast of Lupercal* is more anti-clerical and anti-Catholic than *Judith Hearne*. It is more hostile to the Church as an institution which preserves its own power by maintaining dominance in the educational system. It is not just Devine who is the sufferer, but all the masters, all the pupils; even some priests are the victims of other priests' machinations and tyranny. The novel is an unmitigated condemnation of the kind of Catholicism that denies the freedom of the individual.

Victims of Religion

IN THESE two early works set in Belfast, Moore recreates in considerable detail a society that is the product of a particular set of religious and political circumstances. Thus, the Catholicism that wields power and dominates Belfast society of the 1950s is like Catholicism in the rest of Ireland in its narrowness, its sexual puritanism, its devotionalism and its demand of unconditional respect for the clergy. Moore shows all these aspects at work in *Judith Hearne*. But these qualities, which in themselves would be enough to deny the members of such a Church freedom and dignity are further exacerbated by the particular and perhaps unique political circumstances operating in Northern Ireland. There the Catholic consciousness of being a minority in a state that is politically hostile to Catholicism causes a hardening of these qualities into sectarian righteousness and bigotry and an answering suspicion and hostility to the religion (in reality, religions) of the majority.

Moore's characters are thus the victims of religion, in this case Belfast Catholicism of a particular kind which is repressive in every sense, religiously, socially, sexually, politically. Practitioners of this religion and those who administer it and perpetuate it are depicted with particular venom and even hatred. For the two main protagonists, Judith Hearne and Diarmuid Devine, religion is not a choice, not a gift, not in any sense a joy or a blessing. It has been imposed on them, with all its devotions, its limitations and its prejudices, by their families and their backgrounds. Their belief is not really a belief at all because they only observe this religion by default. Not only does Belfast Catholicism *not* involve the pursuit of true belief, but it also prevents the protagonists from following (or even envisaging in the case of Judith) any personal or deeply held belief of their own. It presents one particular form of fulfilment as the only one that is really necessary and the one that must be observed above all and whatever the cost. Both Judith Hearne and Diarmuid Devine are shaped, made helpless and then broken by the monolithic monster of Catholicism (which is inseparable from Catholic society). Neither is rebellious, and this is their misfortune; circumstances outside their own volition induce them to flout the authority of the Catholic Church, without their ever really having had the intention of doing so. Judith sins by despairing and by making her despair public; Diarmuid Devine by daring to love outside the Church. The Church magnanimously takes them back into the fold, but the cost, in dignity, humanity and in their lost potential as people, is huge.

The plots of these two novels have a great deal in common with the kind defined by Norman Friedman as 'pathetic'. However, having the Church as the prime mover in the novels prevents them from being completely naturalistic in tendency. 'Pathetic' plots, according to Friedman, leave the reader 'with only a frustrated feeling of pity, sorrow and loss in the face of the inscrutably deterministic steamroller of circumstance crushing the mewling kitten of human hopes'.[1] Human hopes are certainly crushed in Moore's early novels, but the steamroller in question is not at all mysterious or inscrutable and the result, in the reader's feelings, is more likely to be anger than unfocused frustration. The 'steamroller' has nothing to do with fate and everything to do with the way a religion can dominate a society.

Moore's focus in the novels is, therefore, on two related elements: society as shaped and maintained by Belfast Catholicism and his protagonists as this society has created them. Moore's hostility and bitterness towards Belfast Catholicism manifest themselves in the style of these early novels in two major ways. Firstly, in order to show his protagonists as victims of the religious and social order, he makes use of a kind of sordid, unselective realism, where everything in the lives of the characters is either ugly or spoiled. He concentrates very much on the physical texture of the lives of the characters and on their physical sensations. Secondly, in order to present the consciousness of these two characters, Moore makes use of free indirect speech, which gives him considerable flexibility as regards point of view. He can show the consciousness of people who have been repressed and victimised all their lives with a degree of sympathy, but keep before the reader's mind, at the same time, that precisely *because* Judith and Diarmuid have been so victimised, their witness is unreliable or fallible. The great virtue of the use of this technique, for Moore, is that by it, he can make plausible at least how people survive and will continue to survive in such inauspicious circumstances. A more romantic or idealistic novelist might have created characters who transcend the limitations and their moment in history; Judith and Diarmuid Devine, Moore makes clear, survive to a greater or lesser degree by self-delusion. Thus the novels are strongly ironic, but without the detachment or satirical intent that the use of that tone usually implies. The irony comes from the gap between reality, in its full horror, as Moore shows it, and the characters' perception of it. Judith and Devine have to perceive their lives in a certain way, if they are to continue to live in this society; the consequences of really looking at their lives are too awful to contemplate. Judith does see the reality of her life, when she is drunk at the end of the novel, and the pain of it literally drives her mad. Diarmuid Devine is spared this agony, despite various happenings that one might think, would dispel his illusions, because he is better at rationalising, because he has much more to lose and because, finally, he enters into a conspiracy with his clerical bosses to preserve the status quo and his own position in the school by means of half-truths and evasions. He surrenders his dignity and his life to them just as surely as if he had been subjected to the most unimaginable torture of Room 101 (in George Orwell's *Nineteen Eighty-Four*). But unlike other, braver men, he does not even try to fight. The Catholic Church and Catholic education have won their battle with Diarmuid Devine long since, probably at an early stage of his own educational experience. That is why he can be treated with such apparent magnanimity. Like Winston Smith in Orwell's novel, he is returned to society, purged and emasculated. His clerical masters are convinced of his harmlessness. Judith Hearne is older and more crushed, so that what in her is withdrawal rather than rebellion lasts far longer, but there is a similar sense in the final pages of that novel that the Catholic authorities (represented by the nurse) are confident that she too will return to conformity.

Novels of Exile and Escape

4

The Search for the Self

A FTER 1960, and after the two Belfast novels, Moore's
writing entered a phase which lasted until the late 1970s
and which therefore encompasses the majority of his works.
The novels of the 1960s and 1970s, in general, are preoccupied with the individual's search for fulfilment and meaning
by following beliefs which are not religious, but which may
perhaps be regarded as spiritual in the sense of being
profound, deeply held, ineluctable, even obsessive. In the
ten novels published between 1960 and 1977, there are two
apparent exceptions to this generalisation, *The Revolution
Script* (1971) and *Catholics*, which followed in 1972. A closer
examination will show, however, that they do not invalidate
the generalisation; they will rather emerge as 'sports', to
borrow Leavis's phrase, borrowed in turn from genetics,[1] or
'aberrations'.

The Revolution Script, a work of political propaganda based
on contemporary Canadian events, has been dismissed by
the author. He considers it not to be a 'serious work'.[2]
Catholics is at once more serious and more problematic. It
does concern itself with belief and in one sense, despite the
focus on organised religion affirmed by its title, it treats belief
as a secular issue. The conflict at the centre of the novel is
twofold: between two different visions of how the Church is
to mediate faith in a secular world and between the different
forms of 'belief' held by James Kinsella and Tomás O'Malley.
Kinsella, according to the new dispensation, believes in a
secularised version of Catholicism, while the sceptical Abbot,
though presiding over the most ritualised and spiritual form
of Catholicism surviving in the new world, is inwardly
conscious that his real role is the secular one of foreman or
manager of the monastery. However, the use of clerical

protagonists in *Catholics* makes it significantly different from those novels with secular characters which address the issue of secular beliefs. Though *Catholics* aroused considerable interest and admiration at the time of its publication, it seems, on sober consideration, not to be among Moore's better novels. The heightened style, the portentous symbolism, the ritualistic simplicity of the confrontation, the lack of depth in the treatment of opposing beliefs, interesting though the protagonists are, show the uneasiness of the author with his subject. There is a sense in which the novel does not belong to the real world; unlike convincing futuristic or science-fiction works, an impression is given that its feeble futuristic basis is an attempt to escape a confrontation with contemporary Catholicism by working on a hypothesis rather than on reality. This, then, would tend to support the assertion that Moore's most serious preoccupation during this period and his most rewarding subject, artistically, is the subject of secular belief.

From this point of view, the eight remaining novels in the period in question, from *The Luck of Ginger Coffey* (1960) to *The Mangan Inheritance* (1979) have a great deal in common; but for the purposes of the discussion of the main theme—the theme of belief—three novels will be treated in detail: *An Answer from Limbo* (1962); *I Am Mary Dunne* (1968) and *The Doctor's Wife* (1976). All of the protagonists of these eight novels have rejected Catholicism; all, with the exception of Gavin Burke in *The Emperor of Ice-Cream*, have left home and country (and despite their truce at the end of the novel, it appears obvious that Gavin and his father cannot coexist in Belfast for very long); several of the protagonists are even in exile from exile, or at several removes from their place of birth, notably Fergus Fadden and Mary Dunne. Movement and rootlessness are features of their lives; they are exiles in more senses than the obvious, as they are likely to move again. Anthony Maloney in *The Great Victorian Collection* goes from California to Canada and back again; Sheila Redden in *The Doctor's Wife* moves from Belfast to Paris to London; Mary

Dunne is about to leave New York for London. The instances abound.

The drama of alienation from family, rejection of religion and the protagonists' sense of the necessity to distance themselves physically both from their families and from Irish Catholicism is played out again and again in these novels, notably in *The Luck of Ginger Coffey*, *The Emperor of Ice-Cream* and *Fergus*. The protagonist in *The Luck of Ginger Coffey* (1960), the novel that immediately succeeds the two Belfast novels, appears to have taken the necessary steps to achieve that freedom that is denied Judith Hearne and Diarmuid Devine: he has left Ireland and he has cast off Catholicism. Like all of Moore's exiled protagonists he sees country, religion and family as being inextricably interrelated, all forces that are repressive and tyrannical. Members of the Catholic clergy, sensing the danger of apostasy, try on several occasions to exercise control over Ginger, but he resists their attempt to reclaim him, not just because he lacks belief, although he does lack belief, but because he is too stubborn and independent to yield to what he considers the bullying tactics of the Church and even of God. Ginger has also challenged the teachings of the Church as regards birth control and on the one occasion in the novel when he visits a church to keep warm, he ends up expressing defiance of what he still perceives as a bullying God. Yet, like everything else about Ginger, his attitude to religion is confused and illogical, more a rebellious instinct that anything seriously thought out. For instance, he has been so busy defying the Church's interdiction on birth control that he has not stopped to consider seriously whether he and his wife would like to have another child.

Perhaps Ginger Coffey is more representative of the common man than Moore's later protagonists. He certainly has very little self-knowledge, whereas Moore's protagonists from this on are intelligent, thoughtful and self-conscious. Therefore, although Ginger Coffey would seem externally to have taken the necessary steps to achieve the freedom to make moral choices, in reality the moral side of his character is very poorly developed. He is a victim, almost as much as Judith Hearne and Diarmuid Devine. If they are victims of religion and of a sectarian and uncaring society, he is a victim of his refusal of responsibility, his pathological lack of foresight, his dependence on luck, whence the title of the novel. Luck is the guiding force in Ginger Coffey's life; choice, which is essential to any concept of morality, is never shown to play a major part. How different this is from the acceptance of the necessity of choice, the embracing of choice, as it were, by characters such as Brendan Tierney and Sheila Redden in novels by Moore written later in this same period and concerning broadly the same themes: the choice of exile and the search for the self.

Ginger Coffey is repeatedly shown as *having* no choice. He is forced to take a particular job, then a second. Admittedly, he grows in stature as the novel progresses, but it is his nature to be unrealistically optimistic. He spends his family emergency money and risks the family's security without even calculating the odds against him. Even as a gambler, and this is how he likes to consider himself, he is hopelessly incompetent. He is a self-deluder who has the freedom to do what he wants with his life, but he does not know what he wants to do. His notion of freedom comes from the pages of a boy's comic or from the imaginary pages of some erotic *Arabian Nights*. Like a boy, he hides to escape the consequences of his irresponsibility; like a boy he finds it hard to articulate his aims in life. Veronica, his wife, bitterly reproaches him for never being willing to admit fault, and at the end, the development in his character is represented in precisely this phraseology: he sees his life (it is expressed in existential terms), as being the responsibility of no one but himself. Neat as this conclusion may be, it is not convincing, and Moore has long since ceased to attempt to represent straightforward moral 'improvement' in his protagonists as he does in *The Luck of Ginger Coffey*. Moore is a much more interesting writer when he is presenting characters who have

to make moral choices, even when all choices have consequences that are difficult, dangerous, even deadly. In most of
the novels of exile, the consequences of the choices the
protagonists have made or are about to make provide the
dramatic interest of the novels, but not in any simplistic or
predictable way.

The protagonist's lack of self-knowledge and understanding of others is emphasised time and again in *The Luck of
Ginger Coffey*. There is a moral and emotional obtuseness
about him. He has lived with a woman and claims to love her,
but he is unable to take her seriously. His self-obsession has
allowed gaps of communication to open between himself and
the other members of his family, so that his daughter, with
whom he is shown to be in very imperfect communication,
has to interpret his wife's wishes for him. Despite the
significant movement away from Ireland into a Canadian
setting, *The Luck of Ginger Coffey* still presents a very confined
scenario. It is relentlessly realistic, even domestic. Echoes of
the Belfast novels are also evident in the unremittingly mundane preoccupations of Ginger as he goes from one job to
another, always threatened by poverty. Ginger moves from
self-delusion to self-disgust to a chastened self-knowledge.
Seamus Deane perceptively sees him at the end of the novel
as having furnished himself 'with a rudimentary ethic of
endurance', no more. Furthermore, Deane marks the real
change in Moore's preoccupations as occurring in *An Answer
from Limbo*: it is here, according to him, that 'Moore begins to
free himself from the *simplisme* of the battle between the
aspiring individual and the stifling social form'.[3]

The Emperor of Ice-Cream (1965), though written after *The
Luck of Ginger Coffey*, is again set in Belfast, from which the
protagonist, Gavin Burke, longs in vain to escape. It follows
that much more attention will be paid to the forces that
restrict him and to his powerlessness. However this novel,
the first to be set in Ireland since *The Feast of Lupercal*, is very
different from the works of the 1950s. It is comic rather than
tragic or fatalistic: the hero is young, resilient, ironic, as well

as iconoclastic. He is too young to be cynical, he has no reason to be depressed and he has not yet realised that even if he were free to do exactly as he pleased, this might not ultimately bring him happiness. He is the complete antithesis of Judith Hearne and Diarmuid Devine. He thinks that people like him will change the world. Therefore, his strongest tendency is to reaction, rather than action. He reacts against all that his parents represent and after a while this also includes the values of his brother, his sister and Sally Shannon.

Gavin, living in his parents' house, which is dominated by Catholic, conservative and nationalistic values, rejects all of these values. He drinks, he thinks about sex, and would, were he free to do so, adopt an openly agnostic outlook on religion and a socialist position in politics. He also has an apocalyptic vision that the world will be changed by war, to support which he quotes to himself Yeats's 'The Second Coming', Louis MacNeice, Clifford Odets and Wallace Stevens, whose strange, visionary and morbid poem provides the title of the novel. This vision is another aspect of Gavin's ineffectual rebellion against his parents—ineffectual because it is cerebral or juvenile delinquent by turn and Gavin is no match, even in cerebration, for his autocratic father—because they subscribe to the nationalist view that war will never reach Belfast.

Gavin Burke has, in common with all of Moore's protagonists from this period, that his rebellion has three root causes and three manifestations: the sexual, the religious and the intellectual. Sally Shannon, despite the allure of her black stockings, merely represents another strain of family life. If Gavin married her, the only way he would be able to have sex with her, they would reproduce the same type of family life as that which he is now desperately trying to escape. Not that this does not have its attractions for Gavin. Just as half of him would like to be a successful student and study law, so half of him would like to be good in order that Sally should love him. That is why he is attracted to her and at the same time, prone to quarrel bitterly and frequently with her. Like the black and white angels, Gavin's treatment of Sally represents the dichotomy of his nature: he feels for her a mixture of pure chivalric affection and lust; he would like to be good and safe, but he also needs to rebel.

The central conflict of the novel is between Gavin and his father, who is one of the few living fathers to feature in any of Moore's novels and who therefore wields actual rather than posthumous power. Gavin's father is the typical Moore *paterfamilias*, a solicitor rather than the usual doctor, to give credence to an even more rational and analytic cast of mind. His values are Victorian, strongly influenced by Catholicism and nationalism. Faced with his son's failure to matriculate, he is unable to suggest any positive course of action, but tries his utmost to maintain control over Gavin, first by proposing that Gavin should go into trade with his Uncle Tom (though he makes it clear that he has the professional's contempt for trade as a way of life), and then by labelling Gavin a failure and ostentatiously washing his hands of him. Gavin *will* be what his father decrees: a solicitor like himself, someone who does his uncle's business like his two lumpish cousins or else labelled a failure, consigned to the ARP scrap-heap. The father is certainly unsympathetically drawn: cold, legalistic, pedantic and unimaginative.

Gavin goes through a long hard struggle against his father and what he represents, quite unlike his mother, brother and sister, who meekly and diligently go about the vocations that are ordained for them. When the big bomb finally comes, Gavin does achieve a victory of a sort: at last his father, humbled and afraid, begins to treat him like an adult. But it is a victory that has its roots in the cataclysmic nature of the bombing — cataclysmic both in its deadly consequences and in its undermining of the most deeply held beliefs of Gavin's parents. None of this derives from Gavin's nature or from a change in the relationship between him and his father. When he refuses to go with the family to Dublin, it is the first real choice of his maturity. This is the reverse of the first confrontation shown between the father and the son in the novel: this time it is the son who dictates, the father who is the child. The relationship is temporarily resolved in the drama of their meeting in the blitzed family home, but at the close of the novel, there is serious doubt in the reader's mind whether Belfast is big enough to hold both Burkes, father and son. It seems too much to hope that Gavin will retain that insouciance that characterises him at the end of the novel. The crisis of the blitz has caused the suspension of normal family activity and hostility, but these will be only too ready to reassert themselves in peace-time.

Not surprisingly, the theme of conflict between father and children and the inescapable influence of parents and fathers in particular, is to feature to a greater or lesser extent in all the novels under discussion in this chapter. In *Fergus* (1970), Moore carries the theme of family influence to an extreme conclusion, although to do so requires him to allow the surreal to have the upper hand. Fergus Fadden, at several removes from Ireland, divorced from Catholicism by his lifestyle as well as by his religious beliefs and living in the great post-Christian nowhere land of near-Los Angeles, is looking very hard for a self. His identity is shaky, sexually, artistically, career-wise. The events of the day, when members of his family and of his past parade in a ghostly fashion for him, point up the dilemma of exile and escape. In the first instance, is it possible really to escape? The novel would seem to postulate that it is not. It seems also that exile is a choice that may calcify the protagonist in perpetual adolescence. Fergus Fadden is made to feel a teenager again, although he is thirty-nine. He relives his lusting after the dentist's wife, his arguments with his father and his rebellion as regards religion and education. All of the apparitions are embodied in the form they took when Fergus was a timorous yet defiant adolescent. Fergus's father, who is the first and last 'visitor' of the day, is again the crucial figure, the father encountered so often in Moore: Catholic, traditional and authoritarian. Though Fergus has come far, he has still, like Brendan

Tierney in *An Answer from Limbo*, an intense desire for his father's approbation. For all his rootlessness, his consorting with movie moguls and girls half his age, the day's events reveal both the hold the family has on Fergus's imagination and psyche and the difficulty he has in establishin., both a secure sense of identity and a stable life style as an exile/escaper from Ireland.

In *The Great Victorian Collection* (1975), Anthony Maloney, already adrift, another victim of the great American/Canadian marriage disaster, is presented with a dream that becomes reality while reality becomes progressively more dream-like. His chances of becoming reconciled with his estranged wife and his bond, already tenuous, with the mother who comes to visit him in California, both fade into a dream. He is an exile now in a way that is beyond any human help; he can never go back to Canada or resume a normal life. Just as the desire to be writers takes earlier Moore protagonists away from Ireland, so Maloney's dream alienates him. *The Great Victorian Collection* is a fable that is never really elucidated, an obscure parable about the nature of art and the possibility of miracles. In theme and setting, it would appear to presage *Cold Heaven*, that other novel of miracles, religious or secular in Carmel, California. But Anthony Maloney fits the mould of Moore's secular protagonists in this middle period of his work: rootless, alienated, essentially unloved. Unique among Moore's protagonists, he finally chooses suicide. The overdose, barbiturates combined with alcohol, is a potent symbol of modern man's *angst* and the spiritual vacuum in which he lives.

Moore has always been regarded as a novelist in exile who writes of exile, but the fate of Ginger Coffey, Fergus Fadden, Anthony Maloney and others is more than simply exile. Movement and displacement are central to the artistic economy of all his novels after *The Feast of Lupercal*. This movement has undoubtedly a metaphorical resonance. None of the characters is grounded or rooted. The consequences of exile for the protagonists of Moore's novels have been amply discussed,[4] but it would appear that exile which begins not out of economic necessity but out of the desire to escape, and becomes the kind of rootlessness that is documented in this period of Moore's work, needs to be examined in the light of its symptoms as well as of its consequences. It is both escape from the self and a search for the self. There is a kind of search evident in all these novels, which is different from the spiritual quest for transcendence which Moore treats of in his later work; it is a search for the self, in the self, in the past, in others, by means of the belief espoused by the protagonists. There are so many ways in which this theme is made explicit that mention of a few will suffice: James Mangan's search for his historical *alter ego*, the *poète maudit* in *The Mangan Inheritance*, Mary Dunne's search in the past for an understanding of herself, and Anthony Maloney's attempts to understand and grasp the essential elements of his great Victorian collection. Ultimately, all of Moore's protagonists are seeking a way of living and an understanding of themselves, in essence an 'intenser distillation of the self',[5] either through following a creative urge which will possibly lead them deeper inside themselves, or through the love of another person, which will possibly enable them to know themselves better.

In *The Mangan Inheritance* (1979), Moore's one excursion into the gothic, James Mangan embarks on a quest: to investigate his lineage, both as a means of re-establishing a sense of himself and as a way of confirming his destiny as a poet through his link with the nineteenth-century *poète maudit*, James Clarence Mangan. Mangan's doubt about who he really is and his lack of a sense of his importance in the world have stemmed from his marriage to a famous film-star, especially as he has become less successful at his writing and more impecunious as she has become richer and more successful. He makes an anguished declaration to his wife, Beatrice Abbott, that he is nothing more than her husband, and the doorman at their apartment block actually calls him 'Mr Abbott'. When Beatrice leaves him, Mangan feels that even this identity is taken away. It is for this reason that he latches on to the daguerreotype of his alleged ancestor, James Clarence Mangan, with an enthusiasm born of despair. Previously, he had no interest in the past, but now to James Mangan at thirty-six, failed writer and failed ex-husband of Beatrice Abbott, the face of the Victorian poet represents the 'cure' for, the 'antidote' to his lack of identity.

The daguerreotype is important to Mangan because it gives him leave, a kind of poetic licence, to reinterpret the past and invest his own future with more hope and significance that it would otherwise have had. He plans a grand future, writing off the years of marriage as if it were the prerogative of genius to strike a few false notes early in its career. He thinks of himself as being in control: he will discover that he is truly the descendant of James Clarence Mangan and return to the New World reformed, to start a truly literary way of life. But almost as soon as he arrives in West Cork and begins to investigate the story and follow leads, he realises that things are not as simple as they seem. Quite helplessly he watches his own life slipping out of control while he remains in Drishane. At the end of his trip to Ireland he discovers that heredity is not what one chooses to take from the past and that the qualities one inherits are quite as much outside one's control as one's appearance. He emerges sane, but can no longer think of himself as a poet without accepting the tainted heritage he discovered in Ireland. Like others among Moore's protagonists, James Mangan discovers that there is no escape from the self, that there is no possibility of forging a new identity in order to escape from the past. This attempt instead leads Mangan deeper and deeper into the past and into an exposure of qualities of his one nature that he would have preferred never to know about.

None of the novels of this period of Moore's writing—the 1960s and the 1970s—is without interest, but all are not equally good. Given the essential similarity of the basic themes, the variety in characterisation, in plot and in technique is considerable. *The Luck of Ginger Coffey*, for instance, belongs from the stylistic point of view with the 'Belfast' novels, in that the protagonist, who for most of the novel lacks even rudimentary self-knowledge, is generally treated ironically by the author. Though this novel is comic in conception and differs from *The Feast of Lupercal* in having a more positive outcome, the basic perspectival technique, whereby the author enters into a conspiracy with the reader at the expense of the protagonist, is similar in both novels. After *The Luck of Ginger Coffey*, though they are presented by many varied techniques, the protagonists come of age and the insight of the reader into their consciousness, whether partial (in the more impersonal third-person narratives such as *The Great Victorian Collection*) or extensive (as in the first-person narrative of *I am Mary Dunne*), is never again shaped by authorial irony. When the increased sophistication of perspectival technique is taken into account, as well as the insight and maturity that are evident in *An Answer from Limbo*, the greatest development in Moore's writing must be seen (as Seamus Deane has remarked in the comment quoted earlier) to have occurred between *The Luck of Ginger Coffey* (1960) and *An Answer from Limbo* (1962).

Three representative novels of this period, *An Answer from Limbo*, *I am Mary Dunne* (1968) and *The Doctor's Wife* (1976) are discussed in detail here. The reasons for the choice of these three novels are: in the opinion of the present writer, they are the most successful, artistically, and the most likely to endure. Secondly, although they are similar enough in theme to be discussed together, they are very varied as regards technique. They represent some of Moore's most innovative work, technically. Thirdly, they span almost the whole period under discussion (1962 to 1976) and can therefore be taken as representative of Moore's preoccupations in the 1960s and 1970s. Finally, *I am Mary Dunne* and *The Doctor's Wife* are of interest as Moore's best and most penetrating efforts to convey the consciousness of a female protagonist. This, in itself, deserves consideration, because it is rare for contemporary male writers to attempt to convey, and very rare for them to succeed in conveying, what it feels like to be a woman.[6]

Moore's use of female protagonists has also contributed to a broadening of the scope of consideration of what passes for belief. An emotional state, the investing of emotional energies exclusively in the loved one qualifies as a 'belief' because it becomes as important as any intellectual viewpoint or artistic aspiration. The loved person becomes something to live *in* and *by*. What emerges from Moore's novels is that it is only for women that sexual love is seen to constitute a viable alternative belief (contrast for instance the crisis of identity suffered by James Mangan when he marries the film-star Beatrice Abbott). Whether this view is valid is quite another matter. The sufferings endured by the women in Moore's novels would suggest that it brings its own dangers.

The three novels exemplify certain key ideas and developments in Moore's fiction: the rejection of religion; exile; the substitution of alternative beliefs and the consequences of following such beliefs. Certain inferences may also be drawn about Moore's attitudes to these beliefs that are adopted by his protagonists as substitutes for religion.

Moore bitterly rejects organised religion in his first two novels. The time and place are particular, the religion is Belfast Catholicism of the 1950s, but the rejection of religion *per se* is total. There is no sense of a possibility of the faith of the individual transcending the social and sexual stultification imposed by Catholicism. The lives of Moore's first two protagonists, Judith Hearne and Diarmuid Devine, are ruined by the consequences of religion in a divided and sectarian society. They themselves do not have a real personal faith that might save them, but maintain merely an observance of Catholicism and of the taboos of Catholic society. Unable to reject or defy religion, they are destroyed by its tyranny. In these early novels, Moore's attitude to religion is expressed as a complete negative in a way that may strike the reader as being melodramatic or adolescent. He sees no value in the kind of Catholicism practised in Ulster. Furthermore, he sees the domination of religion as preventing the development of other means of self-fulfilment. Faith may be irrational, illogical and inexplicable, but formal religion must have a structured and rational basis, and reasons for abandoning Catholicism, apart altogether from any lack or loss of faith (since Catholicism, or any religion, can be, and frequently is, devoutly practised without true personal faith) can be expressed rationally, if simplistically, in the context of Moore's novels. Firstly, in Mauriac's memorable phrase, Catholicism 'makes no allowances for the flesh: it abolishes it'.[7] Judith Hearne and Diarmuid Devine both live their lives under this interdiction and it contributes greatly to the crises which occur to them. In Devine's case it contributes directly to the ruin of his relationship with Una Clarke. For the protagonists of the later novels, the flesh is important; indeed, it plays a central part in their lives. Brendan Tierney's sexual experience with Jane Melville in Spain is an important stage in the process of his liberation and his choice of permanent exile. Much more explicitly, both Mary Dunne and Sheila Redden are shown as regarding sexual satisfaction as being crucial in their lives. This sexual love *is* their belief, while it is shown as being only a small part of Brendan Tierney's life. Sexual passion impels both female protagonists to actions that put them outside the Church to which they once belonged — two divorces in the case of Mary Dunne; adultery and the desertion of her husband and child for Sheila Redden. The difference between Moore's treatment of male protagonists and that of females will be discussed more fully in a later section of this chapter, as it is significant that only for women does sexual love become their *raison d'être*.

Secondly, Catholicism has traditionally made no allowance for intellectual independence. The female protagonists mentioned above drift away from Catholicism, but Brendan Tierney rebels. Such rebellion might seem gratuitous or unnecessary; the question might be asked whether Catholicism really seeks (or sought) to exert as much power over what is essentially the private domain of the mind as it does (or did) over moral and social behaviour. The answer must be in the affirmative. Catholicism tends not to make allowances for dissent. Such a strongly patriarchal, monolithic and hierarchical structure as the Catholic Church tends to call independent thinking arrogant, presumptuous or even heretical when it does not concur with Church dogma. By its very nature and its basis, it cannot accommodate variety.[8] Moore has made reference to the heartening influence which Joyce's 'defiant cry of *non serviam*' had on him as a writer.[9] Ginger Coffey is— comically—accused of that sin of pride in a priest's sermon:

> There's always one boy—Father Cogley said—always one boy who doesn't want to settle down like the rest of us. He's different, he thinks. He wants to go out into the great wide world and find adventures. He's different, you see. Aye, well Lucifer thought he was different.[10]

It is part of the technique of the intellectual autocrat to explode the idea of valid intellectual dissatisfaction, to demean the motives of the rebel, to accuse him of being deviant, irresponsible, worthless. By insisting that his opponent has no worthwhile point of view, the priest can mock his pretensions instead of matching his arguments with rational arguments. The sermon in *The Luck of Ginger Coffey* echoes the homily in Joyce's *A Portrait of the Artist as a Young Man*, although the vision of hell conveyed by the priest in the latter is far from comical:

> [Lucifer] fell and was hurled with his rebellious angels into hell. What his sin was we cannot say. Theologians consider that it was the sin of pride, the sinful thought conceived in an instant: *non serviam: I will not serve* . . . For even they, the very devils, when they sinned, sinned by such a sin as alone was compatible with such angelic natures, a rebellion of the intellect; and they, even they, the foul devils must turn away, revolted and disgusted,

from the contemplation of those unspeakable sins by which degraded man outrages and defiles the temple of the Holy Ghost, defiles and pollutes himself.[11]

(It is interesting to note that, much as the priest in this sermon abhors the sin of intellectual pride, his greatest expression of detestation is reserved for the sins of the flesh.)

Later in *A Portrait of the Artist*, Stephen's confidant, Cranly, injures the artist's pride in asserting just those words 'I will not serve', by saying sardonically '"That remark was made before" (Cranly said calmly).'[12] Cranly is right: there is nothing new in rebellion, but that does not make it any less feared by the Catholic Church. Creating a character like Brendan Tierney, it was difficult for Moore to escape the influence of Joyce. He has said that he chose a female protagonist for his first novel to avoid writing a novel of loss of faith that would be like *A Portrait of the Artist as a Young Man*. *An Answer from Limbo* is far enough from Joyce's novel in its essential theme to allow Moore to acknowledge the influence of Joyce in respect of some aspects of the treatment of that theme.

In the context of intellectual rebellion, Brendan Tierney in *An Answer from Limbo* is the most Joycean figure of all Moore's protagonists: calm, rational, defiant and courageous. When his mother asks him if his children, who are not Catholics, are instead being reared as Protestants, he answers: '"Of course not. As Joyce once said, I'll not forsake a logical absurdity for an illogical one."'[13] (In *A Portrait of the Artist*, what Stephen actually says is: '"What kind of liberation would that be to forsake an absurdity which is logical and coherent and to embrace one which is illogical and incoherent."')[14] It is primarily through Brendan Tierney, also, that Moore expresses the intimate connection between the rejection of religion and the choice of exile.

The impulse felt by the individual to emigrate, which at first may not be very rational or thoughtful, and the forces or desires that impel him to stay away are very complex, especially when emigration is not the result of economic necessity. In the case of Moore's protagonists, exile is both a positive and a negative impulse: it is a movement towards the achievement of some goal, the following of some belief, though both the belief and the goal may at that time be equally nebulous; it is also motivated by the desire to escape from the forces that restrict or stultify. Brendan Tierney sees with clarity the ambivalence and the complexity of his own motives, and expresses in this paragraph, early in the novel, the perception that the rejection of religion and the choice of exile are very closely connected:

> I said I was leaving to become a writer. But now, looking back, perhaps it was not the need to write which made me leave home, so much as the need to run. Wasn't it simply that I was twenty-two, that fifteen and seven made twenty-two, seven years of telling lies to keep the religious peace, seven years of observance without belief, seven years of secret rage at each mention of my 'immortal soul'. (31)

(Moore's own choice of emigration was based on a similar perception. Put simply, 'I stayed away because my parents were religious and I was not.')[15] Traditional beliefs and traditional values are very close to the protagonists who reject them, because (as the above remark by Moore makes clear) they are synonymous with home and family. It is necessary for them to put physical distance between themselves and their families in order to free themselves from the obligation of religious observance. Thus there occurs an immense cultural and physical dislocation within one generation, even though the individual remains attached to his home and family by various other bonds of love and loyalty. Brendan Tierney is the only one of the three protagonists who *specifically* sees his choice of exile in terms of rejecting religion, but for Mary Dunne, the rejection of religion is implicit. The illicit act by which she makes her escape from Butchersville, Nova Scotia, is her marriage to Jimmy Phelan outside the Catholic Church. He too is rebelling against parental expectations and refusing to go to Mass on Sundays. The curious paradox of distance and closeness is frequently emphasised. It is echoed by the contrast between the distance from New York to Butchersville and the immediate closeness of the telephonic contact between Mary and her mother. It is exemplified by the fact that when Mary telephones her mother, the latter has gone to Mass, while Mary is not even aware that it is a holiday of obligation. Brendan Tierney's mother is shocked to find that her own grandchildren have not been baptised and her journey to physical closeness with her son brings them no closer to understanding. Exile has the effect of creating a new world for the people who opt for it, where the values of the old world do not apply and where they cannot be brought to bear. By seeking exile, the individual asserts in the strongest possible way, and also in the most effective way, his independence of the values and beliefs in which he was reared.

The Doctor's Wife presents an interesting variation on this theme of the interconnection between exile and the abandonment of religion. Sheila Redden is a lapsed Catholic living in Ireland. This, in itself, is a reflection of the huge changes that took place in Irish society between the publication of *Judith Hearne* in 1955 and that of *The Doctor's Wife* just over twenty years later (1976). Earlier, the idea of a lapsed Catholic living a respectable middle-class life in Ireland would have been unthinkable. However, Sheila Redden is an exile in Ireland, an exile *manqué*, as it were, who would have left Ireland long since but for her husband, or who ought never to have stayed in Ireland in the first place. She says to her brother: "'I always was at home here. [Paris] I don't feel at home at home.'"[16] The contrast is constantly drawn between the values of Sheila's cosmopolitan Uncle Dan and the traditional values of her conservative, moral father. Sheila appears to have chosen the latter for herself, but in truth is drawn towards the former: 'To sail away from all of the things that hold and bind me, to sail away, to start again in some city like Brussels or Amsterdam.' (40) This aspiration may appear romantic, unreal and unrealisable, but in the climate of Belfast in the Troubles, no longer merely sectarian, but now violent as well, Sheila Redden cannot feel at home. *The Doctor's Wife* shows exile becoming a reality for the aspiring exile. This is necessary if Sheila Redden is to pursue her own version of happiness.

Moore's protagonists reject the Catholic religion and choose exile in order to follow a personal belief. The idea underpinning these three novels is that another belief can be as strong and as influential as religious faith in an individual's life. The religious faith in terms of which these beliefs can be seen is not, paradoxically, anything that has been witnessed or described in any of Moore's prior works. There is no religious zeal in the Belfast novels to equal Brendan Tierney's enthusiasm for the novel he is writing, nor any sense of spiritual ecstasy to compare with the sexual ecstasy experienced by Mary Dunne and Sheila Redden. It is as if these beliefs cause or supply the very qualities that are lacking in religious belief, but that should, in theory, be part of it. To suggest, therefore, that these beliefs are quasi-religious is to yield to an idealised version of religion. It would be more rational to say that these beliefs are to the holders what religious belief is *not*. However, the author's own views and remarks become part of the texture here.[17] Many of these were written or recorded much later than *An Answer from Limbo* and *I am Mary Dunne* in any case, and in them Moore equates religion and belief and claims to treat religion as a metaphor for belief. Perhaps these remarks need to be analysed more thoroughly. The ideals of Christianity may be very different, but religion, as it is practised in contemporary society, rarely manifests itself as all-consuming zeal — zeal to the point of self-forgetfulness, which can be seen even in the essentially egocentric self-forgetfulness of artistic endeavour or of sexual love in the two novels in question. There is no evidence to show, and therefore no reason to believe, that

Moore conceived of religion in this way in the bitterness of his first three novels.

However, it cannot be denied that the protagonists in the three Moore novels under discussion here adopt beliefs with extraordinary enthusiasm, that the beliefs are pursued with zeal, and that finally they could be termed obsessive. It cannot be denied that the pursuit of such beliefs *implies* or *follows* a rejection of Catholicism for the reasons pointed out earlier in this chapter—because sexual love with its surrender to the flesh is, except within very severely defined limits, abhorrent to Catholicism and true intellectual freedom has traditionally been incompatible with Catholicism. Furthermore, the language, the terms and the imagery used by Moore to convey the quality of the beliefs pursued by his protagonists does much to earn them the epithet 'quasi-religious', because the dominant influence on the imagery and symbolism used by the characters and about the characters is the Catholic religion which they and their creator alike have rejected. In this regard, the remark which Cranly makes to Stephen in *A Portrait of the Artist* in one of their many religious discussions could be addressed to any of the three protagonists in question in these three novels:

> It is a curious thing, do you know, Cranly said dispassionately, how your mind is supersaturated with the religion in which you say you disbelieve.[18]

For instance, Brendan Tierney's flight from Belfast and emigration to New York are a result both of his rejection of religion and his powerful urge to be an author. Tierney has an enormous compulsion to write and such a strong sense of destiny that the word 'messianic' comes to mind in relation to him. This impression is deliberately fostered by Moore. It is fortified by the manner in which Tierney describes himself from the beginning of the novel. He knows that he is compulsive, obsessive, driven, and when he describes himself he is pleased to note that others see qualities in him that are congruent with this self-image. At the beginning of the novel, there is a note of self-irony or self-mockery in Brendan's descriptions of himself. This is caused by his rueful sense of his achievement having fallen far short of his aspirations. The irony, which is a feature of the protagonist's perspective and not authorial irony at the expense of the protagonist, is very quickly lost as the novel progresses and Tierney sees his hopes approaching fulfilment. The sardonic, rather indolent tone in which he compares himself to Napoleon ('Napoleonic lock of hair') and remembers that he was once likened to a 'drunken young Calvinist divine' because he had 'a noble guilt-ridden stare' (10) does not survive the end of the first chapter. Once he meets Max Bronstein, he decides that he will no longer be a potential novelist, but an actual writer. It is after this point that Brendan uses religious terms to convey his devotion, his dedication, his 'vocation' as a writer.

A closer examination of the language of religion used by Brendan, apparently to convey his zeal in the service of art, will show that he, as writer, is the God of his own idolatry. The term 'messianic' has a very exact symbolic meaning in relation to Brendan's perception of himself as a writer. Such remarks as:

> I was baptised in a new Communion. (33) That's why I've made writing my religion. (91) My book for me . . . is the belief that replaces belief. (298)

seem innocent enough. Their meaning appears obvious: Brendan has abandoned Catholicism in favour of a new religion of art. However, other remarks made by Brendan at various stages throughout the novel build up a picture of Brendan's vision of himself as, symbolically, the son of God who is God, in other words the Messiah. In a parody of a combination of two biblical appeals, the plea of Christ to God the Father in Gethsemane and the 'Father, forgive them' spoken from the cross, Brendan addresses his own dead father whose approval he never earned during his lifetime: 'O Father, forgive me as I forgive you, Father, I am your son.' (68) Here Brendan is the forgiving God as well as the Son of God, in an echo of a central Christian mystery. Again, at the end of the novel, Brendan thinks of 'some old Dog-God Father who will look down and tell me he is well pleased', (246) because Brendan, like Christ, has 'lost and sacrificed [himself]' (319) and his father is God the Father. For former Catholics, the symbolism and language of their religion are never lost; Brendan Tierney, mockingly, blasphemously, uses it to define his own relation to himself and the goal he is pursuing, summed up in yet another parody, this time of the Jesuit motto: 'my loved ones sacrificed *ad majorem* Brendan *gloriam*'. (53) This is possible because the language of religion fits, metaphorically, his own self-adoration.

Certain other factors enhance the reader's sense that, for Brendan Tierney, the writing of this novel is a religious obsession with himself as the centre or God. It is underlined, conversely, by Mrs Tierney's perception of it and of his whole lifestyle as 'pagan', in other words idolatrous. She uses the word frequently, to describe the children, the Freudian conversation and everything that shocks her by its novelty and irreverence. A closer examination will, however, show, that Brendan rejects all 'paganisms' (in Mrs Tierney's sense of the word) as well as Christianity. His religion is exclusive, monotheistic, unlike the beliefs of his eclectic associates, like Gallery, who look for meaning in buzz-words. Brendan is quick to criticise other cults as cults:

> 'The trouble with analysis . . . is that it's become a reli-
> gion with a Messiah and Holy Writ and even its Judases
> like Ferenczi and Reich—and a whole damn priesthood.
> (137)

One might add that art is also a religion with its Judases and its saints and angels, but for Brendan, art has great advantages over psychoanalysis. Although he recognises members of the artistic pantheon, notably Conrad, Joyce, Zola and Flaubert, he can aspire to join them in their elevated position. Nor is he obliged to pay homage to anything except art in the abstract, which really means the artist who is the human manifestation of art, which, in turn, can be understood really to mean himself, the writer.

The possibility of a religion of sex, a possibility that is realised in *I am Mary Dunne* and *The Doctor's Wife*, is also dismissed in the novel. When Jane and Brendan quarrel and are reconciled, their love-making could be described, to borrow Brendan's own phrase, as 'observance without belief'. It is mere devotion, mere ritual, such as that practised by Catholics without the necessity of belief or in such a way as to hide unbelief from the observer:

> ... the litany of atonement. They made their ejacula-
> tions and responses as devoutly as monk and nun ... as
> though the act itself were an act of communion. (94)

It is not an act of true communion, but merely the outward show of one. Both partners are responsible for the falseness of this moment, but it is a feature of the novel that, as his own writing progresses, Brendan Tierney loses interest in sex, in his wife and in everything outside himself. This casting off and stripping away are revealed by the starkness of language towards the end and by the movement away from imagery. No other 'substitute' religion can be allowed to interfere with the worship of the artistic self. By the end of the novel, Brendan has such a strong sense of his own central role in the universe that, with rare exceptions, he does not need imagery drawn from religion to understand it or to express it.

For the female protagonists in the other two novels under discussion in this section, the situation is less clear cut, though belief, for both of them, in the end becomes passion-ately simple. Both Mary Dunne and Sheila Redden are women of more than ordinary talent, yet their lives hinge on achiev-ing happiness through others, not through themselves. For

both of them, sexual happiness becomes supremely important, in contrast, for example, with the way in which Brendan
Tierney progressively loses interest in sex as his novel nears
completion. For him, his sexual needs and desires are sub-
sumed in the power of his creativity; for the women, on the
other hand, powerless in all other ways, their sexual nature
and their sexual attachments are so important because they
are the manifestation of their power. Their link with the
world is through the men they love.

Mary Dunne's ambitions are theatrical. She leaves
Butchersville, Nova Scotia, because she is 'daydreaming
about joining Catherine Mosca's acting school in Toronto'.[19]
Yet now, twelve years later, though Mary frequently uses
acting imagery in her thoughts and recollections, it is almost
always used in a pejorative sense. The instances are legion: 'I
hate this sickening female role-playing' (41); Hat's wasted
and unhappy life is summed up by her: 'But Hat acted his
whole life' (45); Janice speaks (falsely) 'as though she were
delivering lines from a stage' (54); Mary remembers 'every
line, stage direction, entrance and exit' (79) of the terrible
final few days she spent in New York with Hat, when she
acted a multitude of roles for him and for Terence. Acting, for
Mary, no longer has to do with art, but relates to artifice and
deception in daily life, never more so than when she observes
herself smiling an 'actressy smile' and thinks herself a
prostitute as she is about to make love to Terence. Her
bitterness is due to the realisation, not that acting failed her
by not being worthy of dedication to it as a belief, but that she
failed to follow her belief and her talent in acting, but this
bitterness expresses itself repeatedly in denigration of the art
or the profession of acting. The uneasiness of her attitude to
her former belief in herself as an actress is shown by the
number of different reasons she produces to justify or
rationalise her failure, at various stages throughout the novel.
For instance:

Looking back now, I see that if I'd had the drive, the

self-love, the hardness it takes for success, I would have gone over and thanked her for giving me this start. (169)

(False association of success with qualities she can comfortably say she would prefer not to have.)

If I had not worked hard in acting class, I might still believe I was born to be an actress. (171)

(Dismissal of any serious talent or any sense of artistic 'destiny'.)

Yet, in those days I wanted to become a writer. To become a writer you must want to write. I wanted the condition, not the result. And wasn't that, in some way, true of all my careers, weren't they just roles I acted out. (40)

(Debasing of the 'careers' (both artistic) by again comparing her pursuit of them disparagingly to mere 'role-playing' and highlighting deficiencies in her energy and motivation.) And the final claim to have understood the 'truth' of the matter, but the truth is not where she sees it, but at the end of this passage:

The truth is, I did not succeed as an actress . . . because I lacked the drive, the hard-as-nails self-love it takes. Acting is something I did once, did well, I think, but again it was a role. And when success came, the limited success of that season at East Hampton, followed by the offer of an off-Broadway play in the fall, it came too late. I was mixed up with Hat by then. His career took precedence. (41)

Whatever about the reasons for her failure to make a career in acting, and it seems much more likely to have to do with society's expectations of the roles of women than with any of the other doubtful reasons she gives earlier, it is very clear that, though Mary Dunne began adult life with certain aspirations, she did not follow them in any zealous way, certainly not in a manner that could be described as religious. In this she can be seen in strong contrast with Brendan Tierney. But there is a belief which Mary Dunne follows in a quasi-religious way, and that is her love for Terence. It is here that specifically Catholic and biblical imagery, the imagery of the religion that Mary Dunne has abandoned, is used by her to evoke the power and nature of her new belief. Terence becomes her religion in a way that acting has never done, (and in the same way as writing does for Brendan Tierney), and the depth of her feeling is clear, although there is something perverse as well as blasphemous about the circumstances in which she invokes the most famous of all psalms. Firstly she uses a parody of the psalm as a weapon with which to administer a terminal blow to her relationship with Hat and—it turns out—to Hat himself:

> Terence is my saviour, I shall not want, he maketh me to lie down in green pastures, he restoreth my soul. Yes, that's right. He's my new religion. He's life after death. (122)

It is striking that the beautiful language of the psalm and her evocation of her love are thus turned into weapons of scorn. 'He's my new religion. He's life after death' does not express a sense of reverence for religion, but uses the metaphors of religion to convey her sense that Terence supplies for her what religion never did or never could. The phrase 'he's life after death' contains this element of scorn for conventional beliefs while making use of the despised concept to convey her sense of belief in and dependence on Terence. As Moore said, in another context, religion is a powerful metaphor for belief. Religion certainly supplies powerful metaphorical language for belief, but in Moore's novels of this period it is in the abuse of religion that these metaphors flourish. They seem to say, as it were, not that this ecstasy is what religion is like, but that this is what religion is *not* like, but they say it in terms of religion. It is, therefore, no less than in the case of Brendan Tierney, an attack on the limitations of the real experience of religion, but expressed in the language of religion itself.

Old Testament and New Testament language are used again by Mary when the psalm is combined with images of salvation:

> Terence is my saviour, he restoreth my soul, he has made me happy (183 and, again, 229)

and

> You are my resurrection and my life and out of the depths I cry to you. (186)

Mary Dunne feels guilty partly because so much of her life appears to have been taken up by men and sex. She has been accused of being promiscuous and though, in her rational moments she knows she is not so, when she is in the grip of depression or hysteria she feels that she really *is* Dan Dunne's daughter and that what is said about her is true. Therefore, what Mary Dunne has been looking for, much more than an acting or literary career, is a man to love with whom she can disprove both the theories other people have about her and her fears about herself — that she is promiscuous. Terence is another man and to Hat, who wanted to keep her, he was further proof of her promiscuity and sexual insatiability. But she knows — in moments of reason — that Terence proves to her the validity of her existence. This is why, where Brendan Tierney sees himself as a godlike figure, she sees Terence as her saviour, in the much repeated biblical imagery. Unlike Brendan, she is not looking for something in herself to be developed; as her references to her acting career show, she regards a career now as being unlikely. She has chosen instead to be 'Mrs Terence Lavery'. She has chosen to *be* in him.

For Sheila Redden in *The Doctor's Wife*, Tom Lowry occupies a similar role to Terence Lavery. However there is an interesting development from the point of view of the use of religious imagery. No longer are there explicit statements of belief such as exist in both *An Answer from Limbo* and *I am Mary Dunne*, but it is implied and it is clearly understood by the reader that Tom Lowry is Sheila Redden's new belief. It is clear from putting this novel in contrast with the two earlier works that the change in Moore's attitude to religious belief did not happen only in the novels of the 1980s or suddenly as he was about to write *The Temptation of Eileen Hughes*. That is to say, he did not suddenly conceive of or write about religious fulfilment as a valid aspiration only in his most recent novels. The gradual return to an acceptance of the possibility of faith can be seen as early as *The Doctor's Wife*. Though Sheila Redden's sense of her sexual experience is expressed in terms that are, strictly speaking, blasphemous, they are only so in effect, not in intention. For her the evocation of religion conveys a memory of what religion meant to her at its most sublime moments, when she was an innocent and believing child. That feeling of religious ecstasy, which she believed lost, is restored to her though by other means. This is quite a different attitude to those expressed by Brendan Tierney or even by Mary Dunne, who make use of religious imagery only to mock religion:

> Yet tonight, in the quiet of this moonlight room, that feeling came back to her, that pure Sunday Communion peace. It filled her, shocking her, for wasn't *this* sin, here in this room, committing adultery with this boy, how could this be that same state, that pure feeling of peace? Yet it filled her, it possessed her totally. It was as though wrong were right. Her former life, her marriage, all that had gone before, now seemed to be her sin. These few days with Tom were her state of grace. (101)

No longer is religious imagery used to abuse religion. Instead, Sheila Redden rather makes an effort to *understand* her experience in the light of a religion she once had. She compares spiritual intensity with sexual ecstasy in a positive sense, whereas for Mary Dunne it is a negative comparison.

The other similarity between *The Doctor's Wife* and *I am Mary Dunne* which may be stated briefly, is that Sheila Redden has little confidence in her own abilities and little ability to envisage a life on her own. Like Mary Dunne, a woman of considerable talent, she has never used her talent to develop her own gifts but turned them instead towards domesticity: 'look at me, stuck all these years at home, my M.A. a waste. I don't think I could even support myself any more.' (22) Her belief, the only real belief of her adult life, is a belief not in herself, though it does lead to a greater sense of self, but in another person.

Because the beliefs of Mary Dunne, Sheila Redden and Brendan Tierney take on a quasi-religious significance and are thought of and described in terms of religious ecstasy or messianic zeal, the consequences of such beliefs, as they manifest themselves in the lives of the protagonists, must therefore be enormous. The most serious consequences are charted in relation to the effects on Brendan himself and on other people in *An Answer from Limbo*; in *I am Mary Dunne* and *The Doctor's Wife*, on the other hand, the focus is partly on those affected by the beliefs of the female protagonists but primarily on the psychological effects on the women themselves.

In the case of Brendan Tierney in *An Answer from Limbo*, his obsession with the writing of his novel causes the death of his mother, the alienation of his wife and the abandonment of his children. Because the consciousness of his mother and wife are dramatised, the emphasis is much more on them than on the children. He becomes like Wordsworth's coldhearted scientist who would botanise upon his mother's grave. Neither mother nor wife is free of fault, but it is made very clear at the end of the novel that Brendan deliberately ignores any chance to become reconciled with them. The important point is that nothing that they do—and to an extent both act reprehensibly—could possibly merit the way he treats them. Besides, there is no sense in which he is consciously punishing them; he is simply blind to their needs. The destruction caused to his family is catastrophic; the novel illustrates what the heroine repeatedly thinks in *I am Mary Dunne*, that there is no sin or crime as grave as the sin of indifference.

This aspect is obvious and need not be laboured. What is more subtle, however, is the extent to which Brendan changes in the novel and how he takes cognisance of these changes. In other words, has he changed so much that he can be responsible for such serious effects on the members of his family and yet not feel guilty? The final sentence of the novel, 'I have lost and sacrificed myself' (319) is spoken to himself by Brendan and has been discussed above as the climax of Brendan's messianic self-image. It is worth taking time to interpret exactly the tone of the sentence. Does Brendan regret the loss and sacrifice or regard it as a necessity for a true writer of genius? The choice of the word 'sacrificed' and especially the word 'lost' would suggest the former, but if the sentence is taken in the context of the novel as a whole, the latter seems the more likely interpretation. Brendan, in metaphorical terms, sees the change as a death—he wonders of his former self if he 'was alive only four months ago'. But, like Christ, he has died to be resurrected, to be born into a new life, that of the dispassionate writer/observer, who will not be distracted by emotional demands. He will, like Balzac in the anecdote he quotes in the book, worry more about whom his fictional heroine will marry than about any mere domestic crisis. In the final paragraph of the novel, he takes Ted Ormsby's question of years before: '"But will you sacrifice yourself?"' (25) and perverts it in answering it in the affirmative. In his own sense of the term, a sense perhaps unique to himself, he has sacrificed himself by sacrificing others (which Ted Ormsby has always believed him capable of) and has consequently become a person unable to feel sorrow or guilt. He has, therefore, sacrificed his human feelings and attained the pinnacle of artistic detachment he admires other writers for having reached. At his mother's graveside Brendan repeats to himself in incantatory fashion the drunken, angry words he first utters at the Dortmunders' party: 'He's a writer. He can't feel: he can only record.' (319) To a jaundiced observer it seems very much as if Brendan Tierney has merely given himself leave to feel nothing, least of all any guilt. Inasmuch as Brendan Tierney is throughout the novel an unsympathetic character (though perhaps admirable for his strength of will), the interest of the plot partly lies in the ambiguity of the conclusion. Is Brendan 'punished' for his pride, like Lucifer? Like Faust, he has sold his soul, but has he yet come to regret it? What is certain, however, is that the pity of the reader at the end of the novel is directed towards his victims rather than towards the protagonist himself.

For the heroine of *I am Mary Dunne* the consequences of following her beliefs are more difficult to quantify: her recollections in the novel cover a period of twelve years, between the time Mary leaves Butchersville when she is twenty and the real time of the novel, when she is thirty-two. As discussed in detail in the previous section, Mary's original 'belief', her desire to follow a career in acting, is gradually abandoned and becomes secondary to a quest for an elusive quality in her life, which may be called love or sexual fulfilment. She certainly sees her search as having ended and her present husband as being all that she needs — witness the dramatic religious/sexual imagery. To reach this stage, however, she has had to abandon two husbands after using them both for her own advancement. As everything is filtered through Mary Dunne's consciousness, it is in her own words that this is expressed (in this case about Jimmy): 'I had done a selfish rotten thing just because I wanted to get away to Toronto. But I was not prepared to pay the price for that mistake.' (152) Furthermore, she now never sees her mother or her brother — as far as the reader is concerned she may well have never seen them since she eloped from Butchersville, Nova Scotia, twelve years previously: 'I too wrote "love" but I too wrote tactful excuses, too busy to come this summer, hoping for Christmas, spring at the latest.' (19) She is conscious of her neglect and of her 'crime' of indifference in these areas, but most of all she is aware that she may have been the reason for the failure and premature death of her second husband, Hatfield Bell. The guilt Mary feels about this matter manifests itself in two ways: firstly, she repeatedly relives the final stages of their marriage; secondly, she is, generally speaking, anxious, neurotic and even suicidal. She is sure that she has found in Terence what she has always needed, but she has found it in the first place only at the expense of someone else and she keeps it only at the expense of her own happiness. She has invested too much hope in Terence as her 'Saviour': he is the alternative to her career; he is her assurance that she is not promiscuous. He is made to carry too much responsibility for her life. Under these circumstances her life can hardly be comfortable. The novel certainly ends on a knife-edge, just as Mary trembles on the edge of a parapet, contemplating suicide.

In *The Doctor's Wife* there is another guilty heroine, but there is a great degree of development from the previous novel discussed. For Sheila Redden, loving Tom Lowry means abandoning her husband, her son, her country and the moral traditions of her father. Though she has rejected Catholicism, these values must still be deeply ingrained in her. Where Mary Dunne is thoughtful and guilty *after* the event (as much as twelve years afterwards in the case of her marriage to Jimmy), Sheila Redden is conscious at all times of the choice she has to make, and this despite the short duration of the affair with Tom Lowry. She is conscious on the one hand of the happiness she feels with Tom, but on the other of the impossibility of lasting happiness with him. Therefore, she makes a fully informed and adult choice, which can be contrasted strongly with Mary Dunne's decision to return with Hat to Canada, which she made without intending never to see Terence again. Sheila Redden suffers as much herself as she makes others suffer: indeed, the novel ends with all the parties involved deeply unhappy. But the crucial point is that she does not just pursue her belief at the expense of others, but also, consciously, at her own expense.

Her suffering, in a sense, is willed, or at least anticipated; Mary Dunne's is involuntary. This does not make Sheila Redden's suffering less, but it does make her a wholly responsible individual: 'She knew there was no way in which he could trace her. She did not want him to walk in. And yet she could not help it. She thought of him constantly. She knew that some day she would no longer think of him all the time. But it had not happened yet.' (270)

If these two novels, *I am Mary Dunne* and *The Doctor's Wife* are taken together, they seem to present a very pessimistic view of the possibilities of human happiness: one woman chooses her happiness at the expense of others, but while superficially fortunate, suffers deep psychological disorders. The second chooses unhappiness without being able to prevent the unhappiness of others; her unhappiness is more obvious. Can it not be said, therefore, that the authorial attitude that emerges from these two novels is that unhappiness is the inescapable fact of human existence, or of female existence? (It is not accidental that both protagonists are female; out of all his novels only in *The Temptation of Eileen Hughes* does Moore show a male protagonist investing so much of himself in another person, and Bernard McAuley's passion for Eileen Hughes is a quasi-mystical neurosis.) In a curious way, the sexual love experienced by these female protagonists is half way between the egotism of Brendan Tierney and the self-forgetting zeal of Mother St Jude in *Cold Heaven*. It is both selfish and unselfish. It is certainly not accidental that when, later on, Moore conceived of and wrote of a person full of genuine self-forgetfulness and imbued with a genuine religious feeling quite separate from religious politics, he should have chosen a woman.

These secular people in a secular society, striving to fulfil themselves through their own endeavour or through other people, have rejected religion. But it is as if Moore, even when he entered this humanistic or secular phase, had already lost faith in these values or had never established any faith in them any more than a belief in God. Perhaps it is partly a question of age: 'What we call humanism suits only one moment of our lives', says Mauriac.[20] Forty, it appears, is the significant age, agreed on by authorities as diverse as Mauriac, Jung and Moore himself. For Moore, 'There's a point in life which we all come to, usually in the forties, where you suddenly say, "What am I doing here?"'[21] Mauriac, writing about the conversion of Racine, had the following to say: 'For the fact that he [Racine] was approaching forty is in itself sufficient' [to account for his conversion].[22] Jung has written extensively on this phenomenon. In *Modern Man in Search of a Soul* (a title that could be said to convey the essence of much of Moore's work) he writes:

> We see that in this phase of life—between thirty-five and forty—a significant change in the human psyche is in preparation. At first it is not a conscious and striking change; it is rather a matter of indirect signs of a change which seems to take its rise from the unconscious. Often it is something like a slow change in a person's character; in another case certain traits may come to light which had disappeared in childhood; or again, inclinations and interests begin to weaken and others arise to take their places . . .

> . . . Wholly unprepared, [people] embark upon the second half of life. Or are there perhaps colleges for forty-year-olds which prepare them for their coming life and its demands as the ordinary colleges introduce our young people to a knowledge of the world and of life? No, there are none. Thoroughly unprepared, we take the step into the afternoon of life; worse still we take this step with the false presupposition that our truths and ideals will serve us as hitherto. But we cannot live the afternoon of life according to the programme of life's morning . . .

> . . . I said just now that we have no schools for forty-year-olds. That is not quite true. *Our religions were*

always such schools in the past, but how many people regard them as such today?[23] [my emphasis]

The last sentence of the above quotation from Jung covers precisely the issues raised by Moore's novels of this period: when people reject religion, what are they to put in its place? How are they to live? The novels show protagonists of very different types in very different situations, but what they have in common is twofold: firstly, they reject religion; secondly, they seem to have another system of belief which they can follow instead of religion and which would appear to provide them with a *raison d'être*. But in no case does this belief supply a blueprint for living or a guarantee of happiness. The result is that each individual must act in his own interests at any particular time and must be guided only by his own perceptions of the situation. There can be no reliance either on the prescriptions of religion (though, as was remarked earlier, these often remain subliminally in the mind of the characters and do have some influence, even if that influence is contested), or on the accumulated wisdom of others (such as parents), whose advice has been discredited along with the religion they practise. All the protagonists behave in a manner which is or would be disapproved of by their parents, and the gulf between them and their families is both caused by and symbolised by their geographical dislocation. Yet, they act according to their lights, in their own best interests, in the interests of their own happiness. It is an habitual part of Moore's setting of character against circumstance that while he insists on the ineluctability of choice, he simultaneously puts his characters in the position of being unable to make any choice other than the one they actually make, despite the catastrophic consequences of such decisions. Thus, his protagonists are free and yet unfree. For instance, Mary Dunne is forced to choose between Hat and Terence when Hat wishes to return to Canada. She knows that her choice should be Hat and in theory she is free to choose him, but in practice she is incapable of making that choice; she is unable, in the end, to do other than choose Terence.

Similarly, although the psychology of the characters is completely different and the actual mechanism of choice is not illustrated, Brendan Tierney seems *compelled* to be the artist who has 'lost and sacrificed' himself, as well as losing his mother, wife and children at the end of *An Answer from Limbo*. It is psychologically consistent that the individual will follow the person or the thing which appears most likely to promise happiness and fulfilment—in Brendan Tierney's case, the idea of Brendan as writer, in Mary Dunne's case, the ideal of Terence as lover. 'We have no schools for forty-year-olds.' In their respective novels, Brendan Tierney is twenty-nine, Mary Dunne is thirty-two and Sheila Redden is thirty-seven. There is a progression in the consciousness of the characters: Brendan Tierney is happy and proud to be a monster of selfishness; Mary Dunne is guilty; Sheila Redden, closest to forty, finds it most difficult to choose, is most in need of a 'school' such as Jung envisages, and indeed longs for the kind of certainty that religion might have given her. Seeing most clearly, she is the most aware both of her reliance on herself and of the ultimate selfishness of her act. Though none of the characters express themselves so portentously, they could all be said to share, implicitly, a sense of their lives like that expressed in the remark by Moore quoted above: 'where you suddenly say, "What am I doing here?"'

In the three novels discussed above, Moore has certain common premises. His characters are articulate, intelligent, 'modern' in sensibility in that they are mobile and not willing to be bound completely by conventional wisdom or traditional pieties. They choose to follow beliefs that are apparently serious, in human terms, and valid. Yet the validity of these beliefs and of the whole secular and materialist culture of post-Christian man are called into question in a fundamental manner. The pursuit of these beliefs has unexpected and profound consequences for the protagonists themselves and for those whose lives are influenced by them.

The three novels, *An Answer from Limbo, I am Mary Dunne* and *The Doctor's Wife*, are no less interesting as regards the technique and point of view that Moore uses to develop his themes.

> Given material potentially interesting, concentration and intensity and hence vividness are the results of working within limits, albeit self-imposed . . . Thus the choice of a point of view in the writing of fiction is at least as crucial as the choice of a verse form in the composing of a poem.[24]

The importance of point of view has been indisputably established, in articles and books, from James's *Prefaces*, through Lubbock, Beach, Schorer and Norman Friedman (his article quoted above). One of Moore's greatest artistic accomplishments in the three novels under discussion in this chapter, and to some extent in all his novels, is the variety of perspectival techniques he utilises. The three works share a preoccupation with the belief adopted by people when they no longer believe in religion and appear to have a pessimistic overall view that the idea of secular happiness, whether achieved in oneself or through another, is a snare and a delusion. To dramatise this theme rather than to tell (to show rather than to tell, in Percy Lubbock's distinction: 'The narrative, then . . . is to be raised to a power approaching that of drama, where the intervention of the story-teller is no longer felt');[25] to expose the moral dilemma rather than overtly moralising is Moore's aim in these novels.

Moore has always seen form and point of view as a challenge rather than an onerous duty or a restriction and he seems to delight especially in experimenting in various combinations of third-person narration: 'The whole interesting thing to me about writing is change. It's each book presenting some technical or some intellectual problem that I haven't faced before.'[26] In *An Answer from Limbo*, he uses a combination of first-person and third-person narratives; in *I am Mary Dunne*, he develops a first-person interior language of anguish and near-madness; and in *The Doctor's Wife*, he adopts a perspectival standpoint frequently very far from the protagonist, excludes narration and concentrates almost totally on the depiction of key scenes. It is worth looking at the use of point of view in all three novels in detail, since this is something that contributes greatly to their originality and success.

5

The Giving of Voice —
An Answer from Limbo

IN *An Answer from Limbo* Brendan Tierney's perspective is
not the only one in the novel, but because it alone is
presented in the first person, it is the dominant one. Though
Moore has said that in all his novels, he has tried to capture
the 'voice' of his protagonists, *An Answer From Limbo* is the
first novel in which he entrusts the protagonist with his own
story. He adopts this device not to show a character's
perception of morality and a deep-rooted guilt, as he does in
the later *I am Mary Dunne*, but to show precisely the opposite — the absence of guilt in the ruthlessly egoistic Brendan
Tierney. Moore uses a first-person narrative with Brendan
Tierney, not because he approves of him, or even sympathises with him, but because Brendan can be trusted to tell his
own story. The equivocation — the duality of presenting the
character's 'voice' but in such a manner as to convey authorial
irony — that is associated with free indirect speech is not
needed here. The characteristics shared by all three protagonists of the novels prior to *An Answer from Limbo* are their
anxiety for public approval and their lack of any strong sense
of self which could exist independently of the views of
others. This does not apply to Brendan Tierney. He will not
delude himself or seek sympathy by appearing to be 'nicer' or
more humane than he is. His quest is not for approval but for
glory. It is a brave and risky authorial procedure to have as
the central consciousness of the novel a character as unsympathetic as Brendan Tierney and one who is so little susceptible to guilt, but it is an integral part of the development of
Moore's theme. As his theme changes, so do his characters
move from dependence to independence.

An early paragraph from the novel illustrates very clearly the type of protagonist that Brendan Tierney is:

> For I have not yet become great. I who boasted that I would never settle for the ordinary avocations have settled instead for—what? I have written, yes. Prose, not poetry. Six of my stories have been published in small literary magazines. Yet the novel with which I hope to fulfil my prophesy lies in a drawer in my office, a loved but ailing child, its life endangered by my fitful labours. True, I have escaped from the provincial mediocrity of my native land and now live, in exile, in the Rome of our day. Yet my employment in New York is as an editorial slave on a publication so banal in title and content that I cannot bear to reveal its name, and if asked why I do it I must talk of bills; clothing bills, food and rent bills, medical bills, kindergarten bills, my mother's allowance, those bills in which I monthly drown. And I can tell you that at night, in a harsh, recurring dream, I stand again beside that freezing fountain, reliving that moment when, by their fear of me, my classmates gave me a taste of what my ambitions might bring me, when suddenly, haphazardly, yet with no possible alternative routing, my course was set towards a destiny I have not yet accomplished. In that dream I weep. (10)

This passage is remarkable for its bitterness, its ambition and its force. It is also very self-conscious, as though the speaker imagines the objections of an interlocutor: the 'I have written, yes' and 'True, I have escaped' imply an answer to an inferred question, reminding Tierney that he has gone some way towards realising his goal. He yields to his interlocutor only to reject the implied interjection and to emphasise the limitations of what he has done. This appeal, this demand on the attention of the imaginary listener becomes more insistent towards the end: 'And I can tell you'. The analogy between the work and a child is drawn several times in the novel and suggests simultaneously the passion felt by Brendan for his literary progeny and his relative dispassion about his real living children. Notable also is the control of the passage, which is evident in the style itself, and the control which Tierney here exercises on his life by overviewing it so coldly and so critically.

Mark Schorer, in his influential essay 'Technique as Discovery', characterises 'the use of point of view not only as a mode of dramatic delimitation, but more particularly, of thematic definition'.[1] Thus, in this passage, the technique used by Moore to convey Brendan's thoughts, creates by the very use of the technique itself as well as by the words, images and tone, a means of establishing judgment on Brendan. Schorer's assertion 'not only that technique *contains* intellectual and moral implications, but that it *discovers* them' he applies to a reading of *Wuthering Heights*, in which he seeks to show that the romantic hankerings of Emily Brontë are proven to be pernicious and untenable by the technique and narrative structure of the novel. This is almost to suggest that Brontë's novel was written *in spite* of the author's views or feelings or against the current of her feelings. This kind of interpretation would not be tenable in relation to *An Answer from Limbo* or indeed any of Moore's novels, since there is every evidence that each different stylistic or narrative strategy he adopts is carefully conceived and quite conscious. Moore does create Brendan Tierney for the reader, but by giving him his own voice and avoiding any type of authorial intrusion, he is showing us Brendan creating his life in the past and planning it (therefore creating it) in the future. This is in keeping with the recurrent theme of Brendan as omnipotent God, which was discussed in an earlier section on imagery.

All of Brendan's narrative share of the novel takes the form of interior monologue, but this passage shows how far that form can be from a more natural 'stream-of-consciousness' interiorisation, or even from the type of interior monologue developed by Moore to convey the guilt-feelings of the heroine in *I am Mary Dunne*. The passage is highly rhetorical: it insists that the matter be viewed on the speaker's (or thinker's) terms. Neither doubt nor questioning is allowed, and the addressing of the phantom interlocutor enhances rather than decreases one's impression of Tierney's conviction that only he is allowed to interpret his own life. From the flatness of the opening 'For I have not yet become great', with its suggestion both of the inevitability of greatness and the conviction that because it has not been reached, there is nothing else important in life, there is the careful establishing of the degrees of greatness and of the means by which one achieves it. Thus the lowest form of writing life is in the magazine and tied to it by implication is the lowest form of life, the domestic and familial. Though the banality of the New York publication is emphasised, the mockery is concentrated on the publication itself and Tierney avoids the stigma of association by keeping this magazine at a distance and refusing to reveal its name. In ascending order after this come the stories, then the novel, with the suggestion as well that higher than any other form is poetry, for after all as a teenager Tierney saw himself as a great poet. As well as the literary scale, there is the careful summing up of a hierarchy of places in the phrase 'True, I have escaped . . .'

In the early stages of the novel, the reader is forced to accept, in such paragraphs as this, Tierney's estimate of what he is, his sense of his failure to date and of what he must do to redeem himself. That is not to say that one has to believe in his messianic destiny as a writer, but that one simply has no other evaluation of his literary talent on which to base a judgment. Even later, when Moore introduces the 'voices' of the two other main protagonists, they do nothing to modify the received image of Brendan as a great or potentially great novelist. Their judgment on him is as a man, a husband and a son. To write his novel is more than a desire for Brendan: it is a 'destiny', a nightmare, something that has gone through him and coloured his psyche, 'like wine through water'. And if Brendan Tierney is read accurately at the beginning of the novel, as Moore means him to be read, then what he does will not be a surprise. His depiction of himself is not an exaggeration, despite a style that sometimes appears to mock itself in its self-consciousness.

Brendan Tierney changes a great deal as the novel progresses and a much later passage may be compared with the above. It shows clearly his reaction to the changed circumstances of his life:

> When I leave my workroom I enter into a state of waiting. At home, I walk from room to room, I pick up books but do not read them, I sit in a chair and stare . . . The apartment is blessedly peaceful; no rows, no children, no television. The children are in Saratoga and my mother, of course, is at Finnerty's apartment. She will be going home at the end of next week. That reminds me. I must call her. As for Jane, she is strangely silent. She misses the children, I suppose. She will be going back up to Saratoga again to see them this weekend and I'll have the apartment completely to myself. Peace, it's wonderful. (244)

At the end of the novel, the narratorial voice of Brendan Tierney is made to cast off its self-consciousness and its rhetoric. The style of this passage mirrors the bare intensity and self-dedication of his life. The paragraph provides an extraordinarily succinct summary of Tierney's life and shows that everything he should love has become peripheral to him. His children are absent, his wife is estranged by her silence, his mother, rejected, has left their lives. His life has become intensely simple, or simple in its intensity. The short sentences and the monosyllabic diction mirror this intensity and this simplicity. Yet, for all the intensity, the tone is peculiarly passive, almost vacant, very far from the charged energy and determination which were so evident in the paragraph quoted earlier. This is because what Brendan is describing is the emptiness he feels when he leaves his book to come home, not the elation and almost manic energy that characterises him when he is actually involved in negotiations or discussions with Gerston or Sol Silver. It is the voice of a man who has come near to accomplishing his 'destiny' and from this paragraph can be seen the consequences of his ambition and its near-fulfilment. There is no guilt apparent in this paragraph: only the most cursory attention is given to postponing the visit to his mother. But the passage also completely lacks the rhetoric of Brendan's earlier self-presentation. Though neither here nor in his final speeches in the novel does Brendan articulate a sense of loss for the humanity he has deliberately abandoned, one can infer that loss from the diction and rhythm of this speech. Thus the reader, from looking through the central consciousness of Brendan at the beginning of the novel, is now made by Brendan's own words to look *at* him. As he objectifies his experience, he, in turn, is objectivised.

Mark Schorer discusses the tone and point of view of the final passage of *A Portrait of the Artist as a Young Man* in the essay mentioned above, to illustrate his argument that technique discovers and therefore reveals 'implications'. A similar type of analysis could be applied to *An Answer from Limbo*.

> The final passage of the novel . . . is peculiarly bare. The life experience was not bare, as we know from *Stephen Hero*; but Joyce is forcing technique to comment. In essence, Stephen's alienation is a denial of the human environment; it is a loss; and the austere discourse of the final section, abstract and almost wholly without sensuous detail or strong rhythm, tells us of that loss. It is a loss so great that the texture of the notation-like prose here suggests that the end is really all an illusion, that when Stephen tells us and himself that he is going forth to forge in the smithy of his soul the uncreated conscience of his race, we are to infer from the very quality of the icy, abstract void he now inhabits, the implausibility of his aim.[2]

The question such an approach would raise about Brendan Tierney the writer is, whether a man so dehumanised as Brendan now so proudly is, could be capable of writing the masterpiece which is his aim. All the evidence adduced by Brendan in the novel, in his repeated references to great writers, would suggest that detachment is the essential of greatness. However, it is possible that there are two different messages being given to the reader here: firstly, the obvious, literal one, but, secondly, that the technique is operating independently to give the opposite message about the fitness of the near-automaton Brendan to write a great work of fiction. If this is so, then the final section of the novel, and especially the final lines spoken by Brendan should be examined not just for what they say or how he says them (in the sense of *tone*) but for what they say by virtue of the technique that is used to convey them.

The voices of other protagonists, notably Mrs Tierney and Jane are also dramatised in *An Answer from Limbo*. Moore does not look for any easy method of making either of Brendan Tierney's 'victims' appear more sympathetic or more pathetic to the reader. Nor are their values exalted over his. The magnitude of Brendan's sin of neglect does not need enhancement. Mrs Tierney's values are narrow and parochial; her Catholicism is part traditional piety and part guilt; her baptism of the children against the wishes of their parents is very high-handed. Yet the capacity of Brendan to hurt her, which is shown repeatedly throughout the novel—she does not have the same capacity to hurt him, except when it comes to his artistic vanity—prepares for the final estrangement and the neglect which results in her death. Furthermore, her suffering is not new, but part of a pattern of humiliation that was established by her pious and overbearing husband during their marriage and perpetuated by her poverty and dependence after his death. Sympathy is evoked for Mrs Tierney because she is so palpably a victim and because her suffering is so out of proportion to the extent of her wrongdoing. Moore very skilfully uses free indirect speech to convey Mrs Tierney's thoughts, as in this passage early in the novel:

> They were well named, she decided. The darlings. That was her private name for them, what with their darling this and darling that. Look at those back rests would you. Brendan not thirty and her even younger. Back rests, as if they had one foot in the grave! Bohemians my eye; they were as set in their ways — 'Is it drink time yet, darling?' 'Is it time to do the dishes darling?' — as two old grannies. Bohemians, it's their children not them, who are the Bohemians. Wild savages those children are, but whose fault is that when Jane treats them as equals. 'Never even your wit to the child', as the saying goes. Sure aren't they only children, don't they want somebody to make up their minds for them, is Jane daft that she can't see that? O, well. On Monday I'll have the looking after of them. Then they'll see who's boss. (70)

It is very important in the narrative structure of the novel that the points of view of Brendan, Jane and Mrs Tierney should be presented in different ways. Because Brendan's point of view is presented exclusively in the first person, this distinguishes it from any others that may be shown. In this paragraph, Moore very subtly conveys the thoughts of Mrs Tierney by different means: firstly, through reported thought — 'They were very well named, she decided' — then in free indirect speech for much of the paragraph, on to the final sentence where the pronoun 'I' of direct speech occurs, probably without the reader's noticing it. The central section of the paragraph, in free indirect speech, captures in the idiom and flavour of Mrs Tierney's thought (and speech) her scorn of her son and daughter-in-law, in the inverted syntax of 'Wild savages those children are' and in the colloquial 'Look at those back rests would you.' (70) Mrs Tierney has very little power or independence in the household of Brendan and Jane and this is her way of exercising power as soon as they have left for the evening. In voyeuristic fashion and without their knowledge, she has gained an insight into their lives and thus has gained an element of power. Because she has broken a taboo of privacy, her tone in the quoted paragraph is scornful and rather triumphant. She establishes a superiority over Brendan and Jane by twice comparing them to grannies, as if to assert that it is they, not she, who deserve this appellation. In her mockery of their use of back rests and their—to her—false pretensions to be Bohemians, she is expressing her own realisation of their view of her (which we know from Jane's narrative to be an accurate realisation) as being old, dowdy and dull, and transferring this opinion to them instead. The contempt she expresses for Jane as a mother strengthens her perception of her own competence and experience in the field of discipline and rearing. She even invokes the traditional wisdom of her community to fortify and justify her point of view in this regard. Even the clichéd expression 'Then they'll see who's boss' at the end of the paragraph is an expression of the desire to escape the powerlessness of her position in this family. Under cover of her commentary on the habits of her son and daughter-in-law, the author takes the reader much more deeply into the consciousness of Mrs Tierney than might have been expected from the reticence of the opening 'she decided', which prepares for reported speech or thoughts. No part of this section of the novel presents her as a very honest or honourable person, yet the emphasis on her powerlessness and on her desire to have some role to play in the family brings out the pathos of her position and the cynicism with which Brendan is using her. Powerlessness, despite the competence of her nursing and grandmotherly personality, is the characteristic of Mrs Tierney most strongly and lastingly conveyed; she dies, powerless, unnecessarily isolated, paralysed by a stroke suffered in a futile attempt to reach the telephone.

Jane Tierney, on the other hand, could be said to get in Vito Italiano the lover she deserves, were it not that her fate has somehow the air of a tragedy that must finally be blamed on Brendan, with her as a victim, if not quite an innocent victim. In the third section of the novel, this is our introduction to her:

> Jane Tierney dreamed of dark ravishers, young and fierce, who loomed in her thoughts like menacing yet exciting phalli, their silken white shirts disturbed at the openings by crisp black curls of body hair, who wore suits of impossible cut, gold watch bracelets and religious medals on silver chains, who used cheap cologne, whose olive-complected smiles revealed white predators' teeth. (26)

Jane's fantasy goes on at some length, in half-graphic, half-grandiloquent terms, containing elements of masochism and degradation. As the opening sentences reveal, these may be Jane's fantasies, but they are not expressed in Jane's language. They are expressed instead in a mocking purple passage, in which the author keeps as great a distance as possible between him – and therefore the reader – and the thought processes of Jane Tierney. This is a completely different technique from that used in the passage quoted earlier where Mrs Tierney's thoughts are conveyed in a homely and colloquial Ulster idiom. The key to the ridiculous nature of these imaginings is in the flatness of the final words of the paragraph: 'Men. Not Brendan.' It is as if the plurality of 'olive-complected' lovers could make up for the singular inadequacies of the man to whom she is married.

Moore keeps Jane at a distance, especially at the beginning of the novel. Even in the intimacy of the bathroom, as she sits crying on the toilet seat after a silly quarrel with Brendan, he prefaces her views of herself with phrases which make them reported speech rather than free indirect speech: 'She could see . . . She had her private reservations . . . she worried . . . she knew . . . she'd thought.' (28) There is little compassion for Jane developed in the early part of the novel:

she is shown as being petulant, indiscreet and spiteful. There is also an ironic justice in the appearance of Vito Italiano; he is just the 'dark-complected amoral young man' she has dreamed of. But in her sin, as Mrs Tierney would call it, or sickness, as Jane herself would prefer, (126) she earns compassion, even later on in the novel from Mrs Tierney herself, who suspects Jane's adultery. Her loss of control over her life, the reader's sense of which is further enhanced by insight into Vito's cynical manipulation and subsequent dropping of her, can only be restored by Brendan. Moore presents Jane in an increasingly sympathetic light as the novel progresses; she gains, paradoxically, a dignity in the degradation of her final encounter with Vito. The moral onus is on Brendan to allow her to resign her job and he will be held responsible for the death of his marriage no less than the death of his mother. At the end of the novel, Moore chooses to convey Jane's sense of herself with that equivocal sympathy that comes with free indirect speech and finally through the medium of direct speech. Just before the news of Mrs Tierney's death, the section where Jane thinks of her life and that of her contemporaries begins 'She turned towards the window' (305) and ends 'Pathetic is not tragic. I should go to bed.' (307) The distinction between tragic and pathetic is made by a sophisticated modern person, a self-conscious college graduate, but the irony of being well-equipped to define or label the problem while being completely powerless to solve it, is expressed and understood by Jane in the juxtaposition of the sardonic analysis of the first sentence and the fatalism of the second. Jane is the person who changes most in the course of the novel and it is obvious also that her capacity for feeling at the time of Mrs Tierney's death and funeral sets her apart from and above Brendan and increases the reader's sense of the moral vacuum that now exists in him.

An Answer from Limbo concentrates, not on the making of moral choices or the taking of ethical decisions, but on the consequences of those decisions and choices. By using the technique of giving Brendan's narrative in the first person and changing to either reported thought or free indirect speech in the case of Mrs Tierney and Jane, Moore establishes different depths of field in the perceptions of the reader. But the character to whom one is brought closest in the confidential and conspiratorial 'I' of Brendan's narrative is not closest in terms of sympathy; the author rather chooses to show him in his coldness and egoism. Conversely, the two female characters, though frequently depicted in a critical manner, either implicitly or explicitly, are ultimately the victims of Brendan's immorality, his terrible blankness and restriction of vision. This sort of blankness or moral blindness is shown most startlingly at the end of the novel, not only after his mother's death but in the period around the completion and editing of his novel. It shows how far he has gone and with what damaging consequences, in order to prosecute his belief in his own literary genius. An alternative moral system to Brendan's selfishness is not provided by either of the women: Mrs Tierney is limited to conventional Catholic rituals and pieties and Jane adores instead the modern god of libido and self-gratification. Thus, in terms of the technique of the novel, none of the three central voices is distinguished by having the quality of truth or genuine self-forgetfulness. This quality is most closely approximated to by Ted Ormsby, who is in Brendan's past and miles away from the scene of the novel and whose voice therefore goes unheeded.

6

The Fixed Centre —
I am Mary Dunne

'I am Mary Dunne' focuses on both the making of moral choices and the consequences of these choices. One of the most innovative of Moore's works, this novel uses interior monologue to convey the irrational nature of its heroine's psyche — irrational because she is so much a victim of guilt.

In his preface to *The Ambassadors*, Henry James wrote of the dangers of the use of the first person — 'the darkest abyss of romance this':

> Had I meanwhile, made [Strether] at once hero and historian, endowed him with the romantic privilege of the 'first person' — the darkest abyss of romance, this, inveterately, when enjoyed on the grand scale — variety, and many other queer matters as well, might have been smuggled in by the back door. Suffice it, to be brief, that the first person, in the long piece, is a form foredoomed to looseness, and that looseness, never much my affair, had never been so little so as on this particular occasion.[1]

This looseness is what Moore is contending with in *I am Mary Dunne*, in that the first-person protagonist in interior monologue can say anything, remember at will, move at random from one subject to another and from past to present to future. Mary Dunne has to be allowed what James, in a continuation of the preface quoted above, calls 'the terrible fluidity of self-revelation'. Yet, at the same time, in opposition to this 'looseness', there are at work the inherent constraints of the technique of the single perspective. First-person narration with the 'I' narrator as protagonist is a very limited and limiting technique, but it compensates in intensity for what it lacks in flexibility and variety. In Norman Friedman's schematic classification of different points of view in fiction, he describes the angle of view of the novel with 'I' as protagonist as 'that of the fixed centre'.[2] This is the best perspectival technique to show anguish and paranoia, since a narrator such as Mary must have limited access to, for example the consciousness of others. This is borne out when she suspects the elderly Dieter of being a thief and when she neurotically imagines that Terence is judging her. She has access to conversations, letters, and she can draw inferences, but many of these mental activities, far from calming her or even informing her, serve only to frighten or mislead her. Furthermore, Moore uses in this novel another technique, that of enclosing the real time of the novel in the period of one day, and therefore throwing the narrative weight on memory as experienced, rather than on memory as a merely intellectual activity.IThus he avoids the removal to a distance caused by the use of a retrospective first-person narration. It is the narration of agonised memory, experiential rather than merely retrospective.

Moore's technique in this novel has as its aim the evocation of the intensity and frequent irrationality of Mary Dunne's guilt and memories, not the justification of her guilt. The point is made repeatedly during the novel that it is not necessary for guilt to be justified in order that it should exist. It is enough that Mary should feel guilty for her to be unhappy. The sex of the respective protagonists of *An Answer from Limbo* and *I am Mary Dunne* is not accidental or insignificant, because women have always been programmed by their upbringing and the expectations of society to feel guilt more readily and more strongly. In the context of the theme of this novel (which is also the predominant theme of this period of Moore's work), it would seem that guilt is a necessary corollary of the attempt to establish for oneself a rationally based humanistic form of secular happiness. In *An Answer from Limbo*, Moore is concerned mainly to illustrate the effect of Brendan's selfishness on the two other protagonists, but in this novel, the focus changes to the architect of the unhappiness of others, but who is even more so the architect of her own unhappiness. To show the guilt and the memories of Mary Dunne, Moore utilises for the most part Mary's own 'voice' to tell her story, which is interspersed with dialogue. The novel is in the form, sometimes of coherent, structured narrative, but more often of interior monologue, with all the apparent changes and fluidity (James's 'looseness') implied by that technique.

A circular structure is used to imply that guilt is something without beginning and without end. The novel begins with Mary Dunne in bed remembering the day's events, and ends with the end of that day's events. The beginning could therefore be said to occur after the end. The narrative in the novel as a whole is deliberately made to appear fluid, even haphazard, so that it mimics the workings of the mind. The protagonist, who is the narrator of her own life and the interpreter of her own feelings, draws attention to the apparent randomness by trying to impose coherence and 'usefulness' on her thoughts: 'Far better do something constructive, like try to figure out why I forgot my name this morning.' (11) The appearance of illogicality in the novel, which Moore deliberately fosters, stems from the frequently irrational, even manic nature of Mary's guilt and fear, and also from the mingling of memory and 'reality' in her thoughts. While the novel gives the impression of being based half on reality or present-time and half on memory, there is in fact nothing in it that is not being remembered by Mary, but it is obvious that the events and dialogues of the day she has just lived through will have far greater immediacy than events of several years previously or even of her youth. The reader has to accept that Mary Dunne as narrator, if not omniscient, will have to have almost total recall of the events of her life and certainly of her day. Verisimilitude is sometimes catered for, however, by remarks which draw attention to the effort to remember—here the conversation with her visitor, Dieter or Peters—: 'and the conversation between us went something like:' (24) The actual narrative of her day, this Thursday in New York, is logical: it proceeds through the morning hair appointment, through lunch, to the afternoon, then dinner and the evening.

At the beginning Mary gives a warning that the story she is about to tell will not be sophisticated or structured like a conventional novel: 'I mean if I were to try to tell anyone the story of my life so far, wouldn't it come out as fragmentary and faded as those old snapshot albums, scrapbooks and bundles of letters everyone keeps in some bottom drawer or other.' (10) Her story may give the appearance of randomness, shifting backwards and forwards in time, here and there in location, but the different strands are skilfully interwoven. For instance, the chronology of Mary's life is handled with great care. Moore does nothing so crude as to give her a *curriculum vitae* all at once, but her memories, as they gradually piece together her life, gradually piece together the dates as well.

The novel gives the appearance of naturalness but is, in reality, much more disciplined and at times more expository than if Moore were using a stream-of-consciousness technique. Mary Dunne talks to herself, takes herself to task; she explains herself to herself in her effort to forestall panic and the 'dooms': 'But even as I raged against Ella Mae, I knew it had nothing to do with her, it was my hateful premenstrual tension that put me in a lunatic anger against her, that started the trembling that becomes a shaking, independent of me, as though my heart is an engine which suddenly comes loose inside me and will shake my whole body to pieces.' (25) This sentence, long, loosely structured, appears to present Mary's feelings as she feels them, but in fact moves from analysis, or thinking about the causes for those feelings, to describing them. This is signalled by the change in tense in the middle of the passage: 'that started the trembling that becomes a shaking' and the concurrent move from mind to body. It is with the body that she feels; it is with the mind ('I knew') that she can rationalise her feelings. The intensity of the passage comes from Mary's sense of her lack of control over her body: she can 'know', but she cannot stop her 'lunatic' tremblings. The contrast between Brendan Tierney as first-person narrator in *An Answer from Limbo* and Mary Dunne as narrator of this novel is never more striking than at this point. Where Tierney controls his own narrative in the same way as he controls his life and his feelings, Mary Dunne's lack of control of all these is exhibited by the apparent randomness and the sudden changes of her thought processes.

In *I am Mary Dunne*, Moore also uses the technique, already drawn upon in *The Emperor of Ice-Cream*, of the 'divided self'. 'Mad Twin' is Mary's own recognition of the neurotic, paranoid side of her personality. Its closeness to her and her lack of control of it alike are identified by this appellation: 'See, said my Mad Twin, he's avoiding you, he's not going to answer you: Now stop that, warned sensible self.' (28–29) The fluctuations, the complete unreliability of Mary Dunne's moods during this day are made evident in passages such as this. But Mary's narrative has a dual function in the novel, to narrate her life and to expose her inner suffering self. It is true that she tells the story of her life frequently in terms of guilt: guilt by association with her father, guilt about Jimmy, about Mackie, about Hat. As if it were possible that she does not feel enough guilt, Janice Sloan and Ernie Truelove make her feel more. The novel, however, does contain an 'outer' voice, the voice one would use in telling a stranger or writing the story of one's life. This is narrative about people, interspersed quite naturally with commentary on them. This kind of writing cannot be said to be objective, coloured as it is by the bitterness of her experiences. But neither does it have the quality of frenzy, or desperation, which Moore so ably catches in some of Mary's 'inner discourse'.

George Steiner, writing on inner discourse, describes the inner voice of the individual as the 'conscience', the 'empathic witness', or any of the other 'multitudinous fictions of the self'.[3] Mary Dunne's inner voice is certainly her conscience, but it is also a 'fiction of the self'; her inner voice represents her as actress, as pander, as whore. She does not always lose sight of reality although at times she comes perilously close, but her inner self engages in dialogue with her outward personality: 'Maybe I am not promiscuous, but I have been married three times and I am only thirty-two. Maybe, without my knowing it, I am old Dan Dunne's daughter after all.' (78) There is no greater expression of Mary's sense of her sexual guilt and depravity than her feeling that she may be like her father, that father whose death haunted her adolescence. But this is a 'fiction of the self' that she assumes at the moments of great crisis. When her rational mind takes over, she knows that she is not Dan Dunne's daughter in the sense of the above phrase.

The most intense moments of guilt come at the end of the novel, when the accumulation of memories, meetings and premenstrual tension pushes Mary to the brink of insanity. In this passage, paranoia, rational analysis and irrationality jostle each other:

> I looked at him [Terence] when he said that. Did he know? He sat facing me, smiling, sympathetic, sipping at his coffee. Did he know the Juarez dooms were on me, the electric current dooms which cut me off from everyone else, for in these dooms it is not the world which is at fault, it is me who is at fault, my fault, my fault, my most grievous fault, yet I do not know my fault, the Juarez dooms are not about real things, I do not think about Hat's suicide, I do not know what it is I have done and so, not knowing, I cannot forgive myself. I know only that I have done wrong, that I am being punished, that I will never be happy again. The greatest happiness would be to be as I was a few hours ago before these dooms came upon me. But that will never be, I will get worse, I will end in a madhouse, a vegetable, smeared in my own excrement, unable even to clean myself and once I think of that I know Terence is the one who will be forced to commit me to the asylum and now, I am afraid

to be in the same room with him for he will see how mad I have become and I must be cunning and escape so I say to him, 'Yes, you're right, I have had a hard day. In fact, I think I should take a hot bath and go to bed, if you wouldn't mind too much?' (248)

The central part of this passage comes closest to the stream-of-consciousness type of monologue. The headlong speed and the inordinate length of the third sentence represent the anguish of Mary's fall into the abyss of depression and her relinquishment of rationality: 'I do not know . . . I do not know.' She feels a general and pervasive sense of sin, which is expressed as the only thing real to her in the nightmare of her descent: 'I know only that I have done wrong.' This is why the frantic expression of her sense of guilt is ritualised. 'At fault' becomes 'my fault' repeated twice in the liturgical, perhaps even talismanic terms of the Catholicism she has long since cast off, but whose ritual forms and openness to guilt-feelings she has subliminally retained. The words of the Confiteor are a metaphor for the diffuseness, the formless-ness and finally for the lack of rational basis of her guilt. The Confiteor would normally be recited as a plea for forgiveness, but there is no one to forgive Mary Dunne. Terence was earlier referred to as her saviour, but here he is cast exclus-ively in the role of a judgmental God. Mary's paranoia also leads her to perceive him as the omniscient ('Did he know?') and the omnipotent (he will commit her to the asylum), both of which characteristics are normally associated only with God. Mary's thought carries the characteristic conviction of the depressive, which, though profoundly irrational, is unshakeable: 'I will never be happy again.' Significant too, are the simultaneous existence of the inner and the public self and Mary's awareness of the dichotomy. This time, to continue Steiner's terminology, the 'fiction of the self' is the insanity which Mary embraces and which leads her to visualise herself, vividly and horribly as 'a vegetable, smeared in my own excrement'. Simultaneously, the public self observes ('I looked at him'), sees the consequences of her fictive inner persona ('I know', 'I am afraid'), plans to escape and escapes. This escape is all based on the inner self's conviction that it is mad and the public self translating this conviction into the necessary evasive action. That the outward or public self, which for much of the day is so rational, should have ceased to recognise the unreliability (fictionality) of the inner self's self-perception is the surest indication of the extent of the crisis for Mary. Her sense of guilt leads her to embrace irrationality and isolation. In other words, the duality is dissolved at this point.

The essential, for her, is that she considers herself guilty. By giving her both an 'inner' and a rational voice to use in interior monologue, Moore has entrusted her with the task of telling her own story. The moral resonance carried by the novel is that the individual's perceptions of his own guilt and his own responsibility are formed, not just by the quantifiable, as it were, degree of culpability, but by all the elements that influence the human psyche, including heredity, memory and religion.

The Multiple Perception —
The Doctor's Wife

IF *I am Mary Dunne* and *The Doctor's Wife* are both seen as —
among other things — novels of adultery told from the
adulterous female's point of view, the differences in the way
the stories are told will appear all the more startling. Where
most of the action of *I am Mary Dunne* takes place in the past,
The Doctor's Wife is notable for its immediacy and the *present-
ness* of its action. 'Modern fiction', says Norman Friedman, 'is
characterised by its emphasis on the scene (in the mind or in
speech and action), while conventional fiction is characterised by its emphasis on narration.'[1] Though Moore would not
consider himself a modernist writer, nor would he be considered as such (he has declared himself to be 'anti-anti-
roman')[2] there are ways in which *The Doctor's Wife*, in its
philosophical assumption — which can be seen in the technique of the novel as much as in any overt or implied
authorial viewpoint — its multiple perspectives and its cinematic concentration on scene is one of the most modern and
most innovative of his works. It is, in a different way, as
powerful a dramatisation of the dilemma of modern life,
where no belief replaces belief, where relative truth replaces
absolute morality, in other words of contemporary secularism, as either *An Answer from Limbo* or *I am Mary Dunne*.

The perspectival technique of *The Doctor's Wife* is an
example of what Norman Friedman has characterised as
'multiple selective omniscience'.[3] That is to say, there is no
direct editorialising, no narrator, but neither is the novel
limited to one 'centre of consciousness' as, for instance, that
of Lambert Strether in *The Ambassadors*. James believed that
he could frame the action inside the consciousness of just one

of the characters: 'A beautiful infatuation this', he comments, 'always, I think, the intensity of the creative effort to get into the skin of the creature',[4] but without, as we have seen, running the risk of using first-person narration. Conversely, Moore limits himself to a single narrative focus only when he uses first-person narrative, as in *I am Mary Dunne*. In *The Doctor's Wife*, the point of view is almost unlimited; even minor characters are given voice (or thought). The action is seen from the centre, by Sheila Redden herself, from the periphery, by Mr Balcer and Miss Purdue in Villefranche. Finally, it is seen from the front, in that characters, either literally or metaphorically, look *at* Sheila—Kevin, Owen Deane, Peg Conroy. The one angle from which the story is never seen—or almost never—is that of Tom Lowry. There is, it is true, a short passage in which Tom Lowry is dramatised—'he woke alarmed to stare at a strange ceiling' (157)—but access to his consciousness is very limited and expressed rather in terms of what he does not know than of what he does know or feel. Elizabeth Bowen has written most interestingly on the subject of the 'seeing' and 'seen' characters in a novel. In this novel, most of the characters are both seeing and seen, although the two ageing voyeurs in Villefranche are never 'seen', so little do they impinge on the lovers:

> Where is the camera-eye to be located? . . . In the breast or brow of a succession of characters? . . . It *must*, if used, involve very careful, considered division of the characters, by the novelist in the *seeing* and the *seen*. Certain characters gain in importance and magnetism by being only *seen*: this makes them more romantic, fatal-seeming . . . In fact, no character in which these qualities are, for the plot, essential, should be allowed to enter the *seeing* class.[5]

The effect of multiple perspective, as it is used in *The Doctor's Wife*, is not to dissipate the intensity of one's sense of

character, action and choice, but to enhance one's sense of
the relativity of honour and morality and also one's sense of
the futility of the aspiration to happiness.

The technique of *The Doctor's Wife* differs from a traditional
nineteenth-century novel in that the author *shows* rather than
tells, to recapitulate the distinction formulated and developed
by James, Lubbock and Beach. Location has a very important
role in the novel, and what remains in the memory are
particular scenes in particular places—different houses, different tables, different meals, outside and inside in Villefranche, Paris and Belfast (or indeed, different beds in
Villefranche and Paris). There is a strong concentration on
eating and drinking, but always the day, the occasion and the
location are made specific. Along with this cinematic tendency, there is a corresponding lack of narration. Narration is
difficult to dramatise. In this novel, the reader generally
receives insight into the characters' states of mind only as
they occur. The most extreme form taken by this phenomenon is when Sheila Redden realises that she is going to
reveal her affair to her husband only *as* she does it. It is true
that Sheila Redden occasionally narrates her state of mind—
for instance she tells the priest of her temptation towards
suicide, but then her explanation is so attenuated—even
cryptic—as to reveal very little. The paucity of narrative
emerges very strongly when the novel is contrasted with
either *An Answer from Limbo* or *I am Mary Dunne*. Even Sheila's
past in Belfast is conveyed by dramatic means—the scene of
violence where she is verbally abused by the blonde woman
as a 'Fenian'—or scenically, when Kevin morosely surveys
her room and realises how little he knows her. Such scenes of
narrative summary (conveyed through dialogue) as do
belong to the real time of the novel, for example those
between Sheila and Peg, Peg and Ivo and even Kevin Redden
and Owen Deane, are not essential to the reader (who is
already aware of the real situation), but they shift the point of
view. We hear what the interlocutors *think*, rather than what

they *say*. In other words, these scenes are a means of focusing the camera (the views of others) on Sheila: she becomes the seen rather than the seer. To return to Elizabeth Bowen:

> The cinema, with its actual camera-work, is an interesting study for the novelist. In a good film, the camera's movement, angle and distance have all worked towards the one thing — the fullest possible realisation of the director's idea, the completest possible surrounding of the subject. Any trick is justified if it adds a statement.[6]

By using such cinematic techniques, Moore gives a rounded picture of Sheila Redden. Just as he avoids, by these means, the awkwardness of mirror-view, which he had recourse to so frequently in his early novels (and even in his latest) so he can reveal her mind and her heart without lengthy analysis, retrospection or narrative.

The fragmented and relativistic nature of the techniques used in *The Doctor's Wife* would seem to postulate an underpinning of a quasi-existentialist philosophy (which also emerges from the themes of choice and responsibility in the novel). Sartre insists in his philosophy on the revolutionary freedom man has to determine, not just his actions, but his identity. In the novel this concept is asserted by the title, which gives Sheila Redden an identity derived from someone else (indeed, rather a *profession* than a *person*). The novel, therefore, puts her in a position to forge a different identity. Thus, her choice in the novel concerns not alone what she will *do*, but what she will *be*. Camus has characterised as 'absurd' the gulf between people, other people and things and also as absurd the impossibility of establishing rapport between them. For him, there is no possibility of the human spirit being satisfied by the world. This pessimistic, even despairing viewpoint comes across in the absurdity of Sheila Redden's final fate, as well as in the response of the French priest, who refers, sympathetically at least, if not approvingly, to the view of suicide expounded by Camus in *Le Mythe de Sisyphe*.

Existential theory extends to the theory of the novel and it is on the French novel of the past three decades that it has had its greatest influence. Moore, though he has stated his opposition to the *nouveau roman* and is never likely to write a novel of ideas as opposed to a novel of plot, is a self-confessed francophile. French practitioners of the *nouveau roman* (or *anti-roman*), such as Barthes, Sartre, Robbe-Grillet and Camus himself, insist that the narrator's experience should not transcend that of the protagonist. They reject completely the idea of traditional editorial omniscience in favour of the direct revelation of the actions, thought and feelings of the character, as they happen to him, and conveyed as if it were a surprise to the author. There is a sense in *The Doctor's Wife* in which the author refuses to tell, and therefore refuses to know more than Sheila Redden herself knows. Nor do other people really know anything about her; they may think about her, and they may think they know about her, but Kevin, Peg, Owen Deane, all consistently misjudge her. She creates her life as she lives; the reader, most of all, is surprised by her. Putting Sheila Redden in an existentialist dilemma means abandoning responsibility for her, since authorial control (i.e. full omniscience) is in theory and in practice incompatible with existentialism.

CONCLUSION

Liberty or Banishment?

LIKE Sheila Redden, the protagonists of *An Answer from Limbo* and *I am Mary Dunne* escape the kind of religious domination under which Judith Hearne and Diarmuid Devine suffer in the Belfast novels. They also avoid the hideous fate of these characters. This is partly a result of changing *mores*, but primarily the consequence of an act of will, an act of self-liberation. Exile can be perceived both as an escape from stultifying influences and an escape to greater freedom. The focus of this freedom may not be perceived at first—the actual departure may take the form of an intellectual rebellion, or act of sexual defiance, or a combination of these two—but it eventually crystallises as an alternative belief to Christianity. It is clear that, for Moore, any serious belief will qualify; indeed this chapter treats of two novels in which the belief in question is not intellectual, spiritual or idealistic in any sense: that is the sexual love by which the heroines of *I am Mary Dunne* and *The Doctor's Wife* live. What these beliefs all have in common is the zeal with which they are prosecuted, so that they become quasi-spiritual or 'replacement' religions.

By rejecting their religion and their homeland, with all the ethical and social values implied by those entities, the protagonists of these three novels enter a limbo, step into an abyss of freedom, in which only they can create their own lives, free from the underpinnings or supports of society and religion. With freedom comes responsibility, not only for oneself but for also for others, and it is a considerable burden. Sheila Redden in *The Doctor's Wife* has, effectively, to create a new identity; Mary Dunne, too, has serious problems knowing who she is, on both a superficial and a profound level.

If the conclusions and consequences in the three novels are taken together, Moore appears to postulate a very gloomy view. The movement towards happiness through the pursuit of a dearly held belief, is destructive not only of others, but also of the self. This manifests itself in several different ways, but the conclusion is inescapable; thus, Brendan Tierney becomes a monster of selfishness; Mary Dunne trembles on the verge of insanity; Sheila Redden loses everything and seems to gain very little in return. Taken in conjunction with Moore's more recent novels, these works would seem to put forward the view that it is not in the self or through the self that the greatest fulfilment for the self will be found.

From the technical point of view, emerging from a consideration of these three novels are the skill of the novelist in suiting the style to the theme and his constant willingness to innovate. Just as the ethical stance of the novels is relativistic rather than crudely or simply moralistic, so Moore varies his perspectival technique from novel to novel. In *An Answer from Limbo*, Brendan's point of view is given in combination with that of his victims; in *I am Mary Dunne*, this is not necessary, as the heroine's own guilt condems her more than any other person would do. In that novel, Moore takes on the risky business of interior monologue to convey the inconsistencies, the confusion and the paranoia of guilt and memory. Most interesting, though also most controversial, *The Doctor's Wife* is a novel where the author withdraws almost completely, where the narrative is spare and where the events and consciousness of the heroine are consistently dramatised by techniques which are almost cinematic. Though the themes of this period of Moore's work may be susceptible of consideration together, it is clear that the techniques he brings to the development of these themes are very varied. A recent remark that the author has made about his techniques throws interesting light on this aspect:

> When I decide to write a novel, I think—what is the best way to write this particular story? Should it be a narrative

style like *Cold Heaven* which was a thriller? Or one of emotion?[1]

(*I am Mary Dunne* represents Moore's theme and technique of emotion.)

In the development of Moore's work discussed in the next section of this study, his response to the challenge of form becomes increasingly courageous. Moore prepared for the greater innovation of the novels of faith by his already not inconsiderable level of experiment, especially as regards flexibility of point of view in *An Answer from Limbo*, *I am Mary Dunne* and *The Doctor's Wife*.

Belief in A Secular World

8

The Quest for a Higher Belief

IN Moore's secular novels from *An Answer from Limbo* onwards, his characters tend to know what they believe in and what they want to achieve. Though they may be unfree (as human beings always are) at some deeper level of the psyche, they are free to pursue their beliefs, in a way that would be unimaginable for the protagonists of the early Belfast novels. But gradually in Moore's work, the focus changes to a search *for* something to believe in. Since *The Doctor's Wife* (1976), the theme of searching, of quest, has become increasingly important. In *The Mangan Inheritance* (1979), the novel which immediately succeeds *The Doctor's Wife*, James Mangan comes to Ireland to look for something which, he hopes, will give his life meaning—an 'inheritance', we are told, by the characteristically enigmatic and ambiguous title. It is a search for an identity that goes beyond the individual, into the atavistic and the folk memory. Not alone does Jamie Mangan not know what he will find, but he does not know, except in the most abstract and general terms, what he is looking for (the fact that his search is prompted by and focused on the *persona* of his poetic ancestor is an accidental and extrinsic circumstance). His search is characterised, not by what he wants to find, but by what he wants to leave behind: he is looking for a way to transcend the limitation of the historically and biologically determined individual that he is, at a given moment in time in Canada. This novel signifies a new development in Moore's writing, but one of which hints were already given in *The Doctor's Wife*.

In keeping with an idea of quest which is more spiritual than material, Moore challenges the assumptions of the secular, materialistic world in three of his novels since *The Mangan Inheritance—The Temptation of Eileen Hughes, Cold*

Heaven and *Black Robe*. It is not surprising that in creating fictions in which characters *seek* beliefs—as opposed to following beliefs—Moore should turn or return to religion. His secular novels have prepared the ground for this, by postulating two related convictions: firstly, that secular belief, no matter how personal, how private, even, cannot be pursued as if the individual were alone in the world and that the prosecution of any such belief will involve the sufferings of others as well as the sacrifices of the believer himself; secondly, that even the 'successful' prosecution of such a belief will lead either to a basic loss of integrity, as in *An Answer from Limbo*, or to deep unhappiness (*The Doctor's Wife*) or even to psychic disorder (*I am Mary Dunne*). There is undoubtedly a difference between the personal beliefs treated in these novels and religious belief. Religious faith would seem to provide a means of transcending the self without sacrificing others. All other beliefs are selfish; religious belief, being the ultimate unselfishness, could never involve the kind of immorality from which Moore shows his protagonists and their victims suffering in *An Answer from Limbo* and *I am Mary Dunne*. Religion demands selflessness. In two of the three novels under discussion in this chapter, Moore examines the possibility of a genuine religious faith being able to provide both spiritual fulfilment and a moral framework for life. In *The Temptation of Eileen Hughes*, Bernard McAuley gropes after a quasi-spiritual fulfilment: his obsession is the closest thing possible to spiritual belief and is frequently expressed in mystical terms. It is no accident that this novel, published in 1981, is the bridge crossed by Moore in his literary journey from the secular novels of the 1960s and 1970s to the religious themes of the 1980s.

> It's not that this generation is more materialistic than we were (in fact they are less so in some ways) but they've been denied in a way . . . they've been denied even the great illusory campaign we had . . . so what do we believe in now?[1]

The attitude expressed by Moore in this remark was prepared for by the disillusion of his secular protagonists in the earlier novels and by their notable lack of success in attaining happiness. The casting off of moral guidelines, too, which is associated in Moore's earlier novels with rebellion against the Church, the choice of exile and the assumption of a greater or lesser degree of sexual licence — the very freedom his characters so long for, but which is such a responsibility and frequently a tragedy when it comes, all of this, when surveyed in the context of the recent remarks made by the author, points to a disillusion with secularism and a new interest in religion for its moral as well as its spiritual structure. As early as the time of writing of *An Answer from Limbo*, Moore was conscious of the difficulties likely to be caused by the lack of such a structure in the lives of his secular protagonists:

> It is much easier to live, as the mother does, with a fixed set of beliefs, even if they are wrong ones, than to make up the rules as one goes along. Unfortunately, it is more difficult to live without a faith than with one.[2]

If one examines Moore's present views, it seems as if he has lost some of his earlier humanistic faith in the ability of the individual on his own to formulate a private rubric by which to live. His novels chart the individual unfree to believe and then free to follow belief, but this secular freedom which opens to his characters in the second phase of his work proves to be a disappointment. By the novels of the 1980s, the author and his protagonists alike have become dissatisfied with the secular world. For the protagonists it has yielded all they require in terms of material satisfaction and the power — so lacking for the characters of the early novels — to do exactly as they like. In the early novels, Moore's characters tended to be poor or struggling; now they are financially secure, even affluent. However, in *The Temptation of Eileen Hughes*, Bernard McAuley is profoundly and depressingly conscious of the emptiness of his life; in *Cold*

Heaven, Marie Davenport does not suffer in this way, but she undergoes a different kind of spiritual anguish as she searches for and simultaneously seeks to escape from something she does not understand. Finally, in *Black Robe*, Moore comes full circle from the anti-clericalism of his first novels to admire spiritual zeal, though with many *caveats*.

In order to show how Moore sees religion as offering a framework for the possibility of self-transcendence, it is necessary to examine his own changing attitudes to belief, for it will be obvious that the writer who produced *Judith Hearne* in 1955 had different views from the creator of *Black Robe* in 1985. In Moore's case, spiritual belief or religion can be taken to mean Roman Catholicism, because it is the religion of Moore's upbringing and he was undoubtedly impregnated by its ethos and morality. (There is also expressed in *Catholics*, *Cold Heaven* and *Black Robe* a sense that there is a strenuousness, an excess, a zeal about Catholicism—philanthropic, spiritual, missionary—and a teaching of moral certainty that appeal to Moore.) There are two reasons for Moore's early estrangement from religion: firstly because he hated the repressive and brutal version of Irish Catholicism in which he was reared; secondly, because he felt he had no faith. Now Catholicism has changed greatly; if it is still authoritarian, it at least manages to present a facade of humanity and reasonableness; though the Church is still unwilling to tolerate dissent, at least it is clear that there are many, including members of the hierarchy, who feel the need to express it. The second condition—Moore's personal lack of faith—has not changed, but now the writer, who still asserts his unbelief, is more likely to speak wistfully or nostalgically about his lack of faith. The Church which is more open and less dogmatic and the secularist who is unable to believe, are really the models for *Cold Heaven*, although it is clear that there is a divergence between the author's and the protagonist's views in the degree of their scepticism or hostility to religion. It is instructive, in this regard, to look at the following remarks made by Moore about his own lack of faith, the lack of faith which earlier, in establishing himself as a model for Judith Hearne, he was more inclined to term 'loss of faith'.

> I wasn't religious. I never could believe.[3]

> I never had any faith. I could never forget that my grandfather was a Protestant lawyer who changed his religion to help his business.[4]

> From the time I was very young I had religious doubts. . . . Because of that I began to question my religion.[5]

These remarks, made in various interviews in 1984 and 1985, do not indicate hostility to the idea of faith, but express the feeling of exclusion from it.

Coexisting with his lack of faith and yet a distinct issue — and this is a common phenomenon among Irish Catholics — is Moore's attitude to the Catholic Church. For many years, and for most of his novels, he was unable to separate the *idea* of faith from the *reality* of Irish Catholicism. His early novels reflect both his strong perception of the Catholic Church as being a repressive, bigoted and sectarian force in the society of Northern Ireland and his antipathy to the Catholic Church as an agent of education. The latter feeling has been the most durable element in his hostility to Catholicism.

His views on the subject of Catholic education are strongly testified to both in his fiction and in interviews and autobiographical writings: 'My first two novels were, I would say, anti-clerical . . . they were very critical of the Catholic Church as it was then.'[6]

Moore's experiences at St Malachy's, Belfast's Diocesan College, marked him for life, and he frequently speaks of the repressive and — to him — sadistic system that prevailed under the domination of the Catholic clergy. These are the memory and the vision that inspired the writing of his second novel, *The Feast of Lupercal*. Though the memory of his school days still evokes a bitter and hostile reaction in him, it is evident that radical changes have occurred in Moore's attitude to Catholicism and to belief, which have their roots in two factors. Firstly, the Catholic Church changed markedly during the 1960s. Secondly, Moore has come increasingly to hold the view that people must believe in something. He himself uses the word 'always', but it has not always been *apparent* that belief has been a characteristic of his protagon- ists. The characters of his first three novels suffer instead from the lack of something to believe in or are deprived of the freedom to follow a belief. This, in itself, testifies negatively, as it were, to the importance of belief. But certainly since *An Answer from Limbo*, belief has been the dominant theme of Moore's work: his protagonists must look in others, in art, in the past or, for instance, in the imagined present-cum-past of *The Great Victorian Collection*, for something to believe in, perhaps losing in the process other beliefs which they have held all their lives but have never thought about and which they now find inappropriate or unsatisfactory:

> We go along in life with some belief held in front of us which keeps us going. Most of my novels investigate the period in someone's life when that belief is withdrawn, when they're forced to examine their whole life.[7]

> . . . I found that, while I'm not religious myself, religion is a wonderful metaphor for belief.[8]

Moore may not be religious himself, but the last section of the above remark does not give credit ·to the seriousness with which he has treated religious belief in his recent novels or the increasingly high value he has placed on it. Religion is certainly a metaphor for belief a look at any of the novels where Moore's protagonists abandon religion in order to pursue a secular belief but constantly return to the idea of religion to give a metaphorical structure to their lives, will prove this. But religion is more than a metaphor for belief; it is a different kind of belief. It is a means of transcending the self, a belief without the impulse towards personal gratification and personal fulfilment that other beliefs imply. In his most recent comments, Moore admits to an envy of people who have great faith: 'To be able to believe in something other than yourself is wonderful in this very materialistic society we live in.'[9] For him, religious faith is genuinely altruistic. He also sees faith as a force that makes people better, more moral, although the kind of morality enforced by traditional Catholicism has its negative as well as its positive aspects. This is well expressed in the complex feelings of the following comment:

> The other thing we tend to forget when we denigrate religion in Ireland is that, while it was repressive (and I say this on both the Catholic and Protestant sides; I don't mean it's just a Catholic thing), it tended to make people less materialistic . . . It was fear of sin, but it means that there was some set of values.[10]

In this remark, what he expresses is an inability to 'forgive' the Catholic Church for the fear and guilt ('fear of sin'), the atmosphere in which he was brought up himself and which pervades the Belfast novels of the 1950s, *Judith Hearne* and *The Feast of Lupercal*. He is identifying the result of religion and praising it ('less materialistic . . . some set of values') while deploring the means of enforcing these values ('fear of sin'). In Catholic Ireland of the 1950s, one could not exist without the other and this is the main reason for the pathetic fates of both Judith Hearne and Diarmuid Devine. However, the means employed by the Catholic Church to teach its doctrine have changed greatly in the thirty years since Moore's first novel. In the following remark, he identifies very clearly why religion has again become such a preoccupation with him in his last three novels. In the phrase 'something greater than ourselves', he pinpoints the concept of transcendence which no normal belief can supply:

> I began to see the virtues of faith, even if it is a wrong

faith . . . in *something   greater   than   ourselves* . . . The repressive   Irish   Catholic . . . background . . . often produced people whom we call saints; people who had no sense of self; people who could give themselves up completely for the love of others.[11] (my emphasis)

This altruism is precisely what Moore is writing about in *Cold Heaven* (mysticism) and in *Black Robe* (missionary zeal and martyrdom). The point is that, not believing himself, he believes belief to be, perhaps, 'illusory' ('a wrong faith') but none the less, paradoxically, real and potent. Because of this, he has to make his main centre of interest the secularist viewpoint, such as that of Marie Davenport, though he is more open than she is to a variety of spiritual experiences, and he makes Father Laforgue in *Black Robe* a much more interesting character in human terms, once he is in danger of losing his faith.

The second point raised above and one to which Moore has frequently adverted, is that the Catholic Church has changed so radically since his Belfast youth in the 1930s that it can no longer be seen as repressive and guilt-ridden: 'But then, of course, you had Pope John XXIII and things started to change and then I became very interested . . . One of the greatest revolutions of this century has been the revolution within the Catholic Church.'[12] His 1972 novel, *Catholics*, establishes Moore's attitude towards the changes which took place in the institutional Church during the 1960s and early 1970s.

Catholics is in some ways a paradoxical novel. It is clear from what he has written and said in his novels and elsewhere, that Moore welcomed in theory the relaxation in the Catholic Church that came with Vatican II. However, in this novel, the liberalised Catholic Church is represented by the unsympathetic James Kinsella, 'Catholic priest', to whom the *apertura* with Buddhism is more important than his own faith or the faith of any individual or community. The personal sympathies of the author appear to lie more with the Abbot of Muck Island. This is because, like the author, he is a sceptic who respects the beliefs of others, but also—and here the contradiction arises—because he is a traditionalist in his attitude to the aesthetic and mystery of belief. Unlike Kinsella, the Abbot has a sense of belief as something that cannot be codified, legislated for or modernised by the dictates of the central authority of the Church many hundreds of miles away. For Kinsella, the position of the Church is quite logical: there is no room for romantic deviation if the Church is the 'quintessential structure through which revolution can be brought to certain areas of the globe'.[13] The aesthetic of belief, the irrationality, the 'logical absurdity' will all be lost under the new dispensation. Kinsella perceives all of these qualities as belonging to the past, although he does receive some slight sense from the architecture of the Abbey of 'that bareness which contains all the beauty of belief'. (51) *Catholics* seems to envisage the ordinary Catholic, lay or clerical, merely exchanging a conservative hegemony for a liberal one. Both, ultimately, are equally tyrannical. So, though Moore refers to Vatican II as 'revolutionary', it is not at all clear from a reading of *Catholics* that he sees that institutional revolution in a positive light. In this novel, there is lacking that positive sense of the individual bearing witness to his faith (the monks who have faith are fanatical and dangerous) which emerges so strongly from *Cold Heaven*, from *Black Robe* and from *The Colour of Blood*.

Since he wrote *Catholics*, the direction taken by the institutional Catholic Church as regards doctrine and ritual has concerned Moore no further; he has returned instead to what has always been his central theme, the belief of the individual. In a sense, this concentration on the individual approach to religious faith has been the lasting legacy of the religious liberalisation of the 1960s, though it has not always been encouraged by the institutional Church. In this, Moore was accurate in feeling the great importance of Vatican II. However, as a prophetic or futuristic novel, *Catholics* is very wide of the mark. The conservative backlash has come, but it has come from the hierarchy rather than from the laity, so it is institutionalised rather than rebellious. In the increasing gulf between the institutional Church and the individual, the individual must look for his own salvation.

The Temptation of Eileen Hughes, Cold Heaven and *Black Robe* may be considered as novels of quest; their direction can—very roughly—be stated. They move away from secular beliefs and towards the validation of some kind of religious experience. However, that goal is very nebulous, perhaps even unattainable, and the reader is conducted on the quest by an author whose own views are avowedly ambivalent. This uncertainty is not an unusual phenomenon in modern fiction, although the word 'quest' may have many different meanings. Wayne C. Booth writes of the quest-novel as an extremely common sub-genre in modern fiction and characterises the nature of quest as follows:

> In such works we do not discover until the end—and very often not even then—what the true meaning of the events has been. Regardless of the point of view in the narrowest sense, the moral and intellectual point of view of the work is deliberately confusing, disconcerting, even staggering.[14]

Such a remark could well be applied to any of the three novels by Moore which are under discussion in this chapter (*The Temptation of Eileen Hughes, Cold Heaven* and *Black Robe*), as well as to *The Mangan Inheritance*. The more spiritual Moore's themes become, the more mysterious his treatment and the more tentative the conclusions one is encouraged to draw. *Cold Heaven*, for instance, could be said to defy any attempt at all to reach a conclusion, in the conventional sense of that word.

In Moore's use of perspective in these novels, he applies similar techniques of relativity, so that one no longer has the comfort and security of knowing exactly which character consistently represents the privileged authorial view. There is even ambiguity about which character is presented most sympathetically, from the moral or emotional point of view.

In these three novels, the protagonist is not necessarily the hero, to use an old-fashioned or conventional standard of judgment. To clarify this terminology: it is clear that Judith Hearne is the heroine of Moore's first novel, and Diarmuid Devine the hero of *The Feast of Lupercal*, though they might seem to be very pathetic anti-heroic heroes. In *Cold Heaven* and *Black Robe*, such criteria no longer hold. The central intelligence is shown as a very defective or partial means of understanding, not because of any particular moral or intellectual fault in itself, but because there is a fundamental lack of understanding in its intelligence of all the forces that make up the world and that are experienced by it — and also, very likely, a deep unwillingness to understand. The reader is for much of the time in a similar position to this doubting or uncomprehending protagonist but it is possible for the reader, by virtue of his own experience or his own faith, to transcend in understanding both the limited vision of the central consciousness and even the vision of the author himself. In other words, Moore, in these novels willingly relinquishes his status of omniscient author.

It is significant also that for his most recent novels, Moore has chosen or invented titles that are so extremely enigmatic. Not only are they enigmatic *before* one reads the book, but they remain equally enigmatic after one has finished. They are emblematic of the novels themselves in their reluctance to yield up their secrets. What is one to make of Yeats's phrase, 'cold heaven' in the context of the life of Marie Davenport? What resonance do the words 'black robe' have, beyond the obvious? The title of *The Temptation of Eileen Hughes*, for all its apparent limpidity, poses severe problems as regards the relationship between the title and the main protagonist of the novel, as discussed below. (*The Feast of Lupercal* and *The Emperor of Ice-Cream*, it may be claimed, are similarly enigmatic as titles, but this is not the case: their meaning, in the context of the novels, becomes clear when the works are read.) As Wayne Booth points out, enigmatic titles do not, in general, allow the reader to infer a narratorial point of view.

Moore avoids what Booth calls 'generalised commentary'[15] by eschewing explicit titles. The more sophisticated he has become as a literary craftsman, the more subtle the titles he has used.

In his most recent novels, Moore dares to break one of the cardinal rules in the writing of fiction: that the author must know all, even if he only chooses to tell half. If these novels say anything, it is that the author does not know all and will never know all. Perhaps this accounts for the limited popularity of and the muted critical esteem for these novels: there are those who enjoy the treatment of themes that preclude certainty; there are many others who cannot bear to be left in 'uncertainties, doubts, mysteries'. In many modern novels, it is not clear exactly *what* happens, and the avant-garde cinema in particular has accustomed the discerning viewer to this phenomenon. It is much more difficult and more unsatisfactory not to know the *meaning* of something that does happen, though its physical and contextual reality is clear. Opinion is divided about *Cold Heaven* in particular: for some, the mystery of the apparitions is just that, and therefore not more susceptible to authorial explanation; for others, Moore appears to avoid the issue of faith in the most fundamental sense, by setting his protagonist up as the witness of the apparition and never dealing fully with the link between this spiritual power and the strange but authenticated medical history of her husband. The most famous prescriptions about what a writer should know and what a writer is allowed *not* to know have been supplied by Ernest Hemingway, who was the strongest early influence on Moore's writing:[16]

> If a writer of prose knows enough about what he is writing about he may omit things that he knows and the reader, if the writer is writing truly enough, will have a feeling of those things as strongly as though the writer had stated them. The dignity of movement of an ice-berg is due to only one-eighth of it being above water. A

writer who omits things because he does not know them only makes hollow places in his writing.[17]

but Hemingway allows exceptions to this requirement:

True mysticism should not be confused with incompetence in writing which seems to mystify where there is no mystery but is really only the necessity to fake to cover lack of knowledge or the inability to state clearly. Mysticism implies a mystery, and there are many mysteries; but incompetence is not one of them.[18]

As regards *Cold Heaven* in particular, there is an area of doubt about the depiction of the reality of faith. The apparitions are mysterious for the secular protagonist and for most modern readers; yet they are in some sense real not just for the mystic Mother St Jude but also for the young Sister Anna. The greatest mystery for the reader is not that of the apparitions themselves, but the mystery of the faith that can allow an individual to accept these apparitions. This deeper mystery is mediated through mystery—a double layer of mystery, as it were—because the author himself can express no more than his own sense of helplessness and incomprehension at the workings of faith.

It is the return of religion as a theme in the case of *Cold Heaven* and *Black Robe* and the development of a mystical perception in their forerunner, *The Temptation of Eileen Hughes*, that have both caused and allowed the authorial perspective to occupy such a high ground of ambiguity, an ambiguity of essential or 'fundamental meaning', to borrow the phrase used by Michael Paul Gallagher in a useful essay on Moore.[19] It is also clear that what lies behind the ambiguity of this narratorial voice is the profound ambivalence of the author himself on the subject of religion, his most consistent theme, his most troubling and troubled metaphor even when it is not his theme.

The last word on this subject of authorial knowledge and lack of knowledge may be left to Saul Bellow, one of the age's supreme chroniclers of the joys and sorrows of agnostic and secular man: 'By refusing to write about anything which is not thoroughly familiar', says Bellow, 'the American writer confesses the powerlessness of the imagination and accepts its relegation to an inferior place.'[20] In all three of the novels under discussion in this chapter, Moore does the opposite to the typical 'American writer' deplored by Bellow. Mystical obsessions, spirituality, a crisis of spirituality in a historical setting: all the subjects chosen by Moore are daring in the context of the age, and owe little to his natural or social environment. His recent novels testify to the power of the imagination over knowledge and assert the value and the interest of the unknown and the unknowable. Moore comes to grips with the intractable subject of the spiritual imagination and continues to use a basis of the most convincing realism for subjects that have little to do with the material environment. In *The Temptation of Eileen Hughes*, the quest for spiritual fulfilment takes the form of an obsession or mania: Bernard McAuley makes a god instead of adoring an existing one. In a conventional sense, he is both blasphemous and idolatrous. If, however, as Shelley asserts in *Prometheus Unbound*, we all *create* God in the image we most desire and need, then Bernard is merely taking to extremes a process shared by all believers and the novel can be considered as forming part of the religious pattern in Moore's work, along with *Cold Heaven* and *Black Robe*.

9

Creating a God —
The Temptation of Eileen Hughes

IN *The Temptation of Eileen Hughes*, Bernard McAuley is the archetypal 'modern man in search of a soul'[1] and through his story, Moore illustrates the cruelty of God and of the 'gods'. His story comes closer to tragedy than the fate of most of Moore's protagonists, not just because he dies at the end, but because in his egoism, his failings, his *hubris*, he imitates the tragic hero. However, like most modern heroes, Bernard is at times too close to being ridiculous to qualify truly as a tragic figure.

The decision to take Bernard McAuley as the main protagonist of the novel must be justified, since its title appears to devote the novel to the fate of its heroine. Moore has never before, in a whole series of novels which, by their titles, denote the stories of individuals, thus entitled a novel without intending that novel to 'belong' to that character, but it can be argued that Eileen Hughes's is not the central consciousness of *The Temptation of Eileen Hughes*. To read the novel as if this were the case is an unsatisfactory experience, and such a reading was partly responsible for the confused and mixed reception the novel received when it appeared. For instance, Janet Egelson Dunleavy comments:

> Perhaps Eileen should not have been given responsibility for being the central character of the novel that bears her name, since she is so careless that she can hardly be called tempted. Perhaps this should have been Bernard McAuley's book, in which he might have been probed gradually, with greater skill and art.[2]

Perhaps 'careless' is not the best word to describe the

anxious heroine Eileen Hughes, but the reviewer is right in saying that the book should have been Bernard McAuley's. In fact the novel *is* Bernard McAuley's, in all but name. The interest is focused primarily on Bernard, although the consciousness of Mona and Eileen are also exposed, but in a technical development that for Moore is completely innovative, Bernard is never 'given voice'. He is never the centre of consciousness; his words are expressed, but not his thoughts. In the company of Eileen Hughes, the reader always looks *at* him, never through his eyes. He is apparently cast in the role of the presiding evil genius, the 'tempter' implied by the title, and the other characters react to him. But who is really being tempted in this novel? The most obvious interpretation of the novel is that Eileen Hughes is being tempted, and in an obvious way, this is true. The word 'temptation' has a specific religious connotation as well as a literary and mythic one, suggesting as it does the temptation of Christ by the devil in the gospel of Saint Matthew:

> Again, the devil taketh him up into an exceedingly high mountain, and sheweth him all the kingdoms of the world, and the glory of them;
> And saith unto him, All these things will I give thee, if thou wilt fall down and worship me.
> Then saith Jesus unto him, get thee hence, Satan: for it is written, Thou shalt worship the Lord thy God, and him only shalt thou serve.
> Then the devil leaveth him, and behold, angels came and ministered unto him.[3]

Like Christ, Eileen Hughes is being tempted by material wealth and splendour—the money and acquisitive power of the McAuleys. But unlike Christ, and unlike Faust, that other great model of the tempted, Eileen Hughes is not required to sell her soul or to commit idolatry in order to possess the world, at least not initially. It is part of the plan that Bernard devises and that Mona connives at, that she should retain her innocence, that she should have no idea either of Bernard's adoration of her or of Mona's corruption. If yielding to temptation demands knowledge and consent, Eileen Hughes demonstrates the possession of neither quality. Faust enters into a specific contract with Mephistopheles, and the essence of the biblical story of Christ is that the devil makes sure that Christ knows exactly what he is being offered. He shows him the world at his feet; he establishes clearly for him the conditions under which he will possess the world. Eileen is also being shown the 'world' she will possess: London opens before her — Buckingham Palace, the theatres, the vistas of Kenwood House — but she is not meant to know the condiions under which she can possess all this. Once her eyes are opened, Eileen is never for a moment tempted: she is as yet too ill at ease in the world of luxury, too innocent and, as Bernard accuses her, too conventionally moral. She is too revolted by Bernard's devotion and by Mona's promiscuity even to consider playing a part in the arrangement they offer her.

It would thus appear that it is the nature of Bernard's obsession with Eileen that gives the novel a deeper interest. According to this reading, the title of the novel would mean the temptation offered *by* Eileen Hughes, not the temptation offered *to* Eileen Hughes. Bernard, unlike Eileen, does know from the beginning where this temptation might lead him and he applies considerable cunning as well as his huge material resources to create for himself, for Mona and for Eileen a world where he can adore Eileen without her knowing it and without arousing suspicion. This means yielding to temptation, but only in a very controlled way. The yielding is in the past or in the future envisaged by Bernard McAuley, but in the present or real time of the novel the crisis occurs when Bernard yields to temptation on another level; he experiences an intense need for Eileen to *know* what he feels about her. Because she is a god, in the language of the novel, she need not return his devotion, but because he is a man who adores a god, he must express it to her. The temptation, to risk all in the hope of ecstasy — the ecstasy of mere proximity to the loved one — could only appeal to one who has everything, who has had everything and to whom all means nothing. Bernard McAuley is the person — the limited range of development of his character and his mono-mania would suggest that he is a symbolic or archetypal figure[4] — who has everything, but whose life is empty and who believes in nothing. Or rather he has believed in nothing until the arrival of Eileen Hughes. Bernard uses the 'language' of temptation, in one of the many instances in which he conveys his passion for Eileen in quasi-religious terms:

> I should have resisted temptation this afternoon[5]

and

> But having you here, so close, having you all to myself in London, seeing Kenwood, having you say that you wanted to live in a big house, it was too great a temptation. (77)

Bernard McAuley, who has lived all his life by material things, is here misled by his great material power. Believing that she wants a big house, he knows he can supply her with one. Bernard, ever accustomed to getting what he wants by means of the money he owns, applies the same techniques of buying and selling to the manipulation of the lives of others. Moving is one of the key ideas. Bernard has moved Mona from her pathetic father's dentist's surgery in Kent Street to a big house in Clanranald Avenue. He projects even more dramatic changes in the situation of those he has in his power: Eileen Hughes is to be moved from the humble house in Church Street to a mansion in County Louth; her mother, Agnes, presents no problem as Bernard is prepared to buy her a flat in Belfast or in Dublin.

The Temptation of Eileen Hughes casts a cold eye on the cult of materialism and on those who live by money and see money as being both indispensable and the main means of achieving happiness. In contradiction of this belief in money, however, they seek other sources of gratification, because these lead to obliteration of the consciousness and forgetfulness of the self. Thus, Mona's refuge is sexual encounters with strangers; Derek Irwin's is drink; Eileen's American friend Earl indulges in marijuana as well as alcohol. The surface of Bernard's life is composed of material things: bespoke suits, smoked salmon, expensive hotels and trips abroad. It would appear, furthermore, that this surface is all the depth his life contains. In fact, his most profound feeling, his only authentic feeling, one might say, is dissatisfaction. He appears like the others, except that he has a conscious perception that his life is empty, and he has tried and renounced sensual means of escape: it is explicitly stated in the novel, for instance, that he never gets drunk, and both he and Mona testify to his complete rejection of sexual activity. He has tried and found wanting all the things that money has bought for him — hi-fi, travel, pornography — as well as all the things money cannot buy — sex, drama, history, architecture. He has invested heavily, but has got little return either from material or from cultural things.

Furthermore, not just conventional religion but personal faith has failed Bernard. Because he is a character given to extremes, he envisaged a spiritual life of complete devotion to God; in other words, clerical, monastic, celibate. When Moore said that he agreed with Graham Greene that faith was a gift not given to everyone, he surely applied this concept to the creation of the character of Bernard McAuley. In this case, the concept of 'gift' would mean the only kind of religious existence envisaged by Bernard: his vocation. Because Bernard is 'denied' a vocation, he is denied all faith. Different versions of Bernard's 'vocation' are given at various stages, by Bernard, by Agnes Hughes and by Mona, but the one he himself gives at the end of the novel when he thinks he is going to die from an overdose of drugs can presumably be given credence . . . 'It's all over between me and God. I offered myself to God once. I wasn't wanted.' (158) Moore's

God is harsh: he may want you when you are unwilling; he may reject you when you are willing. It is not for the individual to choose whether to have faith or to have a vocation, although in *Cold Heaven* Moore shows that it is still possible to reject God.

It is fruitful to read this novel and to look at the character and aspirations of Bernard McAuley in the light of Jung's writings on religion and individuation. All beliefs, according to Moore, are synonymous with or analogous to religious belief, but it would not be true to say that sexual love or artistic ambition, typical beliefs explored and developed by Moore, have the same characteristics as Bernard's obsession with Eileen Hughes. In *Psychology and Religion*, Jung describes religion as:

> a careful and scrupulous observation of the *numinosum*, that is, a dynamic agency or effect not caused by an arbitrary act of will. [This is the difference between Bernard's love for Eileen Hughes and the willed beliefs of other Moore protagonists] On the contrary, it seizes and controls the human subject, who is always rather its victim than its creator. The *numinosum* — whatever its cause may be — is an experience of the subject independent of his will . . . The *numinosum* is either a quality belonging to a visible object or the influence of an invisible presence that causes a peculiar alteration of consciousness . . .
>
> Religion appears to me to be a peculiar attitude of mind which could be formulated in accordance with the original use of the word *religio*, which means a careful consideration and observation of certain dynamic factors that are conceived as 'powers': spirits . . . laws, ideals, or whatever name man has given to such factors in his world as he has found powerful, dangerous or helpful enough to be taken into careful consideration, or grand, beautiful, and meaningful enough to be devoutly worshipped and loved.

> ... We might say, then, that the term 'religion' desig-
> nates the attitude peculiar to a consciousness which has
> been changed by experience of the *numinosum*.[6]

Bernard McAuley's *numinosum* is a person, not a power, a
spirit or an ideal, or even a person of particular interest.
Although Bernard McAuley might not recognise it as such,
for Jung, his obsession would be a case of religious pathology
or 'mania':

> It is not a matter of indifference whether one calls some-
> thing a 'mania' or a 'god'. To serve a mania is detestable
> and undignified, but to serve a god is full of meaning and
> promise because it is an act of submission to a higher,
> invisible and spiritual being.[7]

Jung regarded the individuation process as a kind of religious
quest. He thought that a religious attitude was natural to man
and that modern man was at risk of substituting some inferior
kind of worship: 'when the god is not acknowledged, ego-
mania develops, and out of this mania comes sickness'.
Bernard is conscious of a feeling of emptiness and lack of
meaning in his life, but the way he goes about compensating
for or healing this lack is by developing a mania for the
person of a young girl, Eileen Hughes. This is bound to lead
to disaster for him.

Bernard McAuley is for Moore a representative of modern
man, who feels the need for some kind of belief beyond the
ordinary to transcend himself. He has a strong religious sense
which, however, has been unfocused since the 'rejection' by
God of his vocation. His obsession with Eileen Hughes
clearly defies all logic. She does nothing, in human terms, to
deserve such reverence: she is tall, pretty, blue eyed, only
reasonably intelligent and not particularly interesting. Christopher Ricks sees the points clearly:

> ... Brian Moore has himself had to resist temptation.
> There must have been the temptation to make Eileen
> more interesting, more worthy or more plausible a

> precipitator of Bernard's religious adoration than she is here—and yet the point is just this, that (as in *Hamlet* in T. S. Eliot's judgment) the hero's emotions are in excess of their object. Eileen is lovable, no less and no more than that.[8]

This is exactly the point: there need be no rational reason for Bernard's passion for her, any more than there need be a logical reason for sexual love, or for religious belief. As Jung pointed out, without any desire to seem blasphemous, there are correspondences between the delusions of schizophrenics and the visions of mystics. Sometimes the dividing line can be very thin. Is this mania or mysticism? Is it only the subject that makes the difference? Would what is mania when addressed to Eileen Hughes be an admirable expression of spirituality if addressed to God?: 'In true love, to be with the person, to be in their presence, that's everything.' (57–8)

How can there be any possibility for an accommodation, let alone any reciprocation in a relationship that is based, on Bernard's side, on such intensity? There is no way for Eileen to respond to him—neither as a friend nor as a lover. Only by her ignorance, which Bernard has destroyed, or by such a degree of completely exploitative cynicism as she is clearly not capable of, could any arrangement be reached whereby Bernard could continue to see and adore her. Later, in suicidal misery, Bernard is clear sighted enough to see the inevitability of his own failure. He loved God: his vocation was rejected. He loved Eileen; here too he was rejected. It is not enough to love, or rather it is too much to love too intensely. What should Bernard have done? He has tried everything:

> Gods are like the sun. You can't get too close. They'll burn you. Gods don't like you to get cheeky . . . You may not be wanted. You may not be good enough. (159)

In Bernard McAuley, Moore presents an essentially good man but one who, according to Jung's definition, becomes an egomaniac. He uses the only power he knows — the power of money — although, paradoxically, he also realises its power-lessness — to acquire what he wants for himself. Yet it is not altogether a selfish desire. It goes beyond selfishness into the area of deep psychic need. God is not susceptible to persua-sion or temptation — the Bible story tells us that — but it has been Bernard's experience up to now that human beings can be bought.

The Temptation of Eileen Hughes probes the necessity of finding a meaning, a belief, and highlights the emptiness of much of what passes for achievement or happiness in mod-ern life, but it seems to postulate that the process of indivi-duation for modern man is difficult, perhaps impossible. Bernard has tried hard, not just with Eileen but with conven-tional religion and with many substitutes for religion. Yet at the end he is a pathetic wreck — a victim 'even unto death'. Structurally, too, the novel has the elements of 'tragedy': the telescoping of time, the isolation of the hero, the sense in which the decisive action, the 'Crossing of the Rubicon' as Bernard wryly terms his confession of devotion to Eileen, occurs early in the novel, so that everything that happens afterwards is falling action. After the brief period of intensive action, of hope followed by despair, Bernard's attempt to live a 'normal life' can only be in vain. He has tried everything in his quest for a belief by which to live. He has staked everything on Eileen Hughes and when that fails, there is nothing left for him. The essentially egocentric nature of his obsession, the manner in which it falls short of genuine self-transcendence, is shown in this remark to Eileen:

> I'm trying to save myself, not save the world. I told you, when I was twenty I wanted to be a saint, to save my soul, to love God, to do good. But it seems I wasn't wanted in that way . . . until I met you, until that day I saw you standing in the shop, I never knew what real happiness was. (76)

The Temptation of Eileen Hughes can be regarded as typical of the latest stage of Moore's work. Unlike the protagonists of the novels of the 1960s and 1970s, Bernard McAuley realises that material or artistic success or noteworthy achievement are not enough for happiness, or perhaps it would be more accurate to say that he realises this consciously and acts upon it, while they realise it only subconsciously or subliminally. Thus, he embraces a belief that is quasi-religious, that claims to be unselfish and to have the good of Eileen at heart. It is his attempt to escape the desert that is in him and in his life.

Despite the surface realism of this novel, it deals with a highly implausible story. It is not Moore's first venture into the supernormal, but it is his first into such a heightened or mystical psychological state. The author cannot expect the reader easily to identify with Bernard McAuley's state of mind, as it is an unnatural and perhaps even a pathological state, for all that it is understandable in a man of sensitivity whose life has been, perforce, devoted only to material things, and whose impulse towards God has been, according to him, rebuffed. One of Moore's means of overcoming this problem is to focus on the realistic detail of the trip to London and the sightseeing, as if such concentration on the mundane were to disarm the reader into thinking that this is truly a realistic work. Secondly, the time-scale of the novel is extremely short (if the 'epilogue' is omitted); such intensity of feeling as Bernard's or the reception of it by others can obviously not be sustained for very long. It is extremely tightly written; although some of the ideas may be considered preposterous, the writing is never indulgent. Thirdly, Moore never presents the narrative from the viewpoint of Bernard. There are multiple perspectives in use in the thirteen narrative sections, giving voice to Eileen, Mona, Agnes Hughes and one outsider, the chauffeur, Bateman, in the early stages of the novel. All the narrative voices used in the novel express a lack of comprehension of Bernard, thus implying the incomprehension of the world. Fourthly, Bernard's obsession with Eileen is shown repeatedly as having a religious basis. Religion provides Bernard with the language and the means of placing his devotion in some context. To the reader also, this metaphorical underpinning of religion makes Bernard's story more credible.

The central narrative, in which the crisis of the novel occurs, is the sixth of the thirteen sections and is related by Eileen. It begins on the third day of her trip to London, when, for the first time, she is free of the McAuleys and she spends some time alone in that city (37), and ends when she recoils from Bernard. (60)

The narrative is impersonal initially, but that Eileen's is the central consciousness is made evident by the occasional interpolations 'for now she would have a few hours on her own' and 'She felt her voice panicky'. (38) Throughout this section of the novel, the limitations of Eileen Hughes as an agent of perception are highlighted:

> It made her feel afraid, this road, as though she were in one of those fairground mazes that are not frightening at first but become frightening when you start bumping into mirrors and finding yourself trapped. (40)

(as is frequently the case with Eileen, the imagery is drawn from childhood, fair-ground, or comic-strip experiences).

But the author departs from the consciousness and language of Eileen when it is clear there is a need to express a larger concept, a sense of beauty and proportion which would not come without experience of beauty and without the language in which to express it.

> Moments later, as though Bernard had stage-managed it, the sun shone full and sudden on a splendid vista ahead, great green lawns, tall trees, an expanse of water, and, brilliantly white in the light, the long facade of Kenwood House. (49)

Eileen always has a conventional immature response: this is shown immediately after Bernard calls her a god: her god is the Christian God not of an individual or independent faith, but of the catechism learned by rote: 'She wanted to say, But isn't God supposed to care about our sins, to care about every one of us?' (48)

Moore never uses first-person narrative but the narrative is subtly angled from Eileen's point of view, for instance in the final sentence of the lunch scene where her fatal incomprehension is highlighted: 'It's Bernard who's not like the rest of us, she thought.' Even this realisation of her feeling towards him is expressed in terms of its own limitation. It expresses both an unwillingness and an inability to push her discovery any further. It is a profound truth that Bernard is 'not like the rest of us' and yet the most meaningless cliché.

It is not that Eileen does not notice that Bernard is going through a terrible upheaval, but she does not know how to express it, because it has no parallel in her previous experience. The triteness of her similes makes this clear. Eileen does not entirely lack the powers of observation or perception, but is deficient in those of imagination, experience and vocabulary:

> It was as though she had said something terrible. (52) Yet now he kept staring at her as if she had committed a murder. (53)

The first simile is drawn from her own experience of being a young person with the more experienced McAuleys and her dread of making a gaffe; the second from outside her experience, but drawing only on tabloid or comic-strip reactions. In neither case does the simile come near to expressing the reality of the way Bernard is looking at her, though she can observe the outward manifestations of his agitation: 'for a man who was normally tidy and a bit of a dandy, he was suddenly a sight, with his thinning brown hair sticking up behind, showing the bald spot he normally concealed'. (53) (Here her own particular voice can be heard in the colloquialism of this remark.)

In Eileen's 'what do you mean?', her incomprehension not alone mirrors the reader's, but exceeds it. In a fundamental sense, is there any understanding of what Bernard means by saying that he loves her, needs her, adores her? But the reader is encouraged to flatter himself that Eileen's consciousness is remarkably naive. Thus, the author conspires with the reader at the expense of the purported heroine in order to create more sympathy for Bernard. The reader's insight into Eileen's consciousness is, for the most part, an insight into incomprehension. The phrases 'What did he mean?' in Eileen's mind and 'What do you mean?' (55 and 56) expressed by Eileen to him, are, as Christopher Ricks has pointed out, 'pivotal'.[9] These phrases underline Bernard's miscalculation. He cannot tell Eileen half the truth and hope to satisfy her; he must tell her what he means, though at least part of him senses that it will be disastrous for him to do so. His realisation that he must 'cross the Rubicon' conveys this sense of fatality and this phrase, too, is incomprehensible to Eileen, except for a hazy memory of her schooldays.

Bernard's comparison of Eileen with God is a sign of his increasing recklessness and prepares also for the inflated religious language he uses in the afternoon:

> God is an innocent. The gods aren't interested in the sins of mortals, or the loves of mortals. That's one way they differ from the rest of us. (48)

Bernard has language to express his feelings: the language of religion, of imagination and of experience. He can describe very well what he feels (though this does not mean that he can understand it), but initially expresses it more to himself than to her. This is shown in the language of his body ('he turned from her and stared down at his shoes') and in the manner in which what he says to her, far from explaining the matter, only serves to confuse her more: '"I think, maybe, you gave me a sign. It could be an epiphany."' (53) Eileen's response is her conventional memory of the Epiphany as a Church holiday.

When Bernard really tries to explain himself and succeeds,

it is specifically to religious terminology that he has recourse, but in this case to everyday devotional language, beginning with 'maybe I should have kept my vow of silence', (56) and then in this climactic speech:

> Listen, sex isn't love. I know that. It's the opposite of love. Love, real love is quite different from desire. It's like the love a mystic feels for God. It's worship. It's just wanting to be in your presence ... I've worshipped you, In silence. In devotion. (57)

What does he mean? What does he know? Apart from the terminology of religion — 'worship', 'devotion', 'presence', what does this speech express about his feeling for Eileen Hughes? How does Bernard know the 'love a mystic feels for God'? Eileen can understand no more about the nature or the viability of Bernard's love than can the reader. It can only be expressed in the most opaque and elevated terms, highly symbolic, yet difficult to grasp; very familiar yet mysterious. Yet, Eileen knows that what Bernard proposes to her is deeply disturbing. Now it is her turn to 'look at her shoes' (57) in an effort to avoid looking at Bernard.

Moore shows the hopelessness and tragedy of Bernard's aspirations by two means: through his symbolic language of religion and ecstasy, which makes clear the extent of his delusion, and through the incomprehension of the dramatised consciousness, that of Eileen Hughes. Though it takes until the end of the novel for Bernard's fate to be decided, it is undeniable that Eileen's reaction to him in the central section discussed above is final, irreversible and fatal. What she understands of his feelings for her — and she never, for instance, makes a connection between the dissatisfaction and apparent lack of focus she observes in Bernard and this new passion for her — leads her to observe him with disgust and fear. Despite or perhaps because of his extravagant religious symbolism, she never really reaches an understanding of what he means by his love for her or of what she means to him. To her, he is a lunatic; to the reader he is doomed.

The Temptation of Eileen Hughes is certainly much richer in negative implications than it is in optimistic tendency. Of Moore's recent novels, it is the one where all the protagonists, not just Bernard McAuley, are most lost. The author takes away from them, as it were, the right to take comfort in material things; he makes it easy—too easy—for them to achieve success in their chosen areas and then he shows that all the rest remains to be done. What they have is nothing. Bernard is an extreme case, it is true, but the direction his obsession takes points to the importance of the undeveloped spiritual side of the modern individual. This is the direction taken by Moore in his next novel, *Cold Heaven*.

The Temptation
of the Unbeliever—
Cold Heaven

MARIE Davenport, the heroine of *Cold Heaven*, is in several ways very unlike Bernard McAuley. What is wrong in Bernard's life is that he lacks belief and tries to turn Eileen Hughes into the god of his idolatry. He is always painfully aware of this lack. Marie Davenport has a specific area of dissatisfaction in her life—she is about to leave her husband for another man—but this seems to her to be a temporary problem in a privileged and comfortable life. Where he fights for belief, she fights against some inexplicable force which tries to make her believe. As the novel shows, she is free not to believe, but at a deeper level, she is also shown to have the kind of life which suffers from a terrible dearth of spiritual fulfilment. Thus the apparition she experiences in Carmel could be an expression at a much deeper level, of a need which she ignores in her ordinary life.

Marie Davenport is shown as having the shallowest of beliefs. Her life is all surface and no depth. It could be argued that, because Marie is so frequently in the grip of panic, hysteria or anguish, there is little space in this novel to show the added dimensions and the deeper aspects of her character. Fundamentally, however, this novel is pessimistic in the way that only the later Moore novels are. It is not the kind of pessimism that is so bleak and frightful in *Judith Hearne*, because the life depicted this time is of the person who has everything but is nothing. Moore shows Marie Davenport as the typical contemporary woman, the *femme moyen sensuelle*, neither better nor worse, but just as good, just as bad as the average wealthy urban sophisticate of the 1980s. He shows also the superiority of belief in the far greater happiness of Mother St Jude, and it is clear that he feels his own religious agnosticism to be a form of deprivation, in a way that Marie Davenport does not, perhaps because she is only 'about 25' in Monsignor Cassidy's opinion. *Cold Heaven* is a consecutive novel in which Moore has chosen to have a very young heroine and it seems as if his intention was to underline the limitations of the views of these young protagonists rather than subscribe to them fully. When he was younger himself, he tended to choose characters who were closer to his own age. He says of himself: 'It's not the fact that I don't have religious belief that troubles me; it's that I wished I believed in something—that I was a little bit more like the mystics and had a little less sense of self.'[1]

Like *The Temptation of Eileen Hughes*, *Cold Heaven* is very conscious of the limitations of the modern cult of self-gratification and the lack of any real sense of the self except in purely selfish terms. This is not to say that the authorial attitude is narrowly critical of what the priests and nuns call Marie's 'adulterous relationship', but Moore is certainly conscious of the inability of people to believe in much any longer and of their inability to make commitments to other people. In her memory of her meeting with and marriage to Alex, there is a palpable lack of enthusiasm on Marie's part. The reader's impression of the lack of real purpose to her life is increased rather than dispelled by her later account of her meeting with Daniel. There is a strange element of passiveness in the manner with which she recalls her early relationship with her husband, as if she no longer wanted to take responsibility for her part in it:

> She was going around with someone else at the time but all of that changed when Alex decided he was in love with her. She stared now at the sea mist coming in and felt a familiar twinge of guilt. He was the one who was in love. I didn't really care about finishing graduate school.

I didn't know what I wanted to do. When I wrote that paper on Baudelaire, Professor Haines said: 'Obviously Miss Gillan is a hedonist.' I laughed and thought well that's no crime. But after I married Alex, I remembered what Haines had said. Did I marry just to have an easy life? If so, I have paid for it.[2]

The life of Marie Davenport is remarkable for the manner in which surface prosperity is combined with emotional poverty — or indifference. She looks coldly on Alex now and judges him quite dispassionately until she thinks she may have the power to kill him or to save him, and even later, at times, she tends to see him as being not quite human. The displacement and the lack of family ties in the case of Marie and Alex seem to be the fate of urban man. They move from California to New York and back again within a very short period of time. If Moore's early protagonists were rooted in a specific environment from which they found it impossible to escape and tied to families that impeded their movement towards individuality, the wheel has come full circle now. Marie is estranged from her father by an old bitterness and she scarcely knows Alex's people.

Marie's description of her meeting with Daniel is similarly matter-of-fact. Though she contrasts him with Alex, he is in fact, another Alex, who will be able to save her for the moment, and at the expense of his wife and child, from thinking any more deeply about her own life: 'She did not like his wife, a loud stout girl, but remembered the rush of pleasure she felt at the sight of Daniel.' (141) This is not to say that Marie is literally being punished for her infidelity by the 'death' of Alex , but there is an unavoidable contrast between the transcendence of self which is evident in Mother St Jude's mystic adoration and Marie's quest for happiness, which seems, at bottom, to involve little more than changing partners.

Cold Heaven displays, for the first time in Moore's fiction, an attitude towards Catholicism that is not negative or hostile, or even detached and historical (as where he treats of the Church at a certain future moment of time in *Catholics*) but sceptical in a positive way, if such a distinction be allowed. The authorial attitude in the novel may appear to be expressed through Marie Davenport and may thus seem to be wary or even hostile, but the novel, according to Moore himself, is 'in no way anti-Catholic. It is more the opposite.'[3] The novel consciously transcends the limited viewpoint of what is for most of the time the central consciousness, that of Marie Davenport, and is thus less sceptical than might be inferred from an identification of her viewpoint with the author's. The truly happy person in the novel is Mother St Jude. Even Marie Davenport at her most hostile, who represents the more sceptical side of Moore and in turn the sceptical outside world, is moved by her without being able to define or understand her charisma.

Mother St Jude appears only three times in the novel but hers is the character that is universally loved, as she is a person of patent sincerity and innocence. It is difficult to convey the personality of a mystic convincingly in a modern setting, using techniques of realism. Moore successfully does this by relating the other sisters' opinion of Mother St Jude, by showing the extraordinary effect she has on Marie Davenport and by contrasting her with such characters as Sister Anna and Father Ned Niles. Sister Catherine, who interprets the convent life for Marie on her first visit, says, half-reprovingly, half-admiringly: 'Mother St Jude would live off nothing, if we let her,' (82) and later, in awe, 'She has no self.' (85) The 'tall old nun', as she is designated on several occasions, also belongs to a different race from the other chattering sisters. There is a hint of mystery as well as ancient dignity about her 'dark-skinned Mexican or Indian features'. (82) Most striking, however, is the impact this nun has on Marie on the evening of their first meeting: an impact that is, paradoxically, made all the greater by her silence and passivity. Mother St Jude 'stood looking out of the window as though she were alone in the room'. (82) Unprompted, Marie immediately associates her 'seemingly catatonic movements' with spirituality; they 'could be part of an act of silent prayer'. (82)

Mother St Jude is never perceived, by Marie or by anybody else in the novel, as being threatening, deranged or sinister. Marie never resents her. The force of her personality is not used to gain personal power but on the contrary to achieve the self-effacement that is for her a prerequisite for her mystical adoration of God. She is an extraordinarily beneficent force throughout and never more than when Marie experiences her:

> As she hesitated she felt a sudden power in the room, a power that drew her gaze toward the tall old nun . . . Then Mother St Jude raised her bowed head and looked Marie full in the face, her dark luminous eyes intense, her expression one of overwhelming reverence joined to a complete and enveloping love. It was as though, in Marie, she saw one she had waited for all her life and now, praying for her wish to be granted, she gazed in supplication. (83)

Marie immediately yields to her unspoken entreaty. This power of the nun's luminous gaze, which is an expression of intense love for Marie, is also a feature of their second and final meeting.

> Again, as in that first meeting, Marie felt herself enveloped by a look of love mixed with reverence, a look she had never known from any other human being . . . in that moment, mysteriously, her fear of this place and these people was subsumed in a larger feeling, a feeling of peace. (225–6)

Before Marie accompanies Mother St Jude to the site of the apparition, the old nun speaks at some length for the only time in the novel. She claims, 'I am nothing', (227–8) and her language is that of intense devotion to God. Her mention of

St John of the Cross and St Teresa makes it clear that Moore means the reader to see her as a mystic. Her lack of a sense of self is conclusively demonstrated in the contrast drawn between her reaction and Sister Anna's to the occurrence on the cliff: 'her old face filled with doubt, her dark eyes afraid'. (235) She insists: 'You are the one who saw, Anna ' (237) For her, truth is more important than the glory of having seen Our Lady. This contrast is underlined by her final appearance, near the end of the novel. Here the narrative viewpoint is that of Monsignor Cassidy, who questions Mother St Jude about the apparition. The Monsignor as inquisitor is sceptical, faintly weary, and presses her about her recollections. All she is willing to say with any certainty is: 'But I felt the presence of God.' (249) Mother St Jude is shown frequently to hesitate, to repeat 'I don't know', to admit her uncertainty, in contrast with Sister Anna who boldly states, 'It *was* our Lady.' (253) It is Sister Anna's version that survives: it becomes *her* apparition.

The vision of the novel remains sceptical, though infinitely respectful of the rare character of Mother St Jude, who is as attached to the absolute truth as she is to the adoration of God. The two people who actively promote the 'miracle', Father Niles and Sister Anna, are not among the most admirable in the novel. Monsignor Cassidy 'looked into that stubborn face [of Sister Anna] . . . into those almost colorless eyes. Faith is a form of stupidity. No wonder they call it blind faith.' (253) No more than Monsignor Cassidy himself is Mother St Jude stupid—or blind.

Though Moore claims that he (still) does not believe in apparitions, he obviously believes in the belief of others and evinces in this regard a certain degree of wistfulness. These are some of the remarks he has made about his metaphysical theme in *Cold Heaven*:

> Years ago, I started writing something concerning Car-
> mel, became afraid and backed off. Two years ago, while
> visiting my sister who belongs to an order of Catholic

working nuns in England, I was struck by what I sense is true holiness. I wanted to get the idea across because several of the nuns I met there seem to have no self. I tried to convey that quality in my novel.[4]

I was very impressed with the sanctity in some of the older nuns — a feeling that mystics had; they had no sense of self, *solus ad solum* in God. I corresponded with them about what they really felt, but I didn't have the intellectual capability, or perhaps the religious capability, to write about it.[5]

Moore is right in saying that the mystical adoration of God is not susceptible of being understood by 'intellectual capability'. Just as he did not reject faith for rational reasons, so he will not, many years later, admire faith for intellectual reasons. He remains an emotional humanist. The most he can do is accept and admire faith, or perhaps even envy it. However, when the phrase quoted above is used in the novel: '*solus ad solum*, the old nun had called it', (224) Marie Davenport thinks of it, not with admiration but with claustrophobic horror, because she is afraid of its bearing on herself: 'To shut oneself away from the world, alone with God. She felt a panicky impulse to open the door and run out of the convent.' (224) But here, as elsewhere in the novel, Marie's viewpoint, influenced now by panic and a feeling of claustrophobia, is shown as being more limited than the author's. It seems, now, as if Moore genuinely accepts the supernatural as a valid focus of belief and furthermore as a higher form of belief than many he has explored in other novels. This is, perhaps, not just because it is essentially higher, but because it can provide a reason for living, a means of transcending the self that is completely healthy and unselfish, in contrast, for example, to Bernard McAuley's quasi-'mystical' love for Eileen Hughes in *The Temptation of Eileen Hughes*. This sense of dealing with something he cannot understand, but that he cannot disprove the existence of and must therefore accept as a belief of others, is brought out in the following quotation

from an interview with Moore subsequent to the publication
of *Cold Heaven*:

> The book was terribly hard to write. I worried terribly
> about it, because I don't believe in miracles or miraculous
> appearances, but I do believe in and am very interested
> in people who are truly religious, people who are saints.[6]

Against Mother St Jude's capability for mystic adoration in
the novel Moore pits Marie Davenport's freedom to choose
not to believe and her hysterical conviction that she is being
forced by some power which she cannot believe in, but
which, paradoxically, she can feel the power *of*, to bear
witness to something in which she cannot believe. This was a
theme that Moore was very conscious of when he wrote the
novel, and (with the exception of the voracious Father Ned
Niles) none of the representatives of the Church in the novel
tries to force Marie to believe:

> I wanted to point out the element of the supernatural
> . . . that there are things in the world that are not
> understood by us but we also have the choice to accept
> those things or to reject them. My heroine in *Cold Heaven*
> actually rejects [it] . . . and is allowed, quite seriously,
> by the Monsignor at the end of it, to make that decision
> and go away because the Catholic Church has never
> forced anyone to believe in miracles.[7]

As Monsignor Cassidy rightly remarks to himself, Ned
Niles is 'more like a newspaperman than a priest, nowadays'
(155) and later he describes him 'sleuthing around like a
private eye'. (194) Ned Niles combines the appearance of a
fox with the preoccupations and ethical standards of a Fleet
Street newshound. He does try to force Marie, not by using
the authority of the Church, but the far more mysterious and
therefore more impressive power of a mystical figure: '"Remember, the Church doesn't want you to do anything you
don't want to do. But perhaps our Lady does. That's something else."' (183) At the end of the novel, not only does the

official Church in the person of Monsignor Cassidy, release Marie from any obligation, but the experience of the apparition and thus the responsibility for disseminating the knowledge is transferred from Marie to Sister Anna. Marie is thus relieved of moral pressure and responsibility. This relief highlights the changing nature of a religion that can no longer demand belief in apparitions and that can accept the fact of unbelief in others with a certain grace. Moore describes belief in miracles as an aspect of his theme: 'It's the question of free will and the fact that a miracle is a divine interference with our choice.'[8] Mother Paul, in her simplicity and spiritual innocence (the nuns are repeatedly thought of, by Marie, as giggling, schoolgirlish, silly) is taken aback when she hears about Marie's profession of unbelief, but shows her good sense and sophistication by treating Marie kindly and tactfully: 'And who would guess even now, that this politely spoken girl told Monsignor and Father Paul that she hates religion and all it stands for.' (216) How far this is from the negative, harsh and hostile Catholicism of the early Belfast novels. In the Belfast novels the Church controls society while society *is* the Church—that is to say, there is no differentiation between the rules of Catholic society and the rigid rules of a repressive Church.

In *Cold Heaven*, on the other hand, Catholicism treads warily in a secular society. *Cold Heaven*, as well as creating a world of inexplicable apparitions and contemplative ascetics, is the world of sophisticated medicine, of jet travel almost at will, across America and between continents, of motels and car-hire firms. There is no one who better exemplifies a Catholicism that has adapted to the world than Monsignor Cassidy. Moore obviously relished the creation of the character of Monsignor Cassidy whom he christens 'God's golfer' in the novel, admitting in an interview that he was his favourite character. In all of Moore's novels, there is no person he less resembles than Father Quigley of *Judith Hearne*. His lifestyle, though described satirically here by the sharp and vulpine Ned Niles, is genuinely perceived by

Monsignor Cassidy as being 'like paradise': "'Championship golf course, celebrities, beautiful climate, rich parish, well-run school, good curate. And this refectory is like a resort hotel.'" (116) But Monsignor Cassidy has his functions: he is adept at dealing with the spiritual malaises of those (including Marie Davenport) who have everything that money can buy; the Catholic Church, like any business, needs a man with his public relations skills in order to exploit the rich. Though on first acquaintance he may seem almost risible in his madras check trousers and purple golfing shirt, he is shown as being more worthy of respect at the end of the novel. His great virtue is his tolerance, both of mystical belief and of secularist unbelief, and his statement to Marie at the end is impressive exactly because it makes such a limited claim: "'I'm not a very holy man, but I do believe in God. And I believe that God doesn't reveal Himself to us in an unmistakable way.'" (269) In a sense he offers her absolution for her unbelief in his parting remarks, though, significantly, with a secular handshake rather than a clerical benediction.

Usually Moore sets the belief of his protagonist against the unbelief of the world or even that of the people closest to him or her. By 'unbelief' here, is meant the incomprehension, hostility or rejection which is experienced by all his characters at the hands of their families or by society. To give just two examples of many, there is the complete lack of sympathy of Brendan Tierney's mother for his messianic compulsion to write a great novel in *An Answer from Limbo*. Again, Eileen Hughes rejects Bernard McAuley's profession of love for her with fear and disgust in *The Temptation of Eileen Hughes*. In the case of *Cold Heaven*, the unbelief of the protagonist is set against a supernatural power or belief which appears to her to be imposed on her from above. But the difference between Marie Davenport and other Moore protagonists is perhaps not as great as might appear from this outline. She is fighting against something, but she is also fighting *for* the right to live her life according to her own beliefs and her own needs—to leave her husband, to marry the man she loves. There is, however, a value judgment established in this novel about the quality of the ordinary secular beliefs of the protagonist. The superficiality of her guiding principles and of the life she leads is emphasised and constantly juxtaposed with the self-forgetful religious zeal of Mother St Jude. In earlier novels, Moore created female protagonists who literally abandoned the world for love and focused in the loved one all their hopes and aspirations. He created characters like Mary Dunne and Sheila Redden in *The Doctor's Wife* whose emotional and erotic lives took the shape of religious ecstasy for them. Marie Davenport's life has nothing even of this limited selflessness, nor of the guilt which, though it certainly causes suffering, conveys the capacity of those women to feel for others. Much more than Mary Dunne, Marie Davenport is guilty of the crime (or sin—it is variously characterised in *An Answer from Limbo* and *I am Mary Dunne*) of indifference. All her life appears to have been governed by it; at times she appears to be indifferent to herself.

Moore, in an interview previously quoted, claims to have found the novel very difficult to write. Despite his own lack of belief in religious apparitions, he has no difficulty in conveying the sense of one, communicating it as he does always through the consciousness of the sceptic, Marie Davenport. Perhaps this is because the whole area of apparitions is well documented and part of the emotional baggage of every lapsed Catholic. What is not so convincingly conveyed are Alex's repeated 'deaths' and Lazarus-like recoveries of life. This is the medical miracle of the novel, which is the counterpart of the apparitions and Marie feels them to be closely linked and orchestrated by the powers of the supernatural world.

Cold Heaven shows a definite progression in Moore's attitude to faith and to the problem of belief . . . His attachment to the actuality of the modern world seems to get less and less, while he is never able to conquer his pessimism by postulating belief in the other world. It seems that, despite his earlier protestations of his respect for the validity of any kind of belief, in his fiction he has explored all these beliefs and found them lacking. It seems now as if only religious faith in its literal sense (that is, not used as a 'metaphor for belief') can provide that drama, that transcendence, that complete forgetfulness of the self that might lead to happiness. As Seamus Deane says in the following quotation, Moore does put forward the possibility of a world other than the actual, an alternative to the modern world, but it is no more than a possibility. Since he does not believe in it himself, how can it be more?

> It is a radical dissatisfaction with the actual that leads in the end to either the acceptance of or the recognised possibility of miracle . . . Moore's allegiance to the actual world does not waver. Instead, it learns to co-exist with the possibility of another, apocalyptic place, in which the simple can wholeheartedly believe and which the sophisticated dread to accept other than as a psychic disturbance or metaphor . . . Belief remains a powerful force that must be refused, and yet the effects of which in the ordinary run of experience cannot be denied.[9]

In the article called 'Brian Moore's Fiction of Faith', Michael Paul Gallagher has made a serious attempt to detect and elaborate on a consistent theme of faith in the whole of Moore's work in the thirty years since the publication of *Judith Hearne*, up to and including *Black Robe*. Gallagher says 'The expansion of the faith theme from the literal or narrowly religious world into a metaphysical metaphor is the main topic of this article.'[10] Yet, it appears that in *Cold Heaven*, the 'faith theme' has both a literal and metaphorical resonance; it is not just 'something to believe in' any longer: it may instead be something one is denied the gift of believing or that one escapes (apparently) the compulsion to believe, but it is on a different plane to sexual love or artistic ambition as 'beliefs'. Gallagher goes on:

> There is a sense in which Moore . . . is exposing the fragility of religious unbelief just as earlier he had

explored the fragility of religious belief. What he means by 'faith' or 'belief' can equally take the form of agnosticism.[11]

It is certainly true that Marie Davenport's 'unbelief' is akin to the 'belief' of the protagonists in earlier Moore novels, but it is debatable whether this unbelief is so fragile. Marie Davenport is put under extreme pressure to believe, not by the Church authorities but by the corroborated evidence of her own senses and by the extent of the coincidences relating to the 'death' of Alex. She is, in fact, put under much more severe psychological pressure to believe than other Moore protagonists are *not* to believe, yet she resists. To support his point of view, Gallagher puts some of Marie's version of events down to 'neurotic imagination', whereas to a reader who has no interest in making Catholic belief plausible, the 'other-worldly' contact, if one can accept it at all, seems quite natural, convincing, even irrefutable. There is no question of Marie Davenport being neurotic to begin with. If the novel is successful in making the reader accept the possibility of the supernatural, which the reader will possibly do if he accepts the sanctity of Mother St Jude, there is nothing that is beyond belief. Gallagher seems here to be fitting into the position advanced by Monsignor Cassidy, who is relieved to be able to think Marie in the grip of delusion or hysterics. Moore does not create Marie Davenport like that; as the following discussion on technique and point of view will show, she is always a witness whose story is reliable, though her understanding of and response to what she witnesses may be defective.

These are the opening paragraphs of *Cold Heaven* which in setting the scene are a 'symbolic commentary'[12] on a modern sensibility.

The wooden seats of the little pedal boat were angled so that Marie looked up at the sky. There were no clouds. In the vastness above her a gull calligraphed its flight. Marie and Alex pedalled in unison, the revolving pedals making a slapping sound against the waves as the pedal boat treadmilled away from the beach, passing through ranks of bathers to move into the deeper, more solitary waters of the Baie des Anges. Marie slackened her efforts but Alex continued determinedly, steering the *pedalo* straight out into the Mediterranean.

'Let's not go too far', she said.

'I want to get away from the crowd. I'm going to swim.'

It was like him to have some plan of his own, to translate idleness into activity even in these few days of vacation. She now noted his every fault. It was as though, having decided to leave him, she had withdrawn his credit. She looked back at the sweep of hotels along the Promenade des Anglais. Today was the day she had hoped to tell him. She had planned to announce it at breakfast and leave, first for New York, then on to Los Angeles to join Daniel. But at breakfast she lacked all courage. Now, with half the day gone, she decided to postpone it until tomorrow. (9)

This is prose of the utmost lucidity, as limpid as the waters of the Mediterranean which it describes. It conveys a strictly normal, realistic picture, yet even in this realism it gives a foretaste of the themes and issues of the novel. How can a writer convey within a realistic framework that this is to be a novel with transcendent or supernatural themes? The Côte d'Azur is going to be transformed into the coast of California for much of the novel, but despite the commercialisation of the first and the relative inaccessibility of the second, there is much in common between them and this is emphasised here. In the opening sentences, the helplessness of the individual faced with great cosmic forces is expressed. The seats of the 'little' pedal boat, the 'little' underlining its vulnerability, 'force' Marie to look up. The sky is not hostile or threatening, but 'vast' and 'clear'. The movement into danger, a danger from which Marie is only released at the end of the novel, is signified by their passage into the 'deeper, more solitary waters of the Baie des Anges'. What is noticeable is the economy with which Moore depicts not only the scenery and prepares for the fatal accident, but also how he creates the relationship between Marie and Alex, even in the first few lines. At first, they 'pedalled in unison', but very soon their disharmony is signalled by the difference in their efforts: 'Marie slackened her efforts but Alex continued determinedly.' Their first words of communication are words of disagreement, her remark suggestive and conciliatory, his 'I want' assertive and even dogmatic.

Yet one really only establishes the tone of these two remarks and the tenor of the relationship with the help of the gloss that is offered on them by Marie. Already, the first sentence of the novel suggests an identification with Marie as protagonist. She could be alone in the boat on the evidence of this sentence; she is, in fact, alone mentally if not physically, as evidenced by the second paragraph. And it is the beginning of the second paragraph which opens with free indirect speech and furthermore without naming the person on whose consciousness or thoughts it has focused, that makes definite the suspicion of the reader that the central consciousness (limited and ambiguous though the relationship may be between the author and this consciousness) and 'voice' of the novel will be Marie's. Moore slips subtly and imperceptibly into free indirect speech here; he has no need to specify since, if the male person is the object of observation and comment, then the female must be the observer and the female's the 'voice'.

The second paragraph gives Marie's gloss on the two remarks which end the first and in doing so, supplies in a nutshell the whole history of her marriage and her attitude to her companion. It is not clear that he is her husband, but this can be inferred from her decision to 'leave' him. The frustration of an extended period — it could even be years — is implied in her own realisation (it is not the author's observation) that 'she now noted his every fault'. The coldness of her view of him which has developed in response to the coldness of his always 'having some plan of his own' is clear in the deliberateness as well as the metaphorical resonance of the image she thinks of: 'It was as though . . . she had withdrawn his credit.' The paragraph continues in short even sentences, absolutely matter of fact, although the period of Marie's deliberation must be at least several minutes if they reach a point 'far out from the shore' at the beginning of the next paragraph. With each separate sentence, a different mental process is conveyed: observation (She looked back); memory ('today was the day'); rehearsing of her plans ('to announce it at breakfast . . . then on to Los Angeles to join Daniel'); reaching a decision which postpones the decision to tell ('she decided to postpone it until tomorrow'). She thus appears to be in a position of power, she knows something that Alex does not; yet she is powerless to act upon her decision.

These paragraphs have a value as an opening passage of introspection before the period of frenzied activity which begins, not just when the launch hits Alex, but in the very next paragraph, when Alex begins to swim in 'an energetic, erratic freestyle'. With few respites, this activity lasts until the end of the novel. Normality is emphasised here, even in the inertia of Marie's decision not to leave Alex yet, but in this passage, Moore also creates some of the conditions and develops some of the themes that make *Cold Heaven* such a pessimistic novel.

Marie is presented in a relationship that lacks all credibility. Her disillusion is emphasised and there is no attempt made to arouse any sympathy for Alex. Yet her powerlessness also emerges and this is to be a feature of Marie's life until the end of the novel. She is Alex's victim now as she will be his hostage later on and also the victim of other, more powerful forces. She has no power because she lacks 'all courage'; in this, she is contrasted with Mother St Jude who has none of Marie's obvious intellectual or material advantages yet has a tremendous spiritual power.

There is also in this opening passage a sense of a power greater than the individual, in the 'vastness' of the sky and the 'deeper, more solitary waters', an impression that will be retained and intensified when the setting moves to Carmel. It is almost a Wordsworthian setting and description, but lacking any Wordsworthian 'sense sublime' of a benign universal 'spirit and a motion'.

Thirdly, this opening passage presages the remainder of the novel in the manner in which material ease is contrasted with the emptiness of the relationship between Marie and Alex and indeed with the emptiness of her life. 'Beginnings lead off, but they should have the seeds of finality in them.'[13] In *Cold Heaven* this remark has a bearing as regards style as well as character and plot.

The phrase 'seeds of finality' is of significance here if the opening paragraph is compared with the paragraphs that end the novel. Again, the key phrase is that Marie 'looked up at the sky' as she did from the pedalo in Nice:

> She looked up at the sky. No guns were trained from on high, ready to shoot her down. There were only dull gray clouds. Like an old battlefield, once cacophonous with the clash of steel, the roar of cannon, the screams of wounded and dying men, the headland, grassy and quiet, gave no hint of what had happened here. Like a battlefield it had become its history, its truths altered to fit the legend of those who had survived. She thought of Daniel, who would never know about this, of Alex, who had been a part of it without knowing the part he played. She and she alone would remember. She would remember it in silence for the rest of her life.
>
> She thought of that life, that ordinary, muddled life of falling in love and leaving her husband and starting over again: that known and imperfect existence that she had fought to regain against ineluctable forces, inexplicable odds. The priests were gone. It was over. She had been returned to ordinary life, to its burdens, its

consequences. She looked up toward the Point Lobos Motor Inn. She began to walk toward Alex's unit, rehearsing what she would say to him. (270–71)

Unlike the opening scene the sky is clouded. Because of the nature of the supernatural element, the sky has been very important throughout the novel, as well as natural phenomena such as sunlight, thunder and lightning and earthquakes. For instance, Marie relates to Monsignor Cassidy that the sky was cloudy on the day of the first 'apparition' on the rocks. But this time the element of pathetic fallacy, of the ominousness frequently associated with 'dull gray clouds' is weakened by the adverb 'only' before the phrase. In the extended and elaborate similes of the next two sentences, the relief Marie feels at her deliverance from the supernatural forces that threatened to engulf her is highlighted. These images are 'given' to Marie, framed as they are between the two sentences 'she looked up at the sky' and 'She thought of Daniel', yet are so self-conscious and portentous as to test the credibility of that idea. The contrast is made between the activity, the noise, the 'speaking' (in the sense of the communicatiof attempted by the wounded and dying) of the first half of the sentence, signalled by the word 'cacophonous' and the alliterative cacophony of the varied sounds, and the silence, the impenetrability, the anonymity and the uncommunicativeness of the second half ('gave no hint of what had happened here'.) The second simile, on close examination, suggests the rewriting of history or events ('its truths altered'), which the Monsignor has promised to do to protect Marie. Her knowledge is contrasted with the ignorance of others. It was an experience which was vouchsafed to her and, though she has chosen to reject it, it will always be hers. The 'silence' of the final sentence and the 'alone' of the penultimate emphasise her isolation in this experience, which she will communicate to neither of the men, not even to the man she loves. The repetition of the pronoun 'she' returns the concentration to the heroine: it is she alone, with members of the Church merely acting as intermediaries or interpreters, who has had the experience with the supernatural.

In the final paragraph, not just life but existence is postulated in opposition to the essential and incomprehensible: 'ineluctable forces, inexplicable odds'. The use of the word 'ineluctable' is apparently paradoxical. Marie chooses to fight and not to yield to these forces, in so far as belief is concerned. Yet she sees herself, several times, as being forced to negotiate, to do things and go places against her will and she is released from these obligations only by the grace and favour of the Church. Her victory and her loss are conveyed together, both in the banal statement of 'ordinary, muddled life' and in the more thoughtful and philosophical phrase, 'that known and imperfect existence'. The victory of everyday life is thus gained at the expense of the transcendent. In the two flat staccato sentences, 'The priests were gone. It was over.', are contained both the symbols and the 'reality' of the experience she has rejected. 'The priests' is easily understood, but what exactly is meant by the 'it' of the next sentence? The closing stages of the narrative gradually distance the reader from the consciousness of Marie Davenport in a technique that is cinematic. The 'It was over.', which is an expression of lack of comprehension on the part of Marie, is followed by the reader's last moment of access to her point of view. Here it is significant that the subject is placed in the passive voice and thus becomes the object rather than the initiator: 'She had been returned.' The last two sentences are impersonal and reminiscent of the reader's first insight into Marie Davenport's mind in the opening scene in the pedalo at Nice, both in their style and in their content: 'She looked . . . She began to walk.', and though she is also again 'rehearsing what she would say to him', this is the voice of the omniscient narrator rather than free indirect speech.

So the novel ends as it begins, with Marie planning to break the news of her relationship with Daniel to her husband. The novel regains the surface limpidity with which it began. The return to the real world is complete, yet moulds have been broken both in the world of the novel and in Moore's treatment of his subject. To paraphrase Seamus Deane's remark, the possibility of another world, of a different world of experience has been raised and made credible in the person of Mother St Jude. This world is shown as being on a far higher, more sublime level than Marie Davenport's preoccupations — her marriage, her adultery, her impending separation from her husband. So the reassertion of the values of the world by the author at the end of the novel cannot be taken as optimistic. As long as Moore entertains the possibility of faith and a transcendent selflessness, then to regain 'that known and imperfect existence' is a pyrrhic victory. The image of the battlefield on which Marie Davenport turns her back in the closing moments of the novel is thus a very appropriate one, but the novel does not answer the question of whether she is the winner or the loser. It is more likely that she is both.

The moment of greatest tension in the novel and the climax of Marie's fears occur in San Francisco when her husband comes close to death in the hospital there. In order to consider the passage where Moore has to use a technique to convey the immensity of her fears and her helplessness, it is first necessary to look at the character of Father Ned Niles, Marie's inquisitor in this particular scene of the drama. Though there are elements of caricature in the creation of Ned Niles, he is a pivotal character in the plot. He enhances Marie's fears and delusions both by his (apparent) faith in apparitions and by his rapacious desire — the desire of the detective or of the newshound — to follow her story for his publication. It is therefore in his interest that she should believe her own story and that she should feel that she is being made to follow through on the apparitions by reporting them and by making herself available to the Catholic authorities. Father Niles's pursuit of her coincides (although, for Marie, nothing is coincidence) with her moment of greatest anxiety in the novel (once she realises that Alex is not dead), when he is placed under intensive care in the hospital. Medically, there is no explanation. 'It doesn't make any sense', says Daniel, her support in medical as well as in human terms. 'Apparently, something like that happened [something medically quite incompatible with life] on the floor when the nurse checked his vital signs.' (174) The only resource she can now envisage is the spiritual one. She is convinced that she must fulfil some kind of compact with some unknown power which will restore Alex. Ned Niles is the ambassador for the unknown power whom she seeks out and since this is modern America she speaks to him, very appropriately, on the telephone:

> Then he said 'Something happen to your friend?' It was a question that was not a question, it was a statement. He was their agent. He had been waiting for her call.
>
> 'I don't know', she said. 'I'm not sure.'
>
> 'You're not sure? I hope it's nothing serious.'
>
> 'It's serious', she said. 'I wouldn't have called.'
>
> 'I see.' She heard him clear his throat. 'Mrs Davenport. I might as well be honest with you. I've become very interested in your story, especially since we spoke today. I don't want to intrude in your private life, but it occurs to me that it might be a good thing if you could tell Monsignor, or even me, what this other element in your story is, the thing you seem to be afraid of. Does that make sense?'
>
> 'Is that what I have to do?' she asked. It was an order, wasn't it? This was the way they gave orders; they gave them as suggestions, as ways to help you. (175)

Supernatural occurrences are subject to exploitation and manipulation by the unscrupulous – which is why they have become so devalued in the eyes of so many (take for example the Abbot's reaction to Lourdes in *Catholics*) and Ned Niles is certainly unscrupulous. This passage also shows the way in which the 'apparition' and the interpretation of it could be incompatible with Marie's free will, both in the insinuations and suggestions of the priest's speech and in the hysteria of her response. In order to anticipate such objections, Moore deals with them.

Moore has a very good ear for dialogue and in this passage he captures the priest's dishonesty which, typically, masquerades as honesty ('I might as well be honest with you'), the blatant yet hypocritical untruth of his 'I don't want to intrude'. Ned Niles is supremely plausible in his airing of all the clichés. He gives the appearance of casualness ('It occurs to me that it might') and slips in 'or even me' to cover the most rabid curiosity. It is important that he is a disembodied voice, because he could be at a great distance from her, and part of the suggestive power of his speech comes from the fact that they are speaking on the telephone, not face to face.

Marie's response 'Is that what I have to do?' is an apparent *non-sequitur*. Her thoughts are conveyed in free indirect speech immediately after this question. The 'wasn't it?' is merely rhetorical, since she has to her own satisfaction interpreted his suggestion as an imperative. The individual at the other end of the phone line has become 'they'. She has lost all sense of Ned Niles as a man, and fails to respond to his devious and self-interested remarks, especially as she can no longer see the unprepossessing 'foxy' appearance which so repelled her on the previous day. She is incapable of rational thought; he interprets for her what she wants, while claiming to leave it up to her. In his next remarks the appearance of balance, '"On the one hand . . . on the other hand"', hides quite considerable pressure, as does '"then I think you might be wise"'. He continues to manipulate her fears, especially in his choice of the word 'miraculous' whose 'loaded' quality he calculatedly calls upon and which he only pretends to qualify by the parenthetic phrase 'for want of a better word' and by associating it only with her, 'If you do think'. It is as if it were her idea to consider these apparitions seriously as 'miraculous'.

It is part of Moore's intention in the novel to show Marie Davenport under immense psychological pressure, and yet so hostile to the forces of religion that she will not yield to the idea that the apparitions she has seen have a genuine spiritual significance. In this scene her fear and the manner in which she immediately yields to the priest have nothing to do with belief, but are the products of a combination of coincidence and the pressure put upon her by Ned Niles. Her haste to do anything they want is an effort to relieve the pressure on her and on the critically ill Alex. Nobody can be forced to believe if Marie Davenport can go through all these experiences and emerge still sceptical, even hostile. The mystery is why she should even be chosen.

The whole novel remains shrouded in mystery. What emerge from it as regards the development of Moore's attitude to belief and religion are firstly a new sense of the possibility of genuine goodness and remarkable self-forgetfulness, that has its origins in religious belief; secondly, the related concept that there is a possibility of mystical self-transcendence in life which is vouchsafed only to the very few; thirdly, that the individual must be free to refuse to participate in any sort of spiritual life, because any enforced belief is without value (as in the dialogue with Father Niles above); finally, as regards the author's own viewpoint, there is the implicit admission in the novel that there is really no possibility of understanding spirituality other than by experiencing it. Moore creates Mother St Jude with a reasonable degree of success, but all the time he is standing outside the area of holiness, closer to Marie Davenport than to any of the nuns, but far more admiring of them than he is of her.

11

The Cruelty of Belief—
Black Robe

BECAUSE his fictional themes have been so resolutely and consistently contemporary, Moore's one excursion into historical fiction in his 1985 novel, *Black Robe*, is difficult to place in the pattern of his work as a whole. The themes of the novel are familiar: the testing of the individual; the crisis of faith; the 'solving' of that crisis by the resolution to live by the fiction of faith if not the reality, as the Abbot does in *Catholics*. Michael Paul Gallagher makes the point that if one compares *Black Robe* and Moore's first novel, *Judith Hearne*, one finds 'a plot at once amazingly similar and yet totally changed'.[1] And of Father Laforgue's ordeal he writes, quite accurately: 'Like Judith Hearne the extremities of his situation cause his religious bearings to fall apart within himself, and he too enters a lonely passion of darkness, guilt and doubt.' Yet the gap between the novels in other ways is enormous and the gap between *Black Robe* and its immediate predecessor *Cold Heaven* is at least as great. From an examination of the spiritual malaises of modern society, Moore has turned his attention to Quebec province in 1635. He claims that his choice of subject 'was just an aberration. I read this book (Graham Greene's discussion of *The Jesuits in North America*) and I wrote that book. I'm not going to become a historical novelist.'[2]

The effect of the historical theme is at once to enhance the realism of the novel and to dilute its immediacy and impact. That is to say, one presumes a greater fidelity to fact in the texture and detail of the novel, but one has, conversely, to allow for a much greater imaginative leap on the novelist's part in order for him to understand the motivation and

mentality of characters, all of whom live in a different age
from ours and half of whom subscribe to a radically different
set of life-beliefs. If one accepts, however, that Moore
intended the themes of his novel to be universal, not just
limited to Quebec Province in 1635, and indeed chose them
for that reason, in an effort to show that these themes do not
apply just to contemporary society, but to all men, in all ages,
then it becomes possible to see *Black Robe* as an extension or
development of *Cold Heaven* though the former has a mythic
quality which *Cold Heaven* resolutely refuses to permit. There
are two themes which *Black Robe* shares with *Cold Heaven* but
which *Black Robe* develops more strongly in a different
direction. These are admiration for individual zeal and pessimism about the possibility of having or maintaining belief.

As regards the first theme, *Black Robe* moves it in a different
direction. In *Cold Heaven*, Mother St Jude, a character whom,
it is clear, Moore created with a sense of awe and admiration,
remains safely in the convent. It is emphasised in the novel
that she has not left the convent for many years, so the
external face of Catholicism is represented by the much more
practical Mother Paul and by the worldly Monsignor Cassidy.
These are mediators between the world and the transcendent
self-forgetful zeal of the mystic. Father Laforgue is not a
mystic, but he is zealous. His zeal takes the form of a desire
for martyrdom. Because his zeal is externalised and focused
on missionary endeavour, it is much more easily understood
and conveyed. There is no doubt that Moore has, on one
level, created the character of Father Laforgue with the
greatest admiration; he expresses this admiration in the
introduction and elsewhere. It is the extremity of Father
Laforgue's belief that appeals to Moore; people who are
messianically moved or subject to 'Pauline' epiphanies have
frequently provided material for his novels.

Furthermore, Father Laforgue is not a completely invented
or fictional character; he is based on a historical personage.
What is conveyed about him is not merely theological theory
or hagiography, but can be verified by the result of his vow

He proved his faith, whatever one might think about his fanatical desire for martyrdom. This is what Moore read of the historical prototype for Laforgue, Father Noel Chabanel: 'And when the temptation still beset him he bound himself by a solemn vow to remain in Canada to the day of his death.' On this vow, Moore comments: 'A voice speaks to us directly from the seventeenth century, the voice of a conscience that, I fear, we no longer possess.'[3] This sentence is unambiguous: it postulates both the relevance of Father Chabanel's 'voice' or testimony (and, accordingly, that of Father Laforgue) and it expresses Moore's perception that the voice of conscience is lacking in modern life. So far, this seems consistent with Moore's admiration for mysticism in *Cold Heaven*. He has gone further in an interview, and in an image reminiscent of Macbeth's 'doth unfix my hair', he has said of the spirit of zeal and self sacrifice of Father Chabanel/Father Laforgue:

> But it's that spirit—the hair stood up on my head, although I'm not religious. It's that spirit these people had, first of all the dedication they had to do this and the second thing that made the hair stand up on my head was the realisation of the difference between us, I think, even religious people now and religious people then is that they believed in the devil as strongly as they believed in God.[4]

The kind of wonder that makes your hair stand up on your head could hardly be called comfortable or unqualified; it is much more like a horrified admiration. Laforgue is a zealot let loose among Savages and what emerges just as strongly from the novel as his devotion and zeal is his lack of comprehension of the forces he is dealing with. He is repeatedly shown as being physically unfitted to the rigours of the journey with the Savages, yet his determination is extraordinary and he does survive. He is, at first sight, 'a slight, pale man, thin-bearded, intellectual, but with a strange determination in the eyes and narrow mouth'. (18) His deafness, which endures for much of the journey, is symbolic of his incapacity not just to hear but to understand anything of the Savages' language or of their culture or beliefs. He is, as a reviewer pointed out, 'dedicated to the idea of his own martyrdom'.[5] In the scene with his mother in Rouen, a scene that seems somewhat contrived and unconvincing despite the fact that seventeenth-century Rouen still survives and is much closer culturally to the modern reader than seventeenth-century 'Savage' Canada, Laforgue denies being a saint like Joan of Arc, but it is clear that he does see himself as a potential saint or at least a martyr. He has a messianic compulsion:

> he had prayed in nightly vigils that he would be the chosen one ... And now his prayers had been answered. Today he set out for that place where martyrdom was more than just a pious hope. This is my hour. This is my beginning. (34)

Unlike the mystical devotion of Mother St Jude in *Cold Heaven*, this devotion is directed not solely towards God, but towards God through the world. Therein the problem arises. No one could doubt the genuineness of Father Laforgue's desire to do good, or of his eagerness to sacrifice himself in the pursuit of God's work and God's will. Yet he sees only two elements in the work and the life he undertakes in Canada: God and Father Laforgue doing God's will. The work to be done is for the greater glory of God and for the greater glory of Father Laforgue, but the work itself takes a very minor part. Moore seems to be saying, in examining the motivations of Father Laforgue and the whole idea of missionary work, that the goal of converting the heathen is an assumption of the power to do good: genuine self-transcendence such as was seen in *Cold Heaven*, is a relinquishment of all worldly power.

This of course, is not only, and not even primarily the individual's fault, and at this point the scope of *Black Robe* widens and its theme departs from that of *Cold Heaven*. *Black Robe* presents a different view of religion from that of *Cold*

Heaven. In *Cold Heaven*, Moore's admiration of Mother St Jude is unqualified; in *Black Robe*, for the reasons given, his admiration for Father Laforgue may be tremendous, but it cannot be unqualified. Mother St Jude belongs to the institutional Church, but is not really *of* it; Father Laforgue both belongs to it and is *of* it. In *Black Robe*, the Church as an institution is well meaning, but blind. The Savages, as Moore shows them, are not quite so blind; that is to say both that their own beliefs demand extraordinary perception of them and that they are forced into at least acknowledging Christian beliefs by having them constantly before them. Even if they scoff at the absurdity of Christian beliefs and at the blindness of Christians when it comes to recognising the forces of nature and the spirits of animals, they recognise that the Christians have a coherent alternative set of values and beliefs. An old Huron, Ondesson, very pertinently asks of Father Jerome: 'Why do you not respect that we serve different gods and that we cannot live as you do.' (230) Alone among the Christians (apart from the drunken renegade traders who are shown as living only for pleasure) and because he lives with the Savages in a unique set of circumstances, Daniel Davost recognises a coherent Savage belief. It is evident that Moore sees in Christianity and in all institutional religion an infinite potential for division and misunderstanding:

> *Black Robe* is very much concerned with religion. It deals with the inability of the Jesuits, with the best motives in the world, to understand the religion which the Indians had, and the belief on both sides . . . that each side saw the other side as the agent of the devil.[6]

> The only conscious thing I had in mind when writing it was the belief of one religion that the other religion was totally wrong. The only thing they have in common is the view that the other side must be the Devil.[7]

In the introduction to the novel itself the same idea is reiterated:

> This novel is an attempt to show that each of these beliefs inspired in the other fear, hostility and despair, which later would result in the destruction and abandonment of the Jesuit missions, and the conquest of the Huron people by the Iroquois, their deadly enemy. (ix)

Apart from *Catholics*, it is the first time since the early Belfast novels that Moore has really looked at Christianity as a 'system of belief'. In Belfast of the 1950s, Catholicism inspired in other religions 'fear, hostility and despair' and vice versa. This is the spirit — fear of other religions, especially since Catholicism is the minority religion in Belfast — that informs Father Quigley's actions in *Judith Hearne* and that makes the priests at Ardath in *The Feast of Lupercal* so cruel, repressive and tyrannical. In *Cold Heaven*, on the other hand, Catholicism is represented by the easy-going Monsignor, and insofar as belief has any meaning in that Californian world, it is the belief of the individual that is in question. That is to say, Moore largely ignores Catholicism as a social system or as a system of belief in *Cold Heaven* (apart from the viewpoint represented by the discredited Father Niles and discussed above). *Black Robe* seems therefore to see a return to his early view that bigotry and intolerance are endemic in conventional religion. This is a chastening idea and a relevant one: as the reviewer quoted above pointed out:

> *Black Robe* is a fable for our world, insistently contemporary in its exploration of the conflict between religious faiths, or rival sorceries, as they must always seem to each other. In such a world the Christian faith takes its place as one of the many sophistries devised by humanity to interpret or appease what is memorably called 'that mystery which is the silence of God'.[8]

Bigotry and intolerance are not necessarily endemic in the individual, but become so where a religious faith takes power for itself and assumes the right to interpret the world for others. Watching the dying Chomina, Father Laforgue can only feel pity for the Savages, never thinking that they too have their own beliefs in the supernatural and the after-life. He can only think of a god in terms of his own God: 'what mercy does He show to these Savages who will never look on His face in paradise, these He has cast into outer darkness, in this land which is the donjon of the devil and all his kind?' (180) The beliefs of the Savages are the contrary of Christian beliefs, and never are their opposition and mutual exclusiveness expressed more strongly than here, at the moment of Chomina's death. For the Savages, this world is 'the sunlight'; for Christians it is 'the world of night'. For Christians, life after death is 'paradise'; for the Savages it is 'the land of night'. (Dialogue between Laforgue and Chomina, 184)

The irony is that institutional religion will survive, bolstered by law and money. As the fur-trader, Casson, thinks to himself in *Black Robe*: 'The Jesuits were the real rulers of this country. Champlain was completely under their thumb.' (195) But Moore finds it very hard to sustain his own belief in the idea of personal faith. Mother St Jude in *Cold Heaven* has an unshakeable belief, but Moore cannot attempt to understand or analyse that belief. In almost all his other novels, his protagonists have either lost their religious faith or have never had any faith to begin with. Marie Davenport in *Cold Heaven* is in the latter category and the impossibility for her of acquiring or adopting faith is one of the strongest ideas to emerge in that novel. Perhaps, however, it is the Abbot, Tomás O'Malley, in *Catholics*, who comes closest to Father Laforgue. They are priests; their business is faith; their responsibility is not just to have faith but to teach it to others.

Finally, *Black Robe* develops a theme that is shared by none of Moore's other novels—that of cruelty and barbarity as part of a system of belief. This is not a question of pure or gratuitous evil. Moore has never written in any way about evil people, only perhaps about evil tendencies embodied by institutions. Though he has compared this novel to *Heart of Darkness*—'What I actually tried to do is write a *Heart of Darkness* tale, set in the past.'[9]—it differs from Conrad's novel in that it does not focus on any one person's assuming godlike powers of life and death, but instead it focuses on tribal, traditional cruelty. Chomina, who is consistently shown to be a wise and intelligent Savage, explains this to his daughter after he and his group have been 'caressed' by the Iroquois and he has watched his little son being slain and eaten. One of the advantages for Moore of using multiple points of view in this novel is that he can offer this explanation; obviously, for Europeans, such openly ritualised torture and cannibalism would seem like nothing more than barbarism.

> They are not wolves. They are men. They are afraid of each other . . . If an Iroquois sees another Iroquois show pity to a captive, he will make fun of him. The warrior must not show pity. Pity is a weakness . . . Our people do the same if they capture enemies. So do the Montagnais and the Huron. (164)

So do the Normans, he might add, even if they do not employ quite the same means. In the novel, the frequent scenes which show the warriors in council also highlight the fear, the pressure of others' fear and the manner in which the counsel of the most afraid — and therefore the most bloodthirsty — is adopted, because the others, in turn, are afraid of being thought weak or cowardly. Though Moore appears to idealise the Savages in other ways, in writing of their pantheism, their generosity and their patience, their cruelty must also be balanced against these good qualities. Like their virtues, their cruelty is a communal vice which, the novel says, would not exist in the individual to such a horrific extent.

Frank O'Connor once said that no Irishman is of much interest until he has lost his faith. It seems, also, as if Moore is happier with and more interested in protagonists who have lost their faith or who lose their faith. Laforgue may be fanatical, but he is not stupid. After what he has experienced of nature and of Savage society, he is not inclined to attribute the eclipse of the sun to 'God's hand'. Laforgue's crisis of faith is in part a crisis that owes its origin to humanism, which makes him more sympathetic for the reader, as when he thinks about the death of Father Jerome: 'Why did Chomina die and go to outer darkness when this priest, fanatic for a harvest of souls, will pass through the portals of heaven, a saint and a martyr?' (241) Until recently, Laforgue was just such a 'fanatic for a harvest of souls', wanting to force baptism on stillborn babies and on the unwilling Chomina. Now he sees the sophistry of the argument of numbers. In the absence of faith, he can only judge by human arguments. If the Savage leader wants him to baptise the whole village, then he will baptise the whole village, though he knows that it is a mockery of baptism. For Father Laforgue, his earlier zeal and conviction that God meant him for glory seemed like the highest happiness; his doubt is, therefore, the greatest misery. Yet he is a far better person now; so, in a way, his salvation as a human being comes from his loss of faith. At the end of the novel, he is far from the zealot seeking glory by martyrdom. In the resignation of his final remark, he expresses an existential sense of endurance: 'Here, among these Savages, he would spend his life.' (246) He also expresses a genuine sense of Christianity.

If the novel has a specific viewpoint to convey, and it is certainly not an optimistic one, it is that the best hope for honesty and truth lies with the individual. On his own, Father Laforgue learns to lose his faith and then, at the end, he learns to find a different kind of faith. On their own, men are men; in packs, they are like wolves. Again, the novel is critical not so much of individuals, but of society and its institutions.

Like *Cold Heaven*, *Black Robe* puts forward an authorial view that is, with some reservations, admiring of the faith of the individual. It is not easy for the modern secular world to identify with missionary zeal like Father Laforgue's, but it is probably easier to convey this zeal than the intensely inward-looking communion with the 'silence of God' that is the role of contemplatives or mystics like Mother St Jude. Again, despite all that Moore might say about the value of religious faith, there is a hostility to faith as a system of belief still underlying this novel. Obvious parallels can be drawn between seventeenth-century Canada and any of a dozen regions in the modern world that are strife-torn because of differences of faith, not least Northern Ireland. Moore has gone on record as saying that in his opinion the return of religion as a source of conflict and as a basis of political ideology has been *the* great revolution of the present century. Where one might have expected more widespread Marxist revolution, religious revolution has occurred instead. However, along with the durable fanaticism of public and institutional religion, there will always be a parallel current, the vulnerability of personal faith. From the point of this novel, what is perhaps more significant is that the Father Laforgue who loses his faith is a far more sympathetic and credible character to the reader than the man who is secure behind the armour of his belief at the beginning. Until *The Colour of Blood*, Moore never had a convincing protagonist who has faith at the beginning of the novel and who retains it, despite difficulties, until the end.

A study of technique and point of view will help to show how Moore's vision of religion is conveyed in *Black Robe*. The following is part of the passage, set into the account of the first day's journey of the Savages upriver, where insight is given into Laforgue's mind. It follows immediately on his memory of his mother's prayer for him to be a saint, the prayer she made in the market-place in Rouen, the site of the burning of Joan of Arc. The passage analyses the development and intensification of the messianic impulse towards martyrdom in Laforgue, beginning with the surroundings which are so much in contrast with the town of Rouen.

> Now in the silence of the great river, watching a flock of
> geese fly over distant treetops, Laforgue heard again his

mother's words. In the past two years, living in the residence at Quebec, every waking moment had been a preparation for this day: the time spent learning the unwritten Algonkian and Huron tongues, studying the writings of Father Brabant on the customs and language of the Savage peoples, the hours of practice in canoes, a scrupulous diligence in all tasks assigned to him, no matter how onerous or menial, and above all, constant daily prayer, beseeching Saint Joseph and the Virgin to intercede on his behalf and grant him the honour of some greater danger in a lonely place. From the day the Savage, Ihongwaha, brought Father Brabant's letter telling of sickness in the Huron country, he had prayed in nightly vigils that he would be the chosen one. For, indeed, this was a journey like those he had read of long ago in the Jesuit house in Dieppe, a mission worthy of the order's heroic martyrs in Paraguay, a mission to the very place where Father Brabant labored, he whom the Hurons revered, whose letters published in the *Relations* were an inspiration to all at home in France. And now his prayers had been answered. Today he set out for that place where martyrdom was more than just a pious hope. This is my hour. This is my beginning. (34)

The words 'the great river' signify the magnitude of his task. This is 'symbolic commentary' like that used at the beginning of *Cold Heaven*. Now his mother's words have a validity for Laforgue that they lacked in Rouen: there he was embarrassed by their intensity and melodrama; here he is free to entertain the most grandiloquent ideas 'in the silence of the great river'. The impulse to martyrdom, so strong in Father Laforgue, is an intensely private matter, despite the communal purpose of the Jesuits.

The distinction between third-person narrative and free indirect speech is very subtle here, partly because Moore could not hope to catch the cadence of the voice of Father Laforgue, as he would with a contemporary Irish or

American protagonist. The 'voices' of the Savages, as well, tend to be uniform, and notable mainly for their scatological tendency. In his dialogue, as in the expression of his thoughts, there is no great distinction to Father Laforgue's 'voice', so that Moore can slip very easily in and out of free indirect speech, and it is sometimes quite difficult to detect where the change occurs. It is, for instance, the voice of the omniscient author that details the preparation of Laforgue for his great work: the intensity and singlemindedness of the task in which he has been involved is signified by phrases like 'every waking moment'; 'the time'; 'the hours of practice'; 'constant daily prayer'. This long sentence lacks the intimacy of free indirect speech and the phrase 'scrupulous diligence' is not one that the priest would be likely to use to describe his own behaviour. The vocabulary here is that of prayer or devotion, the pre-ordained language of evangelical zeal, which emphasises certainly what Father Laforgue feels, but also the sense in which he is part of a more global concept, part of the missionary endeavour of the Catholic Church militant. The prayer described takes the form of the prayer recited: 'and grant him the honour of some greater danger in a lonely place'. Moore has no ability to internalise this intense desire for suffering and martyrdom in Father Laforgue, so, in describing his fanaticism, he falls back on the conventions of prayer. The next sentence, however, has a different aspect. The language leaves the theoretical and moves into the realm of the immediate and the practical. The letter and the illness which occasioned it have given Laforgue ground for hope in a much simpler and more intense fashion. This hope is now expressed in the excitement of his own language: that 'he would be the chosen one'. Though this is the purest of messianic language, it has been prepared for by the elaboration of the previous sentence. It is also messianic only by the placing of adjective and pronoun; if the order were reversed, it would become simply a matter of being chosen. But it is easy for Father Laforgue, immersed as he is in devotion, to slip into the language of prayer or of the liturgy.

The remainder of the passage alternates between third-person style and free indirect speech. The long periodic sentence with its many dependent clauses is a formal evocation of his journey which does not have the mark of the spoken voice. It is as if the religious heritage of the Jesuits, from the mother-house in Dieppe, were evoked to give the *imprimatur* of sanctity to his journey by comparing it to the great heroic journeys of other missionaries. It is only with the deictic adverbs 'now' and 'today', (always the marks of free indirect speech) towards the end of the paragraph that the reader is returned to the actuality of Father Laforgue's mind and free indirect speech imperceptibly slips into the simplicity of the first person: 'This is my hour. This is my beginning.'

The passage is very effective in conveying the zeal of Father Laforgue, both in the personal simplicity of the final sentences in the first person, and in its calling up of the forces of tradition, of liturgy and prayer and of the desire to emulate other great Jesuit martyrs. The passage shows, therefore, the motivation of Father Laforgue, which is certainly religious, but which also involves a human desire for spiritual fame. The implication is that Laforgue, too, might one day be an example or have his letters published in the *Relations*. This passage also gives an insight into Moore's view that Father Laforgue is not just an individual but part of an institution that sees its function and its glory in the undertaking of danger for the sake of converting the heathen. It is significant that there is no mention of the work Laforgue has to do, or the value of that work. That value is a *donnée*. There is hardly a mention of the Savages, except in connection with their language and with one individual. It is as if the work to be done, the journey, the danger, the hoped-for martyrdom, have all to do with Father Laforgue and his Jesuit confrères, nothing to do with the Savages. There is no mention of God or Christ; there is no mention of Christianity; there is not even a mention of converting the Savages. There is no doubting Father Laforgue's true dedication and zeal; it is clear from what he has undergone already that he is prepared to undergo a great deal. There is no doubt that he is prepared to die a martyr's death. But with all this zeal, both individual and collective, what is lost sight of is the work that is to be done, the goals that are to be reached and the reason why, in the first place, anybody should want to come to christianise the Savages.

It is Daniel who mediates the beliefs of the Savages to Father Laforgue. This dialogue, which takes place when Laforgue tries to remonstrate with Daniel for his sin of fornication, indicates the blindness of both sides, but the greater blindness of the Christians. By using Daniel's viewpoint, Moore is able to show the beliefs of one culture through the eyes of the other. Daniel can 'see' because he loves Annuka and because she interprets her people's culture for him. Any extract from the long dialogue will indicate the huge gulf that lies between the two beliefs and especially the intolerance of the Christians. Perhaps the character of Daniel is too modern for his times; perhaps he is more like a twentieth-century humanist than a seventeenth-century Norman boy. But Moore is showing the bigotry and polarisation of institutions, not of individuals, and even Father Laforgue casts off a great deal of this intolerance by the end of the novel. In this extract, the antagonism between Daniel and Father Laforgue is exacerbated by the fact that Daniel speaks to Father Laforgue like a man, but Laforgue answers him like a Jesuit:

> 'They believe that at night the dead see. They move about, animals and men, in the forests of night. The souls of men hunt the souls of animals, moving through forests made up of the souls of trees which have died.'
>
> 'Is that what she told you?' Laforgue smiled. 'But what childish reasoning! Do they believe that these dead souls eat and drink, as we do?'

The boy looked at him with scorn. 'Is that harder to believe in than a paradise where we all sit on clouds and look at God? Or burn forever in the flames of hell?'

Laforgue felt his anger rise. He clenched his hands together. (102)

All bigotry is ultimately caused by fear. In the case of the Christian missionaries, whose whole lives and endeavours are based upon the conviction that they and only they have the knowledge of and means of access to heaven, they fear any sign of the Savages having an alternative or rival system of belief. Father Brabant, according to Laforgue, has established that the Savages have no concept of an after-life; it is much more comfortable for the Jesuits to believe this, because then they can see the importance of their own role in supplying one. Father Laforgue's reaction to Daniel here is a mixture of Jesuitical sophistry and a mockery which expresses his fear and his unwillingness to believe. He 'smiled'. The smile is a realisation, but an expression of his determination not to fear. He uses all the instant weapons in his power to try to rob Daniel's account of credibility: mockery, the impression that all of this is merely the delusion of the lover 'Is that what she told you?' and finally an 'intellectual' attempt to demolish the opposition. The sophistry of this argument is revealed by the ease with which Daniel demolishes it. What is very effectively conveyed in Laforgue's response is the range of emotions aroused by the thought of the beliefs of others: fear, mockery, scorn, anger. Laforgue *feels* rather than *thinks*. The stock responses of the Jesuits and the psychological pressure he tries to put on Daniel because of his own fear are his way of dealing with the threat of alternative belief.

The key passage that conveys the consequences of Father Laforgue's loss of faith comes almost at the end of the novel. Laforgue is obliged to undertake mass-baptism of the Savages. He goes outside having felt only the silence of God in the tabernacle.

He faced the crowd. Slowly, he raised his fingers, making the sign of the cross, touching his brow, his chest, his right shoulder, then his left. All watched this sorcery. Then, with Daniel carrying the kettle, he went down to the first row of the sick. He took a small ladle from the kettle's rim, filled it and poured a trickle of water on a woman's fevered brow, saying in the Huron tongue, 'I baptise you in the name of the Father, and of the Son, and of the Holy Spirit.' The Savage woman stared up at him, sick, uncomprehending. He moved on, saying over and over the words to make them Christians and forgive their sins. Was this the will of God? Was this true baptism or a mockery? Would these children of darkness ever enter heaven? (246)

The narrative is deliberately objective and dispassionate. The impact of Father Laforgue on the crowd is emphasised, and at the beginning of the passage the attention of the reader is deliberately exteriorised, kept away from the turmoil of the inner man. The reader is watching Father Laforgue and the Savages from a vantage point at a considerable distance. Not until the end of the passage is there a return to Father Laforgue's point of view. The gesture he makes is a fundamental sign of Christian belief, indeed *the* fundamental sign of belief in the Trinity, but in this case it is only a sign. There is no belief behind the sign on Father Laforgue's part. Nor is there belief on the part of the Huron crowd. Moore shows the reader the sign they see, but only in terms of the sequence of actions Father Laforgue makes, as one who was totally unfamiliar with the sign of the cross would observe it being made. To the Hurons it is sorcery; the authorial voice seems to accept the Huron interpretation because there is no other belief to challenge it. In the same way, the meaninglessness of the rubric of baptism is made evident by the laconic nature of the narrative and by the 'uncomprehending' reception of the ceremony by the Hurons, even though it is their language that is being spoken.

The words are spoken 'over and over', but this makes them more meaningless. We see Father Laforgue involved in an empty ritual, a ritual without belief. He is the mediator of belief to the unbelievers, but he himself does not believe in what he is doing. Furthermore, he knows, in a way which would not be possible if he believed himself, that they, too, do not believe. Yet the final words of the novel, in which Father Laforgue's greater love for his flock is expressed as part of his prayer and echoes the earlier question and answer between him and the Huron chief, reassert a return to faith, but a different kind of faith:

> And a prayer came to him, a true prayer at last. *Spare them. Spare them, O Lord.*
> *Do you love us?*
> *Yes.* (246)

At this point Father Laforgue realises what a true prayer is. There is no meaning to faith for him now, stripped as he is of power, of influence, of support in this Huron village, except in private communion with God. It is the fact that he can pray to God that marks his return to some kind of belief. For the reader, it is, furthermore, the true prayer that Father Laforgue has *not* been saying in the novel until now, so preoccupied is he with the possibility of the glory of martyrdom and with the condemnation of Daniel's fornication. True faith is expressed in these final words because in them, Father Laforgue forgets himself completely in the charity he feels for the Savages. The silence of God does not answer, not Father Laforgue, not anyone, no matter how saintly, but symbolically there is an answer in the way the question and answer are echoed to form the final words of the novel. If he loves them, he has faith; he can only love them in God. Earlier he said yes to appease Taretandé; now he says yes because he means it. In the same way, he can mediate the love of God to them, as he is shown to do by his prayer 'Spare them, O Lord' and this may be the only sense in which he will ever again have a belief in God.

As is typical in the group of novels under discussion in this chapter, the outcome of the quest is in the first place mysterious, partial and ambiguous. In the second place, the quest does not lead Father Laforgue where he expects to go, so it is as much a surprise for the protagonist as it is for the reader. He has reached the Huron village that was the object of his journey to Canada, of all his preparation and of all his suffering, but his mental state and his crisis of faith have changed him completely. They have changed his goals; where once he would have been overjoyed merely to baptise any number of Savages, now he draws back. Only for their physical welfare can he pray. His God has changed; the God he prays to is no longer a God to whom duty must be done, who will demand martyrdom, but a God of compassion, a humanist's God, if such a paradox be allowable.

The Silence of God

THREE of Brian Moore's most recent novels, *The Temptation of Eileen Hughes, Cold Heaven* and *Black Robe*, are works that treat of the necessity of some form of spiritual belief in the modern world. This most recent phase of Moore's work was heralded by the disillusionment with secular beliefs which became obvious in the earlier period of his work. Still, as a writer, Moore is convinced that if people are to be kept from despair, some form of belief is essential. It is clear that he no longer thinks it sufficient for the individual to look for that belief in himself, in other individuals or in worldly success. The novels discussed in this chapter investigate the state of mind of people who, instead, and for various reasons, look to their souls.

It is difficult to come to general conclusions about Moore's treatment of the theme of spirituality by examining three novels as diverse as these, since they have so little in common as regards either background or protagonists. *Black Robe* stands out most of all because of the dramatic change in period from the contemporary California of *Cold Heaven* to seventeenth-century Canada. However, a certain number of general premises emerge, which may be stated as follows: Moore believes in the necessity of some kind of belief, not material, not selfish, not political (although he has yet to write the novel where he debunks political idealism). It has become increasingly clear, despite remarks he has made to the effect that all beliefs are equally valid, that, in fact, as far as his novels are concerned, all beliefs are not. There are higher beliefs and lower beliefs. Higher beliefs are harder to believe in, demand more of the individual, may cause suffering, but are fundamentally more rewarding. However, he is more inclined to show the value of such higher beliefs negatively, by using protagonists who are in obvious need of them, but who perhaps do not want to espouse them, or want to, but cannot. The highest belief known to man is religious; religion in the Western world is normally made manifest as some form of Christianity.

For Moore, religion means Catholicism, the faith into which he was born and in which he received his spiritual formation. Since his childhood, he has been wrestling with religion and since his first novel, he has been writing about it, directly or indirectly as the case may be, but always drawing on it metaphorically. In his earlier novels, it signifies repression and bigotry, Belfast-style; later it is something which his articulate and sophisticated secular protagonists reject as part of the process of exile and the movement towards self-expression. In the earlier novels, rejection of Catholicism is seen as a pre-condition of freedom. Increasingly, however, Moore began to see the virtues of religion and this awareness grew in tandem with his disillusion with the modern secular and materialistic consciousness. In the novels under discussion in this chapter, religious faith is a structure which will provide the individual with moral guidelines by which to live and also a form of self-transcendent spirituality, which is of far greater value for those who can achieve it, than any form of worldly or secular belief.

The three novels explore these ideas in different ways. The first, *The Temptation of Eileen Hughes* does not obviously or conventionally even have a religious theme. If Bernard McAuley is taken as the main protagonist, however, it becomes clear that he is just such a man as the hypothetical individual described above, who feels the need for some focus for his spirit that is not satisfied by making a great deal of money in enterprises or by spending a great deal of money in gratifying his whims and desires. Because he is a person of extremes, he is only interested in adopting a wholly religious lifestyle: for him living in God is all or nothing. He considers that God rejects him when he rejects his religious vocation. His mania for Eileen, which he conveys to her in explicit terms of religious and mystical devotion, is his substitute for religion. It is inevitable that this should end in disaster.

Cold Heaven is the first novel since *Catholics* to have a specifically Catholic theme and is very unusual among Moore's novels in having a positive attitude, not just to religion, but to Catholicism. This might appear unexpected given the background of apparitions and mysticism. These are manifestations of an extreme aspect of Catholicism, a belief in which is not even required of those who practise the religion. The hostility of the main protagonist, Marie Davenport to these and to what she (and the author) perceive as an attempt by heaven to deprive her of her free will is, however, only one side of the coin. The other side, made manifest in the humble and unmistakable sanctity of Mother St Jude is the possibility of the most selfless of religious faiths. Marie Davenport explicitly rejects the personal approaches made to her by the old nun and the novel ends with her in a state of unrepentant agnosticism. However, the novel also proposes that this may be her loss, if the possibility of such a faith as Mother St Jude's exists. In *Cold Heaven*, Moore does not spend a great deal of time in describing Mother St Jude; he is always cautious about his ability to understand or convey deep faith. Without understanding, however, Moore is able to accept and admire, and the novel, on its own terms, accepts the religion of Mother St Jude, just as much as the agnostic hostility of Marie Davenport.

The third novel, *Black Robe* looks at an active rather than a contemplative faith, this time from a more ambivalent authorial position but always with a considerable degree of admiration for the zeal of missionary endeavour. The novel undertakes an analysis of much more complex issues, particularly that of 'rival sorceries' which cause division and hatred. In its historical ramifications, this novel throws light on Moore's perception of the reasons for religious bigotry, in the Belfast of the 1950s where he set his early novels, among other places. The interesting aspect of Father Laforgue, far more interesting than his blind desire for the glory of martyrdom, is the way he loses his faith after being exposed to inhuman suffering and cruelty, but gains a different kind of faith, which is certainly more attractive to the modern sensibility. At the end of the novel, he sees in the situation where he will spend the rest of his life, not the possibility of the glory of martyrdom, but the task of caring for a Savage people who are not composed just of souls but of human feelings and frail bodies as well.

There is less technical variety, or perhaps less obvious experimentation in these novels than in earlier periods of Moore's work, apart from the deliberate choice of working within the historical genre in the writing of *Black Robe*. All three novels are on the surface realistic, all three are written in the third person, with one main privileged or pivotal centre of consciousness, but with part of the burden of narration falling on secondary characters: Mona McAuley in *The Temptation of Eileen Hughes*, Monsignor Cassidy in *Cold Heaven* and Daniel Davost in *Black Robe* for instance. The most innovative features are the extreme limitation in the direct presentation of Bernard's point of view in *The Temptation of Eileen Hughes* (Bernard is shown as he is seen and heard, not as he hears, sees and speaks) and the equivocation with which Moore treats all his protagonists. They cannot be seen to present the whole of the authorial viewpoint and yet they are drawn with considerable skill in a manner to evoke the sympathy of the reader. Almost by definition, none of these novels treats of a series of events that is, strictly speaking, realistic since their themes are spiritual, but especially in *Cold Heaven*, there is considerable tension between the surface limpidity and the spiritual mysteries underneath. *Black Robe* is unusual in the extent to which it sets out to capture the texture of life in the seventeenth-century mission-fields. In vivid sensuous detail, hunger, cold, mutilation and death are set in front of the reader.

The three novels taken together mark a considerable development in the consideration of religious faith as a valid form of belief. It seems now, as if Moore has an unerring ear and eye to choose the style and the 'voice' or point of view with which to present his novels. The authorial control on dialogue, narrative and setting are complete, but so natural as to escape notice.

SECTION IV

Politics as Morality

12

A New Engagement with the Actual

THERE are some novelists for whom critics or readers attempt to write their next book, or at least to suggest the direction it should take. This exercise is certainly not to be recommended for a writer like Brian Moore. Who would have predicted a sequence of novels like *Cold Heaven* (1983), *Black Robe* (1985), *The Colour of Blood* (1987) and *Lies of Silence* (April 1990)? Both in their themes and techniques, these last two novels might appear at first to be quite unlike anything previously attempted by Moore, but in fact, others of his novels have had some of the same preoccupations. As regards technique, *The Colour of Blood* is a religious thriller and *Lies of Silence* a political thriller, just as *Cold Heaven* is a 'metaphysical' thriller. The major element of suspense is shared with several of Moore's previous novels; indeed *The Doctor's Wife* is framed like a detective story, with Owen Deane cast in the unlikely role of private eye.

Critics and readers alike might learn from these two novels to expect the unexpected from Brian Moore. In the first place, he has become increasingly interested in exploiting different genres:

> I've become fascinated in recent years by forms I had previously ignored—the historical framework of *Black Robe*, for instance, the Gothic in *The Mangan Inheritance*, and the supernatural thriller in *Cold Heaven*.[1]

Even from his earliest novels, Moore has been willing to experiment with different techniques, some 'literary' (the influence of Joyce and especially of *Dubliners* has been well documented) and some popular, in order to dramatise various characters and events. He fully exploits different settings, motifs and points of view. But the more consciously literary stance of the above remark expresses a greater confidence and also a tendency on the part of the author to see himself in the mainstream literary tradition. In this confidence he is justified; there are few Irish or world novelists who have produced a body of work so varied and yet so consistent in standard as Moore has done.

The Colour of Blood and *Lies of Silence* share a similar pre-occupation with the nature of moral choice in a situation that is politically complex, where the individual is no longer even notionally free to make decisions on the basis of a clear-cut code of ethics. (The essentially notional nature of all choice has consistently been one of Moore's underlying themes.) In both these novels, the prevailing political authority imposes itself without the support of a large number of the people, bolstered, to a greater or lesser degree, by the might of an outside power and by military *force majeure*, whether threatened (in *The Colour of Blood*) or actual (in *Lies of Silence*). Both novels are absolutely contemporary and engage directly with controversial issues. In neither novel is the possibility or the reality of religious belief an issue or 'problem', although personal faith is an important element in *The Colour of Blood* and religion-as-culture an essential aspect of *Lies of Silence*. Taken together, these novels provide an interesting commentary on the modern world, and the second can certainly be seen as a development on the first, not just because they share similar preoccupations, but because the first, although an impressive novels in its own right, lays the foundations for the second.

Therefore, *The Colour of Blood*, though it appears to be set in a strange land, is really not strange or exotic at all. In spite of a setting that would seem to place it very far away from Ireland, it derives much of its power from Moore's Belfast background and is an expression of his preoccupation with the religious and political problems of Northern Ireland. In these qualities, it presages *Lies of Silence*. After the 'dismissive bitterness' (John Cronin's phrase) of his early novels, which conveyed the dismal oppressiveness of Belfast Catholic life and which seemed to lay the blame for this oppression squarely on the Catholic Church, Moore wrote little, directly, about Northern Ireland. These first novels, *Judith Hearne* and *The Feast of Lupercal*, though written by an exile of many years standing, contain nothing of detachment, but instead, the bitterness of a man who felt obliged to leave his country in order to free himself from the obligation to observe a religion in which he did not believe. This bitterness gradually diminished, but in Moore's later novels, when Belfast or even Irish Catholic life is represented, though it is frequently represented in comic vein in *The Luck of Ginger Coffey*, *The Emperor of Ice-Cream* and *Fergus*, it is, all the same, in stock scenes and with stock attributes — sexual puritanism, clerical oppression, nuns, priests, the autocratic and bigoted paterfamilias, the milder and self-sacrificing, but no less religious, Irish mother. In other words, Moore seemed to have little of interest to say about Northern Ireland, once he had highlighted the failure of religion and the absence of true belief there. His attitude seemed to be uniformly negative.

After the outbreak of what are now called the 'present troubles' twenty years ago, Moore, for the most part, avoided the subject of Northern Ireland. This is understandable, given that he has on the whole avoided being a political novelist (with the notable exception of *The Revolution Script*) and that the situation seemed to him, as to many others, to be intractable. Furthermore, because he has been an exile for so many decades, Moore claims that he can write about Ireland now only from the outside or from the point of view of the tourist. In *The Doctor's Wife* Moore does evoke daily life in Belfast since the arrival of British troops and the escalation of terrorist attacks and bombings. Carnage, fear and sectarian hatred are strikingly and economically conveyed, but not at all analysed. The violence of Belfast becomes part of what Sheila Redden is fleeing. In the novel, Northern Ireland is usually not a memory, but a nightmare:

> It was a dream, she was dreaming it, she had dreamed
> different parts of it again and again since the bomb in the
> Swan and the picture in the paper . . . She screamed.
>   She woke in a dark room.[2]

In the novel's terms of reference, religion is a source of
conflict in Belfast, nothing more. It means little to Sheila
Redden. Nor, she thinks, does true belief, nor even observance mean much to people in general:

> It was, she sometimes thought, a bad joke that when the
> people at home no longer believed in their religion, or
> went to Church as they once did, the religious fighting
> was worse than ever. (100)

Sheila Redden finds her true religion elsewhere. In *The
Doctor's Wife*, Moore looks at Belfast life and Belfast violence,
but immediately averts his gaze and focuses instead on
Villefranche, Paris or London, wherever people go to escape.

Even in his more recent novels, where Moore has returned
to the theme of religion (if one includes Bernard McAuley's
mystical obsession in *The Temptation of Eileen Hughes* as a form
of religion), showing Catholicism as a much more positive
force, he has not dealt with institutional religion in contemporary Ireland. He has, deliberately it would seem, chosen
settings as far away as possible from Ireland — contemporary
California in *Cold Heaven* and seventeenth-century Canada in
Black Robe. Yet not one of his novels has a religious theme that
does not cast its own light by positive or negative implication
on his attitude to his own religious origins in Northern
Ireland. Thus, *Cold Heaven* comments by implication on a
religion (Belfast Catholicism) that did not allow its adherents
the freedom not to believe; on the contrary, the Catholic
Church represented in California by Monsignor Cassidy is
aware that it no longer has the right to expect unquestioning
obedience and blind devotion from the modern world. The
Catholic Church which accepts the coexistence of Mother St
Jude's transcendent mysticism and Marie Davenport's hostile

agnosticism in *Cold Heaven* furnishes a blueprint for the way in which the contemporary Church can hope to survive. *Black Robe*, though in appearance the furthest away in time and place, comes closest to representing the political and religious realities of Northern Ireland as Moore sees them. In the following remark, which the author made in an interview, he acknowledges this aspect of the novel, while asserting that such an exposition was not his conscious aim when writing it:

> The whole thing could be a paradigm for what's happened here. Originally I'd have said that wasn't true, but maybe unconsciously I was thinking of it. . . . If you don't believe in the Devil you can't hate your enemy — and that may be one of the most sinister things about Belfast today. We still believe in the Devil. He doesn't have a forked tail. You know him by his name and he went to a certain school.[3]

In *Black Robe*, there is a great cultural gap between the Indians and the French colonists. Even so, Father Laforgue's journey in the company of the Savages shows that as regards physical and emotional needs, the two races are fundamentally more alike than different. The gulf between them, which is caused by the difference in their beliefs and value systems, exists to some degree in any situation of religious or sectarian tension. In *Black Robe*, the Christians are more at fault for not admitting the validity of the beliefs of the Indians. This is the position the Catholic Church has traditionally taken against all other religions, even Christian ones, in boasting itself the repository of the one true faith (and such extremism is shared or even surpassed by other religious groups in areas of sectarian conflict such as Northern Ireland). If one looks back over Moore's writing career from the 1950s, one finds that it is a position which he himself adopted in his strong and bitter hostility to Catholicism and to religious belief in his early novels, but one which he is now very anxious to avoid. Now, despite his own continued and reasserted unbelief, he is very open to the beliefs of others, and indeed, very admiring of them.

Until recently, therefore, Moore remained very circum-spect in his comments and writings about Northern Ireland and has been inclined to leave it to his readers to suggest parallels between his novels and the situation there, as in the case of *Black Robe* instanced above. He did not seem likely to write openly about it: 'I don't feel that a writer of my age or my generation could go back now and write a novel about today's Belfast.'[4] It is all the more unusual and noteworthy that he has been so forthcoming about the resonances of *The Colour of Blood* and that he has finally come to write a novel, *Lies of Silence*, that deals directly with the political, military and terrorist elements of today's Belfast.

13

Faith Versus Materialism —
The Colour of Blood

IN *The Colour of Blood*, the country in question is fictional, reminding one most vividly of Poland, but is not, Moore has said, based on any one country: 'I specifically synthesised a country of my mind, an Eastern European country that could be Hungary, or Czechoslovakia, or Ireland[!]' He goes on:

> When I say Ireland, I'm perfectly serious. I took my descriptions of searches and check-points from my experience in Ireland rather than Eastern Europe. I wasn't trying to make any comparison between the occupation of Northern Ireland and the Russian presence in Poland. But at the back of my mind there are connections. If we cannot live with each other and run our own affairs, someone will be brought in to run things for us.[1]

For a writer who is usually discreet about his moral viewpoint and who is especially chary of being political in his authorial opinions ('You shouldn't confront political issues directly. Otherwise you're competing with journalism.'),[2] Moore is more open in the above statement than he has ever been before, both in political and moral terms.

When Seamus Deane wrote about Brian Moore that he expressed a 'radical dissatisfaction with the actual',[3] without postulating an alternative world, this was true of the trend his novels appeared to be taking, up to the publication of *Black Robe*. The remark was, however, invalidated by the appearance of *The Colour of Blood*. More than anything, it is a novel that engages with the actual. Its thriller technique works in harmony with the grounding of the novel in the real world, whereas in the case of *Cold Heaven*, the thriller technique works in counterpoint to that novel's metaphysical or supernatural preoccupations. *The Colour of Blood* is concerned with the role of the Catholic Church at work in the modern world and it is the first time since the Belfast novels of the 1950s that Moore has dealt with the Church as a contemporary institution: *Catholics* is a futuristic fable; *Cold Heaven* is more concerned with apparitions; *Black Robe* is set in the distant past. The problem confronted in *The Colour of Blood* is how the Church is to live in tandem with the secular authority.

It is clear that Cardinal Bem's solution is pragmatic. There is no doubt that Cardinal Bem is a good man, modest and holy, but above all he is moderate. This is made clear from the opening of the novel, where, in the short spiritual passage he has time to read before the murder attempt, 'reason' is the key concept:

> Do you not think that a man born with reason yet not living according to his reason is, in a certain way, no better than the beasts themselves? For the beast who does not rule himself by reason has an excuse, since this gift is denied him by nature. But man has no excuse.[4]

In Bem's response to this passage written by St Bernard of Clairvaux, the ideal of reason is supported by Bem's longing to escape from the unreason of the world. The one sentence which comes between his reading and the moment when the assassins' car impinges on his vision and his consciousness expresses the following weighty and ambiguous thought: 'Sometimes, reading St Bernard, he could abandon the world of his duties and withdraw into that silence where God waited and judged.' (2) This meditation is deliberately juxtaposed with the violent action which follows it; reason is contrasted with the unreason and fanaticism of the assassins. Moore has used the phrase 'the silence of God' before now.

In *Black Robe*, Father Laforgue fails to interpret 'that mystery that is the silence of God'[5] at the moment of his crisis of faith. In other words, the tabernacle remains silent; God does not communicate with him. Here, 'the silence of God' is not something that Bem fears, but something which he desires. Read in the context of the passage by Bernard of Clairvaux, it appears to signify that the world of his duties is a world of unreason for Bem, given the difficulty of the task of leading his people in a materialist regime, and that the purest spirituality can be sought in closer communion with God in a life of contemplation.

In any case, in order to understand Cardinal Bem it is essential to see him as a man for whom religion and duty to God are intimately bound up with reason and therefore with political pragmatism. His reason is constantly contrasted with the unreason of others: here, in the opening scene with the assassins; later, with the fanatical Archbishop Krasnoy whose intended address reads like an incitement to political revolution and whose intemperate prose the controlled Cardinal Bem refers to as 'dreadful style'. (14) Rhetorical metaphors like those used by Krasnoy are the stock-in-trade of political propagandists:

> The nation in this critical time is like a great forest at the end of a summer of dreadful drought. A spiritual and moral drought. On the floor of this forest are millions of pine needles. It takes only a spark to set them ablaze. (13)

Bem is regarded as a traitor by the members of the fanatical Catholic group that is opposed to him because of his reason and pragmatism. This is why he is in some ways more at home with the security minister and especially with the prime minister. They, at least, speak the same language — the pragmatic language of political compromise, 'for the national good'. (137) In a setting and a dialogue that are, perhaps too consciously contrived, they mirror each other: Urban the supreme civil power, Bem the religious, yet both closely watched and under threat from subordinates; each in the eyes of the other and partially in fact, taking orders from foreign powers—Urban from Russia, despite his papal-sounding name and Bem from Rome. Bem thinks: 'Urban is unmarried: they say he lives an ascetic life. We have this in common: a dog at the foot of our beds.' (148) And much much more, he might have added.

Furthermore, Bem is very clear sighted about the problems that can arise when politics and religion are mixed or confused. For those opposed to the government in Bem's country, Catholicism has become a badge of identity and a statement of political opposition:

> I think our people are using religion now as a sort of politics. To remind ourselves that we are a Catholic nation while our enemies are not. To remind us that we always continued to be a nation even when the name of our country was taken off the map. It's all part of our collective memory and we cherish it. But what has it got to do with our love of God? (166)

Moore has long been interested in the politicisation of religion in our century. Bem's point here no doubt seems particularly apt in the context of Poland, but it also fits the historical situation of Irish Catholicism and the present situation of the minority in Northern Ireland. By compromising with the civil power, Bem tries to prevent the politicisation of religion, but for many of his people this is outright betrayal. It has always been Moore's view, right from his first novels, that faith and belief should be personal and freely chosen, that any one religion should not be allowed to dominate a society and also that religious belief should be an end in itself, not used to further any political viewpoint. The abuse of Catholicism in the name of nationalism is as strong a theme in his early Belfast novels as it is in this most recent one.

Bem's views represent Moore's opinions in this: there is no

distance between the authorial viewpoint and that of the privileged narrator/protagonist. This perhaps accounts for a certain lack of depth and psychological interest in the novel. It could be regarded almost as a tendentious work, if one takes into account the following comment made by Moore upon it.

> I believe, as does Cardinal Bem in my novel, that there are no extreme solutions possible in certain countries: Ireland, Poland, Hungary. The novel is anti-terrorist and anti- the right-wing rhetoric which certain elements in the west spout about Russia and Eastern Europe.[6]

The identification of Moore with Cardinal Bem, the predominantly political theme and purpose of the novel and its thriller technique are probably the reasons why so little attention is devoted to Bem's own personal faith in *The Colour of Blood*. In the work of a novelist who has always been regarded as having a deep interest in the problems of belief and unbelief, this has been viewed as a disappointment. On the other hand, it can be regarded as a thematic progression. It is possible that faith or belief as a *problem* does not interest Moore any longer, but that he is dealing here with faith as a *given* and with the way it works in the world and with the world. A contrary interpretation, and one favoured by criticism hostile to the novel, would be that Moore, in identifying with Bem, is not able to convey in Bem the belief that he has never been able to experience himself. It will be remembered from his earlier novels and especially as regards *Cold Heaven* (an aspect discussed in chapter 9), that though Moore has recently come to accept the religious faith of others and its great power in their lives, he cannot share it and therefore, naturally, finds it very difficult to convey it. Up to *The Colour of Blood*, he has always identified himself, predominantly, with a secular, agnostic or doubting attitude to faith. Father Laforgue in *Black Robe* goes through a crisis of faith. *The Colour of Blood* is the first of Moore's novels to have as a protagonist, a person who has faith, who has apparently always had it and who not only does not lose it, but is never in danger of losing it. Bem has some doubts about his fitness for his high position, but never about God. So his faith tends not to be an issue or a focus of interest in his character. When it is expressed, it is as conventional piety and humility, for example in the following passage, where Bem prays:

> I am Your servant, created by You. All that I have I have through You and from You. Nothing is my own. I must do everything for You and only for You. Tonight at the meeting I was obsessed by politics; I thought of the danger to our nation. I did not think of the sufferings we cause You by our actions. My fault, my own grievous fault. (18)

Bem is doubtless admirable; Moore certainly sees him thus. Bem's sense of spirituality is expressed, but no sense of what his belief entails is conveyed to the reader. In this way he is not as rich a creation, either humanly or spiritually, as the person who doubts his faith but who can be shown, like Father Laforgue, groping for a different but perhaps more honest and valid type of faith.

The problem with Cardinal Bem's credibility and interest as a character arises because he is not really an imagined character, but instead, an actual or composite one. (This could also be argued of the historically inspired Father Laforgue in *Black Robe*, but, perhaps because of the great imaginative leap required of the author in order that he should empathise with him, there is, for the reader, no difficulty in perceiving him as an intensely individual fictional character.) Moore's sources for Bem are Cardinal Wyszynski of Poland, whom he interviewed many years ago, and another prelate, Cardinal Bea, whose memoirs he has studied:

> So I've read memoirs of these good and holy men and so on and I've been impressed, actually, in reading some memoirs of the princes of the Church, by how many of

them came from humble backgrounds (Cardinal Wyszynski was a coal-miner's son), how they rose to these
positions of great power and how they were just like the
rest of us (in uncertainty). They're filled with doubts and
indecisions because, actually, they're truly good people.
They are humble in the best Christian sense.[7]

Bem is all of these things. But Moore admits the difficulty
of writing about a character with whom he has little in
common, from the point of view of spirituality or faith. Bem
is 'a character I really know nothing about. I try to empathise
with him, which I think is what a novelist should do, to get
inside the skin of a character who is not himself . . . you're
not writing autobiography.'[8]

What emerges most strongly from the novel and from all
that Moore has said about *The Colour of Blood* is his admiration
for the everyday heroism of those who believe and continue
to believe. This attitude to the faith of others was already
evident from *Cold Heaven* and *Black Robe*, but in this, his latest
novel, his approval is unequivocal. There are no *caveats* about
the hysteria of miraculous apparitions or the ethics of the
missionary endeavour. A final comment from Moore in the
context of *The Colour of Blood* shows that he has come full
circle from his earlier anti-clericalism and hostility to belief:

> It came as a pleasant surprise to find [of the clerics and
> Cardinals whose memoirs he read] that they weren't like
> the headmaster of the school I'd been to, or they weren't
> like [. . .] parish priests I'd met in Ireland who were
> very much lords of their own domain. These were men
> with a great deal more power and a great deal more
> human responsibility.[9]

The change in attitude to belief and believers, the most
striking manifestation of which is expressed in the above
quotation, occurred gradually between the writing of Moore's
first novel in the 1950s and this recent novel of 1987. His
protagonists, lacking real faith to begin with, though forced

into observation of religion, successively put their faith in artistic creativity, in love, in sex, having, through the choice of exile, abandoned the pretence of religion and the *mores* of Catholic Ireland. Moore moves his characters through disillusionment, alienation, existential anguish, into mystical mania (*The Temptation of Eileen Hughes*), and finally back into religion. *The Colour of Blood* confirms Moore's admiration for religion, and the fact that he has invested a clerical protagonist with unflinching faith without at the same time showing him to be domineering or self-seeking, is very significant. His own ideal, expressed in his admiration for the religious protagonists in all his recent novels, is the possession of a true spiritual and selfless faith.

It is likely, at least, that Moore will continue to use religion as a theme or as a metaphor for belief. If his work as a whole is looked at, even now it seems likely that he will endure as a novelist of belief, faith and finally, possibly, even of Catholicism.

In *The Colour of Blood*, Moore uses the thriller genre more extensively than ever before. The positive aspects of this form are its immediacy, its drama, its impact and the speed with which the plot unfolds. The opening sequence, consisting of Cardinal Bem's reflections in the car and then the shocking unexplained attack on the car, is masterly in its economy and precision. The best thrillers have maximum action and minimum interiorisation, and Moore is conscious of the limitations of the genre, given the nature of his theme. He has remarked that a character in a novel like this cannot take time off to engage in philosophical speculation while someone is just about to shoot him or some other sensational action is about to occur. It is not that thrillers do not have serious themes: most of them do have serious moral preoccupations, but there is little room for development of character. Interestingly, in the case of a thriller-writer like John Le Carré (whom Moore definitely does not regard as a 'serious' writer), the more Le Carré becomes interested in the psychology and motivation of his characters, the less his novels are favoured by the aficionados of the thriller genre. *The Colour of Blood* is a novel of 'static character', according to Wayne C. Booth's classification: 'The changes which go to make up the story are all changes in fact and circumstance and knowledge, never in the essential worth and rightness of the character himself'.[10] Bem is just such a static character, and the pace of the narrative allows very little time for retrospection or introspection. This is noticeable not so much while one is reading the novel, but after one has finished reading it; Moore has not overestimated his ability to absorb the reader and maintain attention and suspense. Besides, for the whole of the novel, the reader's consciousness *is* Cardinal Bem's. The point of view is uniform: there is no change from third-person narration with Bem as the centre of consciousness. The reader is caught up in the life of the protagonist in the opening paragraph and this identification is intensified immediately by the attack on Bem's life. The reader feels as Bem feels, sees as Bem sees, knows only what he knows. The reader travels with him and depends on him completely for his understanding of the rest of the novel. Bem has to be accepted as good and reliable, but since there is no ambiguity in the author's view of him, this is easily done. The nearest Moore ever came to this type of narration was in *The Doctor's Wife*, where Sheila Redden, although not a victim of violence or subversive forces, only comes to know what is going to happen to her as it is happening. With her, this is caused by her state of mind, whereas Bem is caught in a tornado of political and religious events. In *The Doctor's Wife*, Sheila Redden's is not the only point of view dramatised; other characters provide both retrospection and analysis. These qualities are almost totally lacking in *The Colour of Blood*. In the extremely brief time-scale of the novel, there is no room for them.

Looking at *The Colour of Blood* in the context of Moore's work as a whole, it would therefore appear that he has at his command many different novelistic techniques, and that he is willing to diversify into genres other than those he has previously used. However, it would seem that the thriller form used in *The Colour of Blood* is not the most revealing or rewarding for the development of richness of character or for conveying the subtleties or complexities of faith. The modified thriller-form, with multi- rather than single-perspective technique has been used to greater effect by Moore, for instance, in *Cold Heaven*.

The political thriller with a basis of moral choice or dilemma is a genre superbly handled by Moore, as *The Colour of Blood* and *Lies of Silence* show. But the form, accessible and relevant as well as thought-provoking, carries its own dangers: in September 1987, when *The Colour of Blood* was published, who could have foreseen the cataclysmic changes that took place in so many Eastern European countries during 1989? There is no longer a possibility of any Eastern European country—however synthetic or composite—providing the setting for a novel such as *The Colour of Blood*. In the same way, Northern Ireland's problems, no matter how often they are perceived or described as insoluble, are also part of a political and historical continuum that is intrinsically fluid and subject to change. For Moore to explore the dilemma of an individual in such a context shows an author at the height of his powers and confidence.

14

The Killers' Choice —
Lies of Silence

*L*IES *of Silence*, published in April 1990, is set for the most part in contemporary Belfast, concerns itself with the political situation in Northern Ireland and has among its themes the ineluctable nature of moral choice and the randomness of fate that picks one human being rather than the next. In the novel a young hotel manager, Michael Dillon, is forced to make choices, knowing that the consequences of any decision he makes may well be disastrous. In the politically realistic Belfast world of the novel, crisis is endemic beneath the surface of normal life, and for the duration of the novel this crisis erupts into Michael Dillon's life.

Many of the motifs and techniques of earlier Moore novels are evident in this work. Like Marie Davenport in *Cold Heaven*, the protagonist is faced with a choice that he thinks will threaten the life of the partner he is about to leave. As in almost all of Moore's novels, notably, *The Feast of Lupercal*, *The Doctor's Wife*, and *The Temptation of Eileen Hughes*, there is a desperate search for love. As everywhere in Moore's work, there are strong women, interestingly drawn. In technique, *Lies of Silence* most resembles *The Colour of Blood*. Both novels are thrillers in which the action takes place in a politically unstable country over a very short period of time. Talking about *The Colour of Blood*, Moore said that it could be set in any Eastern European country — or in Ireland! In both *The Colour of Blood* and *Lies of Silence*, the narrative vehicle is the mind of a single protagonist, the form a third-person narrative. In *Lies of Silence*, the reader sees only what Michael Dillon sees, experiences only as he experiences, knows other characters only through the filter of his responses, opinions and prejudices. At the same time the author is able skilfully to interpolate opinions — mainly on the political situation in his own country, a country he left many years ago — which appear, on superficial reading, to be the opinions of his protagonist, Michael Dillon, but are in fact more profound, more thoughtful and more far reaching than his protagonist would be capable of under such circumstances.

Lies of Silence is an ambitious new departure for Moore because in it he develops a theme that is absolutely contemporary and squarely *of* Northern Ireland. The thriller form allows him to incorporate a political theme into a novel that is still predominantly of human and moral interest in a way that was not possible with the reportage technique he adopted in his earlier excursion into Canadian politics, *The Revolution Script*. In *Lies of Silence* Moore dares to do two things: he comments on the current political situation in Northern Ireland and he writes about the country and city he left almost forty-five years ago and in which he has not lived since. Nor does he attempt to remain neutral about Northern Ireland: he does not adopt a sectarian or 'nationalist' position, but neither does he limit himself to the depiction of, for instance, the plight of the helpless individual faced with the twin horrors of institutional violence and paramilitary violence of both the orange and green variety. Moore once wished a plague on both houses in the Catholic/Protestant conflict in Northern Ireland. While he has no sympathy for IRA violence and is intolerant of hypocritical justifications of it, he expresses clear opinions about the causes of the current problems. Descriptions of the city of Belfast and of the political situation are slotted neatly into the texture of the novel, as if they were part of Dillon's consciousness or of his train of thought. For instance, on the first evening of the novel's action:

> He turned up towards Millfield, driving through those parts of Belfast which had become the image of the city to the outside world: graffiti-fouled barricaded slums

where the city's Protestant and Catholic poor confronted each other, year in year out, in a stasis of hatred, fear and mistrust.[1]

On the morning of the second day, a little before Dillon is forced to drive his bomb-laden car to the hotel, he sees his neighbour, Mr Harbinson, and the tension, fear and anger he feels, a specific anger because of the treatment he and Moira have received, spreads into a more general anger which is expressed in the following passage. It is at the core of the book and sums up much of what the novel stands for, as well as justifying its title. The passage, highly structured, rhetorical, repetitive though plausibly interiorised, is clearly an authorial interpolation.

> And now . . . Dillon felt anger rise within him, anger at the lies which made this, his and Mrs Harbinson's birthplace, sick with a terminal illness of bigotry and injustice, lies told over the years to poor Protestant working people about the Catholics, lies told to poor Catholic working people about the Protestants, lies from parliaments and pulpits, lies at rallies and funeral orations, and above all, the lies of silence from those in Westminster who did not want to face the injustice of Ulster's status quo. Angry, he stared across the room at the most dangerous victims of these lies, his youthful, ignorant, murderous captors. (49)

Again, as he drives from north Belfast towards the Clarence Hotel, Michael Dillon sees, 'those Protestant and Catholic ghettos which were the true and lasting legacy of this British province founded on inequality and sectarian hate'. (59)

Lies of Silence takes as its subject matter, a week—the final week—in the life of a Belfast hotel manager, Michael Dillon. The action begins in Belfast (this is stated very precisely) at 8.45 p.m. on Monday and ends (this is not stated but can be inferred with absolute accuracy) with the protagonist's death just after 5 p.m. on the following Tuesday, in London. Until

Friday afternoon the action takes place in Belfast, then there is a very clear shift to London by means of an early afternoon flight from Aldergrove to Heathrow. The plotting and structure of the book are so good that the pace seems to be uniformly crisp, but, in fact, most of the novel is devoted to the early part of the week, especially the first night and then the two days in which Michael's life is changed irrevocably, Tuesday (chapters 3 to 5) and Wednesday (chapters 6 to 8). Thereafter the action speeds up considerably, with the two final chapters, 9 and 10, encompassing all of Friday, the move to London and the last four days of Michael Dillon's life which he spends in London. The novel is set (although this is never stated directly) in a hot mid-July, the marching season, the time of greatest sectarian tension in Northern Ireland.

All the action of the novel is rooted in the real world. It is a realistic novel *par excellence*, whose imaginative universe is created by the names of streets, the broadcasting and news media, peopled by characters who could just as easily belong in documentaries—policemen, soldiers, clergymen—people like those whom anyone familiar with the Northern Ireland situation sees constantly on TV screens or reads about in newspapers. The novel is structured around action. Never once in the novel is Michael Dillon on his own for more than a few minutes; his nights after the first night are spent with Andrea. All the introspection he has time for takes place during these sleepless nights (his only respite from sleepless anxiety is at the weekend in London when he is temporarily able to forget his problems, able to pretend that he has started a new life). During the day he is plunged into activity, crisis, damage containment. His thoughts are often panic-stricken, his actions usually reactions to events.

Michael Dillon's character is not developed by reference to the consciousness of any other character. He is the protagonist whose point of view alone must carry the narrative. There is no time for description in a thriller like this. However he must be a character the reader can identify with and trust. He must be sympathetic and moral or at least moral enough to take moral choices seriously. Michael Dillon is not shown as being a man of great courage in his everyday life. He is rather ashamed of his profession, though he has achieved considerable success in it, and he looks back nostalgically to his college days when he wrote poetry and published articles and read the serious books that he still keeps on his shelves Though he is in his mid-thirties (his age is not made precisely clear: he was born in 1952, is twelve years older than Andrea who graduated a year previously and his wife, Moira, is thirty-three) he is conscious of a feeling of insecurity and inferiority. Because he was 'once a poet', (5) he thinks Andrea might despise him for having become a hotel manager. 'But what was it she saw in him?' (7) and 'Tonight she might end it.' (5) Before he leaves Belfast, Michael has 'a vision of himself as a head flunkey in morning clothes, a glorified servant condemned to smile and turn the other cheek to the condescension, bad manners and arrogant assumptions of people who could pay hundreds of pounds for a night's lodgings'. (117) Though Michael loves Andrea he does not feel secure about her love for him. Nor does he show great courage in this affair: even though he decides to leave Moira he does not tell her of his decision. Admittedly a larger crisis intervenes, but even afterwards he still does not tell Moira. In fact, he never tells her. She finds out when she sees him and Andrea together on the morning of the second day. It is this point that brings the public plot or crisis and the private plot of the novel together. In anger and defiant self-assertion Moira broadcasts her and Michael's involvement with the terrorists to the world and mentions to a journalist that Michael has seen the face of one of the terrorists. So Michael's lack of courage in private matters could be said to cause or at least to contribute to the testing of his courage in the wider public matter. In his private world, Michael Dillon has a sense that his life is out of control. He feels he was wrong to think he was a poet, wrong to have married Moira, wrong not to have left her earlier: 'Once again his life had taken a wrong turning. Once again, he had acted too late.'

(34) This perception is true on a wider scale: his life is out of his control and in the hands of terrorists.

The crisis prepared for in the opening pages of the novel is a romantic one: will Michael leave his wife for Andrea and what will the consequences be? In this opening dilemma, the novel echoes *Cold Heaven*, but this crisis is resolved almost incidentally when Moira sees Michael and Andrea together and a far more serious public/political/moral crisis takes over.

In terms of the novel, Michael's character is conveyed to the reader—created, as it were—by the views of others as well as by his own reactions to people and events. These views may not often be expressed directly by the other characters, as Michael himself is always the centre of consciousness, but they may be inferred: others love him or have loved him, notably Andrea, but also his parents, Moira, Moira's parents and the staff of the hotel. Though he is not altogether happy with himself, he must be a likeable person. He is shown facing dilemmas and it is very important for the tension and fabric of the novel that these be complex dilemmas and that their outcome should remain in doubt for as long as possible. Which individual, reading the novel, would be sure how he or she would react in a similar situation, when the choice is between public and private good, when the duty of a citizen seems in direct opposition to the instinct of the individual. Michael Dillon's first choice is in Belfast: whether to alert the police to the bomb in his car and risk his wife's life. It is no conscious act of heroism on his part when he telephones the police. Some instinct to preserve human life impels him, an instinct that is aroused by the chatter of French tourists and even by the sight of the old demagogue, Alun Pottinger and his minders, although he despises Pottinger's bigotry. He acts in the best possible way under the circumstances and though he is, it is true, about to leave the wife he no longer loves for another woman, and this adds to the moral complexity conveyed to the reader, it is not in the end a factor in his decision. There is a valuable human instinct that the lesser of two evils be chosen: for Michael Dillon, it is the lesser of two evils to prevent *certain* carnage than to risk *possible* death.

The second decision Dillon has to make is much more complex and because he has so much time to think about it, relatively speaking, he cannot let his instinct decide for him as in the case of the bomb. In a sense he does not finally make this decision at all; he could only have made it by declaring to Inspector Randall his decision not to testify (or to testify). At the moment he is killed he has decided not to testify, but he misses Inspector Randall's call. But it is already too late: the defiance he expressed on the two occasions that he met the priest, Matt Connolly, has made his death inevitable. To identify or not to identify Kevin McDowell? If Dillon were to testify against the youth, it would mean one IRA member less on the streets at the very least. Furthermore, Moore is careful not to make Kev out to be a good terrorist. He is nasty, brutish, potentially sexually violent, and enjoys torturing his captives. Neither Michael nor the reader is convinced by the protestation of his uncle, the priest, that he is a good lad, misguided but willing to learn his lesson. Kev will do violence again. Yet when Michael Dillon is in London, he decides rationally, with the support of Andrea, that he is no longer part of that 'moronic bloody mess' (177) that is Belfast. He would be risking his life now for the uncertain good of putting one terrorist behind bars, but he is torn between his desire to save his own life and Andrea's, and his wish not to yield to IRA pressure. The priest's plea is counter-effective. Subliminal anti-clericalism, disgust at the clerical presumption of authority and the priest's ability to equivocate with terrorism harden Michael's resolve to identify Kevin McDowell. 'He was not afraid of them. To hell with them.' (189) The final decision of his life is *not* to testify, but there is no knowing whether this would have been his ultimate decision had he lived. Michael's changes of mind do not lose him the sympathy of the reader although he is ashamed of his own weakness. Logically he knows that no one has the right to demand heroism of him, when he never sought the occasion himself. Still, another part of him wishes that he could supply that heroism:

> He had, instead, been put to the test by accident, a test he had every right to refuse. And yet as he unlatched the gate and went up to the front door of the house he knew that the moment the phone rang and he answered it, the moment he told them he was afraid, he would lose for ever something precious, something he had always taken for granted, some secret sense of his own worth. (192–3)

Sinister, unpredictable, a place where appearances are deceptive, Belfast in *Lies of Silence* is radically different from the city of Moore's early novels. In the thirty-year span from *The Feast of Lupercal* to *Lies of Silence* dramatic changes are perceived to have taken place, changes which are not just to do with the boiling over of what was previously simmering sectarian tension and Catholic dissatisfaction. In the 1980s, Catholic and Protestant alike may well be less religious, the middle classes apolitical and gathered in enclaves in north or south Belfast where they may have more in common with each other than with their co-religionists in the Falls or the Shankill. During the long night of captivity, Michael thinks: 'He did not believe in God, in religion, or in any order or meaning to this world.' (43) This has a relevance for the novel beyond Michael's personal life. Then, early in the morning, when he sees his neighbour, Mr Harbinson, he reflects:

> Mr Harbinson was, by the sound of him, almost certainly a Protestant, but, equally likely, he was no more a religious Protestant than Dillon was a religious Catholic: . . . Mr Harbinson, like ninety per cent of the people of Ulster, Catholic and Protestant, just wanted to get on with his life without any interference from men in woollen masks. (49)

Perhaps this, at least, is an improvement on the earlier Belfast, although it would appear unfortunate that agnosticism is a prerequisite for religious tolerance. Another striking change is the casual manner in which Catholics like Michael and Moira accept the reality of divorce. Both mention the dissolution of their marriage as a legal matter to be put in the hands of their solicitor. Even Michael's mother, who is a devout Catholic, accepts that he intends to remarry.

Belfast presents a picture of a much more cosmopolitan city than in the earlier novels. There is at least the possibility of escape, of movement to and from Canada and London. The media and the attention of the outside world have at least ensured that Belfast will not regress to the state of religious primitivism that obtained there in the 1950s.

Where *Lies of Silence* shows not change but similarity to *Judith Hearne* and *The Feast of Lupercal* is in its anti-clericalism. As regards the opinion of the author, it is clear that the admiration be expressed (albeit equivocally) for missionary zeal and martyrdom in *Black Robe*, for secularist tolerance (Monsignor Cassidy in *Cold Heaven*), for mystical self-abnegation (Mother St Jude in *Cold Heaven*), or for the pastoral integrity of Cardinal Bem in *The Colour of Blood*, does not extend to the clergy or the Catholic educational system of Northern Ireland. Even before the despicable Father Matt Connolly comes on the scene, this is made clear by Michael Dillon's reflections on and recollections of the clerical education he received. The anger he feels on the morning he drives through Belfast with a bomb in his car is directed partly at St Michan's, his alma mater (St Malachy's Diocesan College):

> the red brick façade of the Catholic school where for eleven years he had been a boarder, a school where teaching was carried on by bullying and corporal punishment and learning by rote, a school run by priests whose narrow sectarian views perfectly propagated the divisive bitterness which had led to the events of last night.

> Look at me, Look at me, he wanted to shout as he drove

past those hated gates. See this car on its way to kill innocent people, see my wife in a room with a gun at her head, and then ask your Cardinal if he can still say of those killers that he can see their point of view. (58–9)

The priest who intervenes in the later stages of the plot and does much to determine Michael Dillon's fate is all the more unattractive because he has a patina of bonhomie. He is not severe or Olympian like Father Quigley, the Belfast preacher in *Judith Hearne*. That would be out of keeping with the present age, so the priest masks his authoritarian presumption under a pretence of egalitarianism. There is clear authorial intervention when, at the moment the priest comes into Andrea's flat: 'The priest, with the confidence of his kind, sat down proprietorially in the best chair and took out cigarettes.' (156) Michael Dillon's reaction to Father Matt Connolly is extremely hostile:

He looked at the priest's raw, red face, his ice-blue eyes, his confident smile. He knew that 'Wee Father Matt', in the authoritarian way of most Irish priests, thought of himself as someone special, a person of a higher calling than the laymen he dealt with. He would have no idea that, to Dillon, a priest was at best a fool who believed in something totally false, at worst a dangerous meddler in other people's lives. (156)

Certainly, Father Matt is very unattractively drawn, dishonest, disingenuous, ambivalent about murderous violence:

I'm not saying I agree with these kids . . . This boy I'm talking about, he's only nineteen. He's not a murderer or a criminal. Maybe he's misguided; I'll grant you that. But we're talking about him being locked up in a place like Long Kesh for maybe as long as fifteen years. That's shocking waste of a young life. And I'm thinking of his mother, too. Of her life from now on, if that happens. (158)

Not until later does Michael find out that Kevin McDowell is the priest's nephew. At this point, as in the second meeting with the priest in London, Michael is outraged, provoked into declaring a position that will eventually cause his death. The contempt expressed in his 'vicious little bastard', (56) (of Kevin McDowell) and in his ironic emphasis on '*Father*' is enough to condemn him. To be fair to the priest he would prefer Michael not to be killed. He knows that the IRA can stop Michael testifying in any case but he would call off the killers were he to get an undertaking from Michael. Although he is drawn so very unsympathetically in the novel, he too is a victim of circumstances: 'So when I went back and was asked what you'd said, I had to tell them the truth.' (188) and 'if anything happens to you because of something I said, I'd have it on my conscience for the rest of my life'. (189) The priest seals Michael's fate not by betraying him to the IRA, but by provoking him into declaring his defiance.

As always in his novels, Moore excels in *Lies of Silence* in his depiction of female characters. The three women who are important in Michael's life, Moira, Andrea and his mother are all drawn skilfully and memorably, but it is Moira who stands out as a major, almost tragic figure. She is not in any sense a bad woman, but men have taken advantage of her all her life, men including Michael. In his case, he went as far as to marry her in order to possess her. Moira is neurotic and bulimic because she is a victim of society's expectations of her and of her own upward mobility. Most of all she is the victim of men. She, tall, beautiful, apparently powerful, but she has always been a victim, although Michael realises it only when he has decided to leave her. 'Now she was no longer his enemy. She was his victim.' (17) But he never pursues this thought to realise that she can only be someone else's victim when he is finished with her. To ease his guilt he thinks, 'she would have no trouble finding a second husband'. (19) He thinks he knows what she needs: 'she wants to be loved. If only I'd been able to love her, to love *her*, not just her looks.' (21) but in fact Moira has always kept men at a distance by flaunting her sexuality and her flirtatious behaviour.

Moira, who is bored and frustrated with her life, well educated but under-utilised, immediately rises to the challenge of the gunmen, whose arrival distracts her completely from her unhappy self. She shows no fear, engages in dangerous repartee, 'You're just a bunch of crooks', (43) paying no heed to Michael's discomfiture. Part of this courage reflects her lack of care for her own life. Bulimics, as the doctor tells Michael, often become suicides. Moira does have a death wish. On their wedding day she told Michael,' 'I don't want to get old and ugly and nobody will look at me any more. I'm going to die young when men still want me. While I have the power.' (74)

Moira is very destructive; perhaps this is why she and the gunmen, particularly the nasty Kev, can communicate in their negative violent way. Michael is excluded from this conversation and horrified by the overtly sexual response of the young gunman. In general, Moira is angry and no one can help her, so she causes more destruction. It is on Michael that the reader depends for an understanding of Moira until near the end of the novel when she expresses, forcefully, her sense of herself. This is how Michael describes her:

> Her angers were fevers. She fought them alone, running out of the house, sometimes taking the car, sometimes on foot, but always wandering restlessly, aimlessly, until her rage fell, like mercury in a thermometer. (105)

and later as 'an angry, sentimental, discontented girl who used the sword of her beauty to assure her the indulgence of the men with whom she dealt'. (110)

The bombing and the gunmen give Moira's life a purpose. She becomes hysterical, dangerous (very dangerous to Michael) but she has a purpose—peacemaker, martyr, campaigner; she is not sure what, but something. In a long outburst to Michael, she complains with justification: 'What do you think my life's been until now? . . . you don't care whether I have a brain or not, you don't know me, you don't want to know what makes me tick—.' (137)

Her *cri de coeur* is quite justified, but Michael and the other men could never have had a chance of knowing her because she kept them at bay with the same 'sword of her beauty' that she used to attract them. She says 'I hope they shoot me' but she manages instead, not consciously or deliberately, to punish Michael.

Andrea, though much more thinly drawn than Moira, is nevertheless convincing as the person whom Michael loves and needs. She is his passport to a new life and soon becomes his means of escaping Northern Ireland. Young, free, Canadian, she is not burdened by a complex and violent past. She takes her history lightly, came to Belfast by accident, and stayed there for fun. She is not carrying the weight of the 'Northern problem' as all people *of* Northern Ireland must do. 'Past history', she says of a previous boyfriend. 'Doesn't matter.' (10) Michael associates her with unalloyed happiness, chooses her because he thinks she is everything his troubled, unhappy wife is not, looks at her enviously as an older, world-weary, battle-scarred person might look at a carefree child, 'seeing that world of spontaneous gaiety from which he was now shut out', and realising, 'she was more open, more honest than any other girl he had known'. (110) For a brief period near the end of the novel, Andrea creates for him a London idyll in leafy Hampstead. The last Sunday of his life is his happiest day ever: 'It was like a time long ago, the time of his childhood. He did not want to close his eyes. He did not want this day to end.' (170)

When Michael goes to London he leaves behind and says goodbye to his mother. Perhaps her function is to show that remoteness is the best means to survival and sanity. She is remote in Donegal and somehow mysterious. Michael says he does not know her, but there is warmth and affection between them. All the parents who feature in the novel — and it is a work where ties of family, loyalty and community are very important — are of quite a different type to the autocratic Irish parents who featured in the early Belfast novels.

Although *Lies of Silence* marks a new departure for Moore,

this novel shares with others the idea, expressed here by Michael Dillon, that life has no order. A series of accidents and errors leads to his death in what appears to be an entirely arbitrary fashion. Traditionally, religion imposes order, helps people to understand the incomprehensible. A political structure normally imposes order of a different kind, but Northern Ireland is a country without an effective political structure, and Belfast, a city where disorder is likely to break out in certain areas and at certain times, and to affect uninvolved 'neutral' individuals like Michael Dillon. This situation is highly suitable material for Moore to mine for his sixteenth novel on his governing passion, his sixteenth variation upon a single theme: what is man to believe and if he believes nothing, how is he to live? The lasting image of *Lies of Silence* is a bleak one: nothing remains to explain Michael Dillon's death or to show how his life could have been made more meaningful.

Notes

Introduction (pp ix–xvii)
1. John Wilson Foster, 'Question and Answer with Brian Moore', *Irish Literary Supplement* 4 (Fall 1985), 44–5.
2. Cited by Robie Macauley and George Lanning, *Technique in Fiction* (New York: Harper and Row, 1964), 6.
3. Hallvard Dahlie, *Brian Moore* (Boston: Twayne Publishers, 1981), 150.
4. John Wilson Foster, 'Crisis and Ritual in Brian Moore's Belfast Novels', *Eire–Ireland* 3 (Autumn 1968), 67.
5. John Wilson Foster, *Forces and Themes in Ulster Fiction* (Dublin: Macmillan, 1974).
6. Jeanne Flood, *Brian Moore* (Lewisburg: Bucknell University Press, 1974).
7. Christopher Ricks, 'The Simple Excellence of Brian Moore', *The New Statesman* 71 (18 February 1966), 227.
8. Michael Paul Gallagher, 'Brian Moore's Fiction of Faith', *Gaéliana* 5 (1985), 93.
9. Interview with Ray Comiskey, 'Moore's Almanac', *Irish Times*, 1 November 1983, 10.
10. ibid.
11. RTE Radio, 'Dialogue', 20 February 1986, Brian Moore in conversation with Andy O'Mahony.
12. Joyce Andrews, 'Education through the Writer's Eye' (M.Ed. dissertation, University of Dublin, 1984), 157.

Chapter 1 (pp 3–15)
1. John Cronin, 'Ulster's Alarming Novelists, *Eire–Ireland* 4 (Winter 1969), 27.
2. Hallvard Dahlie, *Brian Moore* (Toronto: Copp Clarke, 1969), 3.
3. RTE Radio, 'The Gay Byrne Show', 24 September 1987, Brian Moore in conversation with Gay Byrne.
4. John Wilson Foster, *Forces and Themes in Ulster Fiction* (Dublin: Gill and Macmillan, 1974), 159.
5. RTE Radio, 'Dialogue', 20 February 1986, Brian Moore in conversation with Andy O'Mahony.
6. Cited in Donat O'Donnell, *Maria Cross* (London: Burns and Oates, 1963), 23.

7. Joyce Andrews, 'Education through the Writer's Eye' (M.Ed. dissertation, University of Dublin, 1984), 134.

8. 'Dialogue'.

9. O'Donnell, *Maria Cross*, 109.

10. John Wilson Foster, 'Question and Answer with Brian Moore', *Irish Literary Supplement* 4 (Fall 1985), 44.

11. Tom Adair, 'The Writer as Exile', *The Linen Hall Review*, 2 (Winter 1985), 5.

12. Andrews, 'Education through the Writer's Eye', 154.

13. 'Out of the Air: Pentecostal Backlash', *The Listener*, 88, 2 November 1972, 596.

14. John Stuart Mill, *Autobiography* (London: OUP, 1971), 26–7.

15. As detailed in the interview with Ray Comiskey, 'Moore's Almanac', *Irish Times*, 1 November 1983, 10, cited on page xiii of the Introduction.

16. Adair, 'The Writer as Exile'.

Chapter 2 (pp 16–45)

1. Robert Sullivan, 'Brian Moore: A Clinging Climate', *London Magazine* 15 (December 1976/January 1977), 63.

2. Brian Moore, *Judith Hearne* (London: André Deutsch, 1955), 58–9. Subsequent references to this edition in parentheses.

3. Foster, *Forces and Themes*, 156.

4. Cronin, 'Ulster's Alarming Novelists', 30.

5. Terry Eagleton, *Exiles and Emigrés* (London: Chatto and Windus, 1970), 13.

6. ibid, 73.

7. Brian Moore, 'Old Father, Old Artificer', *Irish University Review* 12 (Spring 1982), 16.

8. ibid, 15.

9. Derek Mahon, 'Webs of Artifice', *The New Review* 3 (November 1976), 43.

10. Kerry McSweeney, 'Brian Moore: Past and Present', *Critical Quarterly* 18 (Summer 1976), 55.

11. ibid, 56.

12. James Joyce, 'A Painful Case', *Dubliners* (Harmondsworth: Penguin, 1971), 105.

13. Michael P. Gallagher, 'Brian Moore's Fiction of Faith', *Gaéliana* 5 (1985), 94.

14. James Joyce in a letter to Grant Richards, 1906, cited in '*Dubliners*' and '*A Portrait of the Artist as a Young Man*': a Casebook, Morris Beja, ed, (London: Macmillan, 1973), 38.

15. Michael J. Toolan, 'Psyche and Belief: Brian Moore's Contending Angels', *Eire–Ireland* 15 (Autumn 1980), 100.
16. David Daiches, *The Novel and the Modern World* (London: The University of Chicago Press, 1970), 73.
17. François Mauriac, *Thérèse Desqueyroux* (Paris: Livre de Poche, 1980), 9. (My translation)
18. George Orwell, *A Clergyman's Daughter* (Harmondsworth. Penguin, 1978), 16.
19. Sullivan, 'Brian Moore: A Clinging Climate', 70–71.
20. Stephen Ullmann, *Style in the French Novel* (Oxford: Basil Blackwell, 1964), 94–120.
21. Roy Pascal, *The Dual Voice: Free Indirect Speech and its Functioning in the Nineteenth-century European Novel* (Manchester: Manchester University Press, 1977), 9–10.
22. ibid, 17.
23. Derek Oldfield, 'The language of the novel: the character of Dorothea' in *'Middlemarch'*: *Critical Approaches to the Novel*, Barbara Hardy, ed, (London: The Athlone Press, 1967), 63–86.
24. Ullmann, *Style in the French Novel*.
25. Philip French, 'The Novels of Brian Moore', *London Magazine* 5 (February 1966), 90–91.
26. Moore, 'Old Father, Old Artificer'.

Chapter 3 (pp 46–59)
1. 'Dialogue'.
2. Brian Moore, *The Feast of Lupercal* (London: André Deutsch, 1958), 44. Subsequent references to this edition in parentheses.
3. Brian Moore to Mordecai Richler, 3 January 1958, cited in Hallvard Dahlie, *Brian Moore* (Boston: Twayne Publishers, 1981), 52.
4. Anne Haverty, 'The Outsider on the Edge', *Sunday Tribune*, 3 November 1985, 17.

Conclusion (pp 60–63)
1. Norman Friedman, 'Forms of the Plot', in *The Theory of the Novel*, Philip Stevick, ed, (New York: The Free Press, 1967), 159.

Chapter 4 (pp 67–104)
1. Used of *Wuthering Heights* in *The Great Tradition* (Harmondsworth: Peregrine, 1967), 38.
2. Patrick F. Walsh, 'Technique as Discovery: A study of Form in

the Novels of Brian Moore' (Ph.D. dissertation, University College Dublin, 1973). Brian Moore in conversation with the author.

3. Seamus Deane, *A Short History of Irish Literature*, (Hutchinson: London, 1986), 220.

4. Notably by John A. Scanlon in 'States of Exile: Alienation and Art in the Novels of Brian Moore and Edna O'Brien' (Ph.D. dissertation, University of Iowa, 1975), and in 'The Artist-in-Exile: Brian Moore's North American Novels', *Eire–Ireland* 12 (Summer 1977), 14–33.

5. Brian Moore made the comment that failure leads to an 'intenser distillation of the self' in an interview with Rochelle Girson, *Saturday Review*, 13 October 1962. Cited in Murray Prosky 'The Crisis of Identity in the novels of Brian Moore', *Eire–Ireland* 6 (Fall 1971), 106–18.

6. Moore, who is repeatedly questioned on this matter, asserts that it is *not* extraordinary for a man to be able to write sensitively of women. As he says, two of the world's greatest novels, *Madame Bovary* and *Anna Karenina* were written about women by men.

7. Cited in Donat O'Donnell, *Maria Cross* (London: Burns and Oates, 1963), 23.

8. This tendency in Catholicism, which was in abeyance during the liberal post-Conciliar years, has re-emerged strongly in the current conservative pontificate with the silencing of dissident Catholic theologians.

9. Brian Moore, 'Old Father, Old Artificer', *Irish University Review*, 12 (Spring 1982), 16. See chapter 1.

10. Brian Moore, *The Luck of Ginger Coffey* (London: André Deutsch, 1960), 19–20. Subsequent references to this edition in parentheses.

11. James Joyce, *A Portrait of the Artist as a Young Man*, in *The Essential James Joyce*, Harry Levin, ed, (London: Jonathan Cape: 1948), 262 and 267.

12. ibid, 355.

13. Brian Moore, *An Answer from Limbo* (London: André Deutsch, 1960), 39. Subsequent references to this edition in parentheses.

14. Joyce, *A Portrait of the Artist as a Young Man*, 359.

15. 'Ciarán Carty talks to Brian Moore', *Sunday Independent*, 2 June 1985, 14.

16. Brian Moore, *The Doctor's Wife* (London: Jonathan Cape, 1976), 178. Subsequent references to this edition in parentheses.

17. Especially Gallagher (*Gaéliana*), 'Dialogue' and Andrews.

18. Joyce, *A Portrait of the Artist as a Young Man*, 356.
19. Brian Moore, *I am Mary Dunne* (London: Jonathan Cape, 1968), 137. Subsequent references to this edition in parentheses.
20. Cited in O'Donnell, *Maria Cross*, 23.
21. 'Robert Fulford interviews Brian Moore', *Tamarack Review* (Spring 1962), 14, 16, cited in Michael Gallagher, 'Brian Moore's Fiction of Faith', *Gaeliana* 5 (1985), 92.
22. Cited in O'Donnell, *Maria Cross*, 23.
23. C. G. Jung, *Modern Man in Search of a Soul* (London: Routledge and Kegan Paul, 1978), 120, 124–5.
24. Norman Friedman, 'Point of View in Fiction: The Development of a Critical Concept' in *The Theory of the Novel*, Philip Stevick, ed, (New York: The Free Press, 1967), 132.
25. Percy Lubbock, *The Craft of Fiction* (London: Jonathan Cape, 1921), 122.
26. Foster, John Wilson, 'Question and Answer with Brian Moore', *Irish Literary Supplement*, 4 (Fall 1985), 44.

Chapter 5 (pp 105–116)
1. Mark Schorer, 'Technique as Discovery', in *The Theory of the Novel*, Philip Stevick, ed.
2. ibid, 76–9.

Chapter 6 (pp 117–124)
1. Henry James, Preface to *The Ambassadors*, *The Bodley Head Henry James*, vol 8, 24.
2. Friedman, 'Point of View in Fiction: the Development of a Critical Concept', 125.
3. George Steiner, 'The Distribution of Discourse', *On Difficulty and Other Essays* (London: OUP, 1978), 81.

Chapter 7 (pp 125–129)
1. Friedman, 'Point of View in Fiction: the Development of a Critical Concept', 121.
2. Mentioned in Kerry McSweeney, 'Brian Moore: Past and Present', *Critical Quarterly* 18 (Summer 1976), 53–66.
3. Friedman, 'Point of View in Fiction: the Development of a Critical Concept', 127.
4. Henry James, *The Art of the Novel: Critical Prefaces*, R. P. Blackmur, ed, (New York: Scribners, 1962), 37–8.
5. Elizabeth Bowen, 'Notes on Writing a Novel', in *The Theory of Fiction*, James L. Calderwood, ed, (New York: OUP, 1968), 224–5.

6. ibid, 225.

Conclusion (pp 130–132)
1. Anne Haverty, 'The Outsider on the Edge', *Sunday Tribune*, 3
   November 1985, 17.

Chapter 8 (pp 135–148)
1. Joyce Andrews, 'Education through the Writer's Eye' (M.Ed.
   dissertation, University of Dublin), 1984, 157.
2. Michael P. Gallagher, 'The Novels of Brian Moore', *Studies* 6C
   (Summer 1971), 186.
3. Anne Haverty, 'The Outsider on the Edge', *Sunday Tribune*, 3
   November 1985, 17.
4. Philip Oakes, 'The Novelist who Listens to Women', *Sunday*
   Times, 4 October 1981, 44.
5. RTE Radio, 'Dialogue', 20 February 1986, Brian Moore in conversation with Andy O'Mahony.
6. ibid.
7. Interview with Ray Comiskey, 'Moore's Almanac', *Irish Times*, 1
   November 1983, 10.
8. ibid.
9. RTE Radio, 'The Gay Byrne Show', 24 September 1987, Brian
   Moore in conversation with Gay Byrne.
10. Andrews, 'Education through the Writer's Eye', 155.
11. ibid, 157.
12. 'Dialogue'.
13. Brian Moore, *Catholics* (London: Jonathan Cape, 1972), 21. The
    second reference to this edition is in parentheses.
14. Wayne C. Booth, *The Rhetoric of Fiction* (London: The University
    of Chicago Press, 1961), 287.
15. ibid, 198–9.
16. Attested to in numerous articles and interviews. Moore quickly
    became disillusioned with the Hemingway hardboiled 'macho
    style (Moore's phrase) and turned for inspiration instead to the
    Joyce of *Dubliners*.
17. Ernest Hemingway, *Death in the Afternoon*, cited by Larry W
    Phillips, *Ernest Hemingway on Writing* (London: Granada, 1985)
    85.
18. ibid, 80.
19. Michael P. Gallagher, 'Brian Moore's Fiction of Faith', *Gaéliana* 5
    (1985), 93.

20. Cited in David Madden, *A Primer of the Novel: For Readers and Writers* (Metuchen, New Jersey: The Scarecrow Press, 1980), 196.

Chapter 9 (pp 149–163)
 1. The phrase is borrowed from Jung's seminal work of that name (first published in 1933). The novel yields a great deal to a Junglan reading, as developed in this chapter.
 2. Janet Egelson Dunleavy, 'Brian Moore's New Woman', *Irish Literary Supplement* 1 (Spring 1982), 10.
 3. Matthew 4:8–11.
 4. The one-dimensional nature of his character cannot be accidental in the work of a writer who excels at making even his most minor characters vivid.
 5. Brian Moore, *The Temptation of Eileen Hughes* (London: Jonathan Cape, 1981), 75. Subsequent references to this edition in parentheses.
 6. Carl Gustav Jung, *Collected Works* 11, par 6–9, in *Jung: Selected Writings*, Anthony Storr, ed, (London: Fontana, 1983), 239–40.
 7. ibid, 13, par 55.
 8. Christopher Ricks, review of *The Temptation of Eileen Hughes*, 'The Virgin's Story', *Sunday Times*, 4 October 1981, 44.
 9. ibid.

Chapter 10 (pp 164–186)
 1. Interview with Ray Comiskey, 'Moore's Almanac', *Irish Times*, 1 November 1983, 10.
 2. Brian Moore, *Cold Heaven* (London: Jonathan Cape: 1983), 103. Subsequent references to this edition in parentheses.
 3. Maureen Connelly, 'Miracles in *Cold Heaven*', *Irish Literary Supplement* 3 (Fall 1984), 8.
 4. ibid.
 5. Comiskey, 'Moore's Almanac'.
 6. Interview with Marie Crowe, 'Marie Crowe talks to Belfast writer Brian Moore', *Irish Press*, 21 June 1983, 9.
 7. 'Dialogue'.
 8. Comiskey, 'Moore's Almanac'.
 9. Seamus Deane, *A Short History of Irish Literature* (London: Hutchinson, 1986), 221.
10. Gallagher, 'Brian Moore's Fiction of Faith', 92.
11. ibid, 94.
12. Adapted from the phrase, 'symbolic significance', as used by Wayne C. Booth in *The Rhetoric of Fiction*, 73.

13. Macauley and Lanning, *Technique in Fiction*, 17.

Chapter 11 (pp 187–204)
1. Gallagher, 'Brian Moore's Fiction of Faith', 89.
2. 'Dialogue'.
3. Brian Moore, *Black Robe* (London: Jonathan Cape, 1985), viii. Subsequent references to this edition in parentheses.
4. 'Dialogue'.
5. William Kelly, 'Imaginative Initiation', *Irish Literary Supplement* 4 (Fall 1985), 45.
6. 'Dialogue'.
7. Tom Adair, 'The Writer as Exile', *The Linen Hall Review* 2 (Winter 1985), 6.
8. Kelly, 'Imaginative Initiation'.
9. John Wilson Foster, 'Question and Answer with Brian Moore', *Irish Literary Supplement* 4 (Fall 1985), 44.

Chapter 12 (pp 213–217)
1. Philip French, 'The Novel Tamer: Philip French Examines the Cult of Brian Moore', *Harper's and Queen*, September 1987, 68.
2. Brian Moore, *The Doctor's Wife* (London: Jonathan Cape, 1976), 92–3. The second reference to this edition is in parentheses.
3. Tom Adair, 'The Writer as Exile', *The Linen Hall Review* 2 (Winter 1985), 6.
4. John Wilson Foster, 'Question and Answer with Brian Moore', *Irish Literary Supplement* 4 (Fall 1985), 44.

Chapter 13 (pp 218–228)
1. French, 'The Novel Tamer', 68.
2. Ciarán Carty, 'Ciarán Carty talks to Brian Moore', *Sunday Independent*, 2 June 1985, 14.
3. Seamus Deane, *A Short History of Irish Literature*, (London Hutchinson, 1986), 221.
4. Brian Moore, *The Colour of Blood* (London: Jonathan Cape, 1987) 2. Subsequent references to this edition in parentheses.
5. Brian Moore, *Black Robe* (London: Jonathan Cape, 1985), 242.
6. French, 'The Novel Tamer', 68.
7. RTE Radio, 'The Gay Byrne Show', 24 September 1987, Brian Moore in conversation with Gay Byrne.
8. ibid.
9. ibid.

10. Wayne C. Booth, *The Rhetoric of Fiction* (London: University of Chicago Press, 1961), 276.

Chapter 14 (pp 229–242)
1. Brian Moore, *Lies of Silence* (London: Bloomsbury), 10–11. Subsequent references to this edition in parentheses.

Select Bibliography

Bibliographies

McIlroy, Brian, 'A Brian Moore Bibliography', *Irish University Review* 18, 1 (Spring 1988), 106–33

Stanton, Robert J, *A Bibliography of Modern British Novelists*. vol 1 New York: Whitston, 1978, 535–67.

Studing, Richard, 'A Brian Moore Bibliography', *Eire–Ireland* 10 (Autumn 1975), 89–105.

James Vinson, ed, *Contemporary Novelists*, London: St James's Press New York: St Martin's Press, 1976, 977–9.

I am also indebted to the bibliography in an unpublished MLitt thesis by Seamus Hosey, 'Crisis and Identity in the Novels of Brian Moore' (University of Dublin, 1983).

A. WORKS BY BRIAN MOORE

1. Novels

Judith Hearne, London: André Deutsch, 1955. (Published as *The Lonely Passion of Judith Hearne*, Boston: Little, Brown & Co 1956.)

The Feast of Lupercal, Boston: Little, Brown & Co, 1957; London André Deutsch, 1958.

The Luck of Ginger Coffey, Boston: Little, Brown & Co, 1960; London André Deutsch, 1960.

An Answer from Limbo, Boston and Toronto: Little, Brown & Co 1962; London: André Deutsch, 1963.

The Emperor of Ice-Cream, New York: The Viking Press, 1965; London André Deutsch, 1966.

I am Mary Dunne, Toronto: McClelland and Stewart, 1968; New York The Viking Press, 1968; London: Jonathan Cape, 1968.

Fergus, New York: Holt, Rinehart and Winston, 1970; Toronto McClelland and Stewart, 1970; London: Jonathan Cape, 1971.

The Revolution Script, New York: Holt, Rinehart and Winston, 1971 London: Jonathan Cape, 1972.

Catholics, Toronto: McClelland and Stewart, 1972; London: Jonathan Cape, 1972.

The Great Victorian Collection, New York: Farrar, Straus and Giroux, 1975; London: Jonathan Cape, 1975.

The Doctor's Wife, London: Jonathan Cape, 1976; New York: Farrar, Straus and Giroux, 1976.

The Mangan Inheritance, London: Jonathan Cape, 1979. (Originally published as *Family Album*, New York: Farrar, Straus and Giroux, 1979.)

The Temptation of Eileen Hughes, London: Jonathan Cape, 1981.

Cold Heaven, London: Jonathan Cape, 1983.

Black Robe, London: Jonathan Cape, 1985.

The Colour of Blood, London: Jonathan Cape, 1987.

Lies of Silence, London: Bloomsbury, 1990.

2. Articles

The Writer as Exile', *The Canadian Journal of Irish Studies* 2 (December 1976), 5–16.

The State of Fiction', *The New Review* 5 (Summer 1978), 52–3.

Old Father, Old Artificer', *Irish University Review* 12 (Spring 1982), 13–16.

B. INTERVIEWS WITH BRIAN MOORE

Adair, Tom, 'The Writer as Exile', *The Linen Hall Review* 2 (Winter 1985), 4–6.

Anon, 'Out of the Air: Pentecostal Backlash', *The Listener* 88 (2 November 1972), 596.

Carty, Ciarán, 'Ciarán Carty Talks to Brian Moore', *Sunday Independent*, 2 June 1985, 14.

Comiskey, Ray, 'Moore's Almanac', *Irish Times*, 1 November 1983, 10.

Crowe, Marie, 'Marie Crowe Talks to Belfast Writer Brian Moore', *Irish Press*, 21 June 1983, 9.

de Vere White, Terence, 'Brian Moore: A Compulsive Novelist', *Irish Times*, 7 September 1977, 8.

Foster, John Wilson, 'Question and Answer with Brian Moore', *Irish Literary Supplement* 4 (Fall 1985), 44–5.

French, Philip, 'The Novel Tamer: Philip French Examines the Cult of Brian Moore', *Harper's and Queen*, September 1987, 62, 68.

Gallagher, Michael Paul, 'Brian Moore Talks to Michael Paul Gallagher', *Hibernia*, 10 October 1969, 18.

254 Brian Moore: A Critical Study

Haverty, Anne, 'The Outsider on the Edge', *Sunday Tribune*, 3 November 1985, 17.

Jones, DAN, 'Brian Moore: A Profile', *The New Review* 2 (November 1975), 47–50.

McAuley, Liam, 'Brian Moore: an Exile's Late Arrival', *Irish Times*, 26 September 1987, Weekend Supplement, 11.

Oakes, Philip, 'The Novelist who Listens to Women', *Sunday Times*, 4 October 1981, 44.

Interviews on Radio

RTE Radio, 'Dialogue', 20 February 1986, interviewer: Andy O'Mahony.

RTE Radio, 'The Gay Byrne Show', 24 September 1987, interviewer: Gay Byrne.

C. ABOUT BRIAN MOORE

1. Individual Studies

Dahlie, Hallvard, *Brian Moore*, Toronto: Copp Clark, 1969.

Dahlie, Hallvard, *Brian Moore*, Boston: Twayne Publishers, 1981.

Flood, Jeanne M, *Brian Moore*, Lewisburg, Pennsylvania: Bucknell University Press, 1974.

2. Collection of Critical Articles

Christopher Murray, ed, *Irish University Review*, (Brian Moore Issue), 18, 1, Spring 1988.

3. General Criticism

Bourden, Patricia, 'No Answer from Limbo: An Aspect of Female Portraiture', *The Crane Bag* I (1980), 95–100.

Brown, Terence, 'Brian Moore', *Ireland Today*, 1020 (1985), 11.

Cronin, John, 'Ulster's Alarming Novels', *Eire–Ireland* 4 (Winter 1969), 27–34.

Dahlie, Hallvard, 'Brian Moore and the Meaning of Exile', in *Medieval and Modern Ireland*, Richard Wall, ed, Gerrards Cross: Colin Smythe, 1988, 91–107.

Deane, Seamus, *A Short History of Irish Literature*, London: Hutchinson, 1986, 220–21.

Foster, John Wilson, 'Crisis and Ritual in Brian Moore's Belfast Novels', *Eire–Ireland* 3 (Autumn 1968), 66–74.

Foster, John Wilson, *Forces and Themes in Ulster Fiction*, Dublin: Gill and Macmillan, 1974, 122–30.

French, Philip, 'The Novels of Brian Moore', *London Magazine* 5 (February 1966), 86–91.

Gallagher, Michael Paul, 'The Novels of Brian Moore', *Studies* 60 (Summer 1971), 180–95.

Gallagher, Michael Paul, 'Brian Moore's Fiction of Faith', *Gaéliana* (University of Caën) 5 (1985), 89–95.

Henry, Dewitt, 'The Novels of Brian Moore: a Retrospective', *Ploughshares* 2 (1974), 7–26.

Mahon, Derek, 'Webs of Artifice', *The New Review* 3 (November 1976), 43.

Mahon, Derek, 'A World of Signs', *The Irish Times*, 11 June 1988, Weekend Supplement, 11.

McMahon, Sean, 'The Black North', *Eire–Ireland* 1 (Summer 1966), 67–8.

McSweeney, Kerry, 'Brian Moore: Past and Present', *Critical Quarterly* 18 (Summer 1976), 53–66.

Prosky, Murry, 'The Crisis of Identity in the Novels of Brian Moore', *Eire–Ireland* 6 (Fall 1971), 106–18.

Rafroidi, Patrick, 'The Great Brian Moore Collection', *The Irish Novel in our Time*, 221–36, Maurice Harmon and Patrick Rafroidi, eds, Lille: Publications de l'Université de Lille, 1976.

Ricks, Christopher, 'The Simple Excellence of Brian Moore', *The New Statesman* 71 (18 February 1966), 227–8.

Scanlan, John A, 'The Artist-in-Exile: Brian Moore's North American Novels', *Eire–Ireland* 12 (Summer 1977), 14–33.

Simmons, James, 'Brian Moore and the Failure of Realism', *The Honest Ulsterman* (March/April 1970), 8–14.

Toolan, Michael J, 'Psyche and Belief: Brian Moore's Contending Angels', *Eire–Ireland* 15 (Autumn 1980), 97–111.

Walsh, William, *Commonwealth Literature*, London: Oxford University Press, 1973, 84.

Woodcock, George, 'Away from Lost Worlds: Notes on the Development of a Canadian Literature', in *Readings in Commonwealth Literature*, 209–20. William Walsh, ed, Oxford: Clarendon Press, 1973.

4. Studies of Individual Novels

The Feast of Lupercal

Hirscberg, Stuart, 'Growing up Abject as Theme in Brian Moore's Novels', *The Canadian Journal of Irish Studies* 1 (November 1975), 11–16. (*The Feast of Lupercal* and *The Emperor of Ice-Cream*)

The Emperor of Ice-Cream
Hirscberg, Stuart, 'Growing up Abject as Theme in Brian Moore's Novels', *The Canadian Journal of Irish Studies* 1 (November 1975) 11–16. (*The Emperor of Ice-Cream* and *The Feast of Lupercal*)
Raban, Jonathan, *The Technique of Modern Fiction: Essays in Practical Criticism*, London: Edward Arnold, 1968, 60–6.

I am Mary Dunne
Brady, Charles A, '*I am Mary Dunne*', *Eire–Ireland* 3 (Winter 1968) 136–40.
Dorenkamp, JH, 'Finishing the day: Nature and Grace in Two Novels by Brian Moore', *Eire–Ireland* 13 (Spring 1978), 103–12. (*I am Mary Dunne* and *Catholics*)

Catholics
Dorenkamp, JH, 'Finishing the day: Nature and Grace in Two Novels by Brian Moore', *Eire–Ireland* 13 (Spring 1978), 103–12 (*Catholics* and *I am Mary Dunne*)
Porter, Raymond J, 'Mystery, Miracle and Faith in Brian Moore's *Catholics*', *Eire–Ireland* 10 (Autumn 1975), 79–88.
Shepherd, Allen, 'Place and Meaning in Brian Moore's *Catholics*' *Eire–Ireland* 15 (Fall 1980), 134–40.

The Doctor's Wife
Flood, Jeanne A, '*The Doctor's Wife*: Brian Moore and the Failure of Realism', *Eire–Ireland* 18 (Summer 1983), 80–102.

5. Reviews of Individual Novels

Judith Hearne
Farrington, Conor, *Irish Writing* 31 (Summer 1955), 62–3.

Fergus
Cronin, John, *Eire–Ireland* 6 (Summer 1971), 179–80.

Catholics
Brown, Terence, 'Brian Moore: Parables of Change and Pain' *Hibernia*, 1 March 1974, 14.
Mahon, Derek, *The Listener* 88 (2 November 1972), 610.

The Great Victorian Collection
Dahlie, Hallvard, *Ploughshares* 3, (1975), 149–53.

Healy, John, *Queen's Quarterly* 58 (Winter 1976), 688–9.

Lenoski, Daniel S, *The Canadian Journal of Irish Studies* 1 (November 1975), 41.

The Doctor's Wife

de Vere White, Terence, 'Every Trick of the Trade', *Irish Times*, 13 November 1976, 8.

Johnston, Jennifer, 'Madame Bovary—Irish Style', *Hibernia* (19 November 1976), 16.

The Mangan Inheritance

Ricks, Christopher, 'A Novel without a Hero', *The London Review of Books* 16 (6 December 1979), 11.

Sealy, Douglas, 'Man and Superwoman', *Hibernia*, 22 November 1979, 14.

The Temptation of Eileen Hughes

Allen, Walter, 'Moore's Mystery', *Irish Press*, 29 October 1981, 6.

Dunleavy, Janet Egelson, 'Brian Moore's New Woman', *Irish Literary Supplement* 1 (Spring 1982), 10.

Gallagher, Michael Paul, *Irish University Review* 12 (Autumn 1982), 242.

Ricks, Christopher, 'The Virgin's Story', *Sunday Times*, 4 October 1981, 44.

Cold Heaven

Breslin, Sean, 'Women Psyche', *Irish Press*, 19 November 1983, 9.

Casey, Kevin, 'Wife's Tale', *Irish Times*, 5 November 1983, Weekend Supplement, 5.

Connelly, Maureen, 'Miracles in *Cold Heaven*', *Irish Literary Supplement* 3 (Fall 1984), 8.

Gallagher, Michael Paul, *Irish University Review* 14 (Spring 1984), 131–4.

Black Robe

Barry, Sebastian, 'The Jesuit Father and the Savages', *Irish Times*, 1 June 1985, Weekend Supplement, 5.

Kelly, William, 'Imaginative Initiation', *Irish Literary Supplement* 4 (Fall 1985), 45.

The Colour of Blood

Bailey, Paul, 'Lamb in the Middle', *Observer*, 27 September 1987, 26.

de Vere White, 'Cardinal Red', *Irish Times*, 26 September 1987 Weekend Supplement, 5.

O'Toole, Fintan, 'Catholicism in a Godless Community', *Sunday Tribune*, 20 September 1987, 21.

Vansittart, Peter, 'Worldly Skills and Threatened Faith', *Sunday Times*, 27 September 1987, 65.

6. Dissertations

Andrews, Joyce, 'Education through the Writer's Eye', MEd dissertation, University of Dublin, 1984. (Brian Moore is one of the writers interviewed.)

Hosey, Seamus, 'Crisis and Identity in the Novels of Brian Moore' MLitt dissertation, University of Dublin, 1983.

Scanlan, John A, 'States of Exile: Alienation and Art in the novels of Brian Moore and Edna O'Brien', PhD dissertation, University of Iowa, 1975.

Walsh, Patrick Francis, 'Technique as Discovery: A Study of Form in the Novels of Brian Moore', PhD dissertation, University College Dublin, 1973.

D. CRITICISM OF FICTION:
A SELECTION OF WORKS CONSULTED

Booth, Wayne C, *The Rhetoric of Fiction* . . . London: University of Chicago Press, 1961.

Bowen, Elizabeth, 'Notes on Writing a Novel', in *The Theory of Fiction*, 224–5, James L Calderwood, ed, New York: OUP, 1968.

Calderwood, James L, ed, *The Theory of Fiction*, New York: OUP 1968.

Daiches, David, *The Novel and the Modern World*, London: The University of Chicago Press, 1970.

Eagleton, Terry, *Exiles and Emigrés*, London: Chatto and Windus 1970.

Forster, EM, *Aspects of the Novel*, Harmondsworth: Penguin, 1970.

Friedman, Norman, 'Point of View in Fiction: The Development of Critical Concept' in *The Theory of the Novel*, 108–37, Philip Stevick, ed, New York: The Free Press, 1967.

Friedman, Norman, 'Forms of the Plot' in *The Theory of the Novel* 145–66, Philip Stevick, ed, New York: The Free Press, 1967.

Grant, Damien, *Realism*, London: Methuen, 1970.

James, Henry, *The Art of the Novel: Critical Prefaces*, RP Blackmur, ed New York: Scribners, 1962.

Lubbock, Percy, *The Art of Fiction*. London: Jonathan Cape, 1921.

Macauley, Robie, and Lanning, George, *Technique in Fiction*, New York: Harper and Row, 1964.

O'Donnell Donat, *Maria Cross*, London: Burns and Oates, 1963.

Pascal, Roy, *The Dual Voice: Free Indirect Speech and its Functioning in the Nineteenth-century European Novel*, Manchester: Manchester University Press, 1977.

Phillips, Larry W, ed, *Ernest Hemingway on Writing*, London: Granada, 1985.

Scholes, Robert, and Kellogg, Robert, *The Nature of Narrative*, Oxford: Oxford University Press, 1966.

Schorer, Mark, 'Technique as Discovery', in *The Theory of the Novel*, 65–84, Philip Stevick, ed, New York: The Free Press, 1967.

Sternberg, E, ed, *Stream of Consciousness Technique in the Modern Novel*, New York: Kennikat Press, 1979.

Stevick, Philip, ed, *The Theory of the Novel*, New York: The Free Press, 1967.

Index